FIGHTING THE WRONG ENEMY

Antiglobal Activists and Multinational Enterprises

FIGHTING THE WRONG ENEMY

Antiglobal Activists and Multinational Enterprises

E D W A R D   M.   G R A H A M

INSTITUTE FOR INTERNATIONAL ECONOMICS
Washington, DC
September 2000

Edward M. Graham, senior fellow, was associate professor in the Fuqua School of Business at Duke University (1988–90), associate professor at the University of North Carolina (1983–88), principal administrator of the Planning and Evaluation Unit at the OECD (1981–82), international economist in the Office of International Investment Affairs at the US Treasury (1979–80), and assistant professor at the Massachusetts Institute of Technology (1974–78). He is author or coauthor of a number of studies on international investment and technology transfer, including *Global Competition Policy* and *Competition Policies in the Global Economy* (1997) with J. David Richardson, *Global Corporations and National Governments* (1996), and *Foreign Direct Investment in the United States* (3rd ed. 1995) with Paul R. Krugman.

INSTITUTE FOR INTERNATIONAL ECONOMICS
11 Dupont Circle, NW
Washington, DC 20036-1207
(202) 328-9000   FAX: (202) 328-5432
http://www.iie.com

C. Fred Bergsten, *Director*
Brigitte Coulton, *Director of Publications and Web Development*
Brett Kitchen, *Director of Marketing*

Typesetting by BMWW
Printing by Kirby Lithographic, Inc.
Cover photograph:
  © *Steve Rubin/The Image Works*

Printed in the United States of America
02 01 00   5 4 3 2 1

Library of Congress Cataloging-in-Publication Data

Graham, Edward M. (Edward Montgomery), 1944–
  Fighting the wrong enemy : antiglobal activities and multinational enterprises / Edward M. Graham
    p. cm.
  Includes bibliographical references and index.
  ISBN 0-88132-272-5

  1. International business enterprises—Social aspects. 2. Globalization—Social aspects. 3. Investments, Foreign—Social aspects. 4. Investments, Foreign (International law) 5. Social responsibility of business. I. Title.
  HD2755.5 .G722   2000
  332.67′3—dc21   00-040997
                                      CIP

Dedicated to the memory of
RAYMOND VERNON
an extraordinary oarsman

Contents

Figures

Preface

This book has had an unusual history. It was originally intended to evaluate the Multilateral Agreement on Investment (MAI) that was to be negotiated at the Organization for Economic Cooperation and Development (OECD). The book would then have been similar to other Institute publications such as *NAFTA: An Assessment* by Gary Hufbauer and Jeffrey Schott and *The Uruguay Round: An Assessment* by Jeffrey Schott.

The MAI negotiations of course ended in failure. Thus the focus of Edward M. Graham's book shifted from an evaluation of the agreement itself (although remnants of such an evaluation remain) to an analysis of why it failed and the broader implication of that failure for global governance. A particular focus is whether the organized opposition of antiglobalists, to whom the MAI became the focal point for opposition to increased economic integration, was the main reason for the failure. Graham concludes that it was not but, rather, that the MAI negotiations were in deep trouble much earlier because of fundamental policy disagreements over foreign direct investment itself among some of the key OECD governments. However, while concluding that specific aspects of the publicly available draft of the MAI that created some potential for harmful effects (e.g., on the environment) could have easily been rewritten, he also concedes that the opposition created something like a coup de grace to the MAI.

The main purpose of the book, however, is to draw lessons from the MAI episode for international approaches to foreign direct investment and globalization more generally. Graham thus examines whether foreign direct investment is contrary to the interests of workers and the environment, as claimed by the antiglobalists. He reviews a considerable number of empirical studies and concludes that, on many issues, the evidence supports the opposite of antiglobalist claims. For example, there is strong evidence that foreign direct investment improves the welfare of workers in developing countries (though the evidence is more mixed with respect to workers in developed nations where skilled workers gain but some unskilled workers may lose).

With respect to the environment, there is no evidence of any "race to the bottom" where governments, in order to attract or retain direct investment, lower environmental standards; in some cases, there might even be a "race to the top." There is, to be sure, little question that economic growth in developing nations will place additional stress on the world's environment. Growth, however, is essential to relieve poverty in these nations and further integration into the world economy provides their best hope for attaining growth. The issue is thus how to reduce and eliminate poverty without further befouling the air and water of the planet. Graham praises environmental groups for raising these issues but finds fault with at least some of them for not confronting the tradeoff between environmental goals and reduction of poverty, where globalization contributes positively to the latter.

Graham's main policy conclusion is that the MAI episode underlines the likely futility of new international efforts to improve the global framework for foreign direct investment in the near future. He thus counsels against including a comprehensive investment agreement in any new multilateral trade negotiations in the World Trade Organization, for example, as proposed by some of its key members. He concludes that foreign direct investment is likely to continue to grow rapidly, and to make a significant contribution to the world economy, without new intergovernmental efforts to create multilateral rules. This conclusion modifies some of the Institute's earlier views on the topic, including in Graham's own *Global Corporations and National Governments* (1996) and Theodore Moran's *Foreign Direct Investment and Development: The New Policy Agenda for Developing Countries and Economies in Transition* (1998).

The Institute for International Economics is a private nonprofit institution for the study and discussion of international economic policy. Its purpose is to analyze important issues in that area and develop and communicate practical new approaches for dealing with them. The Institute is completely nonpartisan.

The Institute is funded largely by philanthropic foundations. Major institutional grants are now being received from the William M. Keck, Jr. Foundation and the Starr Foundation. A number of other foundations and private corporations contribute to the highly diversified financial resources of the Institute. About 26 percent of the Institute's resources in our latest fiscal year were provided by contributors outside the United States, including about 11 percent from Japan.

Partial funding for this project was provided by the Toyota Motor Corporation under the Institute's new program of studies on the backlash against globalization, a topic of central interest in both the United States and Japan. The program was created in 1998 to analyze the nature and significance of the backlash, and the resultant need for improved understanding of both globalization itself and policy responses that can improve its contribution to the world economy. Support for this program is also being provided by Stephan Schmidheiny, a director of the Institute, who has helped shape our research program as well as provided generous funding for it.

The Board of Directors bears overall responsibility for the Institute and gives general guidance and approval to its research program—including the identification of topics that are likely to become important over the medium run (one to three years), and which should be addressed by the Institute. The Director, working closely with the staff and outside Advisory Committee, is responsible for the development of particular projects and makes the final decision to publish an individual study.

The Institute hopes that its studies and other activities will contribute to building a stronger foundation for international economic policy around the world. We invite readers of these publications to let us know how they think we can best accomplish this objective.

C. FRED BERGSTEN
Director
August 2000

Acknowledgments

This book was a long time in the making—too long, in fact—and, to the extent that the book makes a contribution to an understanding of the issues it attempts to cover, this contribution is the product of inputs from many persons. Some of these persons wish, or must, remain anonymous. These include specifically numerous persons working within governments of a number of nations who agreed to talk with this author about the MAI negotiations or related matters on condition that these talks would remain "off the record" to the extent that neither the names of the individuals nor the governments would be revealed. I am grateful to all of you who agreed to talk with me under these conditions.

I am also very grateful to many individuals who work within the secretariats of the OECD and the WTO and, in addition, the staff of the World Bank who were willing to talk with me about the relevant issues. Again, most such persons spoke on the condition that their contribution would remain anonymous. Even so, however, I would like to thank William Witherell, head of the Directorate for Financial, Fiscal, and Enterprise Affairs at the OECD, and Gerhardt Abel, former head of the Directorate for International Trade at the OECD, for opportunities extended to me to participate in public fora and internal symposia organized by and within OECD. In both cases, it was understood that I was on public record as not favoring OECD as the correct venue for negotiation of multilateral rules on investment,[1] and it was to their credit that they allowed me to speak at these events knowing that on some matters, I would speak against the OECD position.

---

1. See my *Global Corporations and National Governments*, Washington, Institute for International Economics, 1997.

Numerous persons provided substantive guidance on early versions of the book manuscript. Special thanks go to IIE colleagues, including C. Fred Bergsten, Kimberly Elliott, J. David Richardson, and Jeffrey Schott. Two IIE research assistants worked on this book, and their contributions were invaluable: Hiroko Ishii and Erika Wada. Ms. Wada is, of course, coauthor of Appendix B of this book. Special thanks also go to Joel Bergsman of the World Bank, Merit Janow of Columbia University, Theodore Moran of Georgetown University, and Pierre Sauvé of Harvard University, all of whom read and commented extensively upon the full manuscript, and to Daniel Esty of Yale University and Steven Charnovitz of Wilmer, Cutler, and Pickering, who commented upon the environmental chapter. Isiah Frank of Johns Hopkins University read an early version of the manuscript, and his comments too were invaluable.

Raymond Vernon of Harvard University, to whom this book is dedicated, had wanted to read and critique the manuscript, but he passed away before this could happen. Beginning as supervisor of my own doctoral dissertation, Ray has tirelessly and selflessly critiqued virtually everything I have ever written, and his many valuable suggestions will be long appreciated.

I benefited from discussions with a number of representatives of nongovernmental organizations as well. Special thanks in this regard go to Konrad von Moltke of Dartmouth College and the World Wildlife Federation, who went to special lengths to explain the positions of various environmentally oriented NGOs on the MAI and on international investment issues in general.

Publication of this work would not have been possible without the very fine contribution of Mike Treadway, who served as editor, doing as always a superb job with a manuscript that left much to be desired. Thanks also go to Marla Banov, Kara Davis, and Brigitte Coulton of the IIE publications department for their very fine efforts.

FIGHTING THE WRONG ENEMY

Antiglobal Activists and Multinational Enterprises

Introduction

The Dog That Did Not Bark

In a well-known Sherlock Holmes story, the great detective deduces the identity of a murderer from the failure of a dog to bark. Holmes reasons that the perpetrator had to have walked past the dog in order to carry out the crime. But this dog always barked at strangers. Therefore, that the dog did not bark indicated that the perpetrator was known to the dog. Hence the crime was committed by an insider. This observation narrowed the list of suspects considerably, for had the dog barked, the murderer could have been almost anyone. In a sense, therefore, the fact that the dog did not bark conveyed more information than if it had barked.

The history of the Multilateral Agreement on Investment (MAI), an international treaty that sought to bind the member countries of the Organization for Economic Cooperation and Development (OECD) to certain rules pertaining to international investment, in some ways resembles the story of the dog that did not bark. Negotiation of the agreement ended in failure—the MAI itself, as it were, failed to bark—in late 1998. Also, why the negotiations failed is something of a mystery, with both insiders and outsiders as suspects. Who really killed the MAI? Did it fall under the weight of its own internal problems? (Was the agreement also a "dog" in that sense?) Or was it pushed, by opponents outside the proceedings? And, arguably, the talks' failure will turn out to be in some ways more informative than would have been their success. This book explores the various reasons why this may be so.

Negotiations to create the MAI were formally launched at a meeting of trade ministers of the OECD member countries in May 1995, at the OECD headquarters in Paris. Largely at the instigation of the United States, the OECD countries agreed to begin these negotiations the following autumn. The new rules to be established under the agreement were intended to limit the powers of governments to pursue interventionist policies aimed at affecting international flows of investment and the commercial operations of investments under the control of foreign investors. For the most part, the new rules were meant to be liberalizing, that is, to remove existing governmental barriers and controls on foreign investment. And although the rules were meant to cover all types of international investment, including portfolio investment, they were mostly aimed at long-term foreign direct investment (FDI), about which more below.

The new rules would have been quite complex (chapter 3 delves into some of their details) but, broadly speaking, would have done four things. First, they would have established the principle of national treatment in the investment domain. Under this principle, governments would obligate themselves to treat foreign investors and their investments "no less favorably" than they would treat domestic investors and their investments under like circumstances. In something of a departure from current practice, this principle was meant to cover preestablishment as well as postestablishment investment.[1] That is, had it been fully implemented, the agreement would have forbidden OECD governments from unfairly raising barriers to foreign investors seeking to establish subsidiary operations in their countries, and from discriminating against those investors and their investments once established. Second, the MAI would have created certain standards for investor protection, by specifying under what conditions a government could expropriate a foreign investment and what obligations to the investor the government must then fulfill. For example, investors would be entitled to compensation for the value of any investments thus seized. Third, the MAI would have prevented governments from requiring foreign investors to meet certain onerous conditions before allowing them to enter or remain in the country. Such conditions might include the use of local suppliers, the achievement of a minimum level of employment, or the export of a minimum percentage of output, or the investor might have been required to set up the investment as a joint venture with domestic investors. Arguably, such performance requirements would have been ruled out anyway, as violations of national treatment, but the MAI would have removed any ambiguity by banning these and certain other such requirements specifically. Fourth, the MAI would have set up a dispute settlement procedure to which both governments and affected private investors could seek recourse if any OECD government acted so as to violate its obligations under the MAI.[2]

---

1. The North American Free Trade Agreement (NAFTA) also covered preestablishment investment, so the MAI would not have set an entirely new precedent.

2. As chapter 3 details, a number of provisions in the draft MAI do not really fall into any of these categories, but these four include the most important provisions.

Had they been implemented and enforced unconditionally, these provisions would generally have acted to reduce the ability of governments to intervene to affect foreign investment flows or to modify the behavior of international investors or their investments. The MAI would thus arguably have generated significant economic benefits by reducing or eliminating government actions that have the potential to reduce the economic benefits created by international investment.[3]

The MAI, however, would not have addressed all such government actions. One major gap in its provisions, for instance, was a failure to address investment incentives, that is, subsidies and subsidy-like concessions that governments offer to foreign investors to induce them to invest in areas under the government's jurisdiction. As chapter 3 discusses in some detail, such measures can also have adverse effects on economic welfare. Chapter 3 discusses why, in spite of the likely negative impact of investment incentives, the MAI negotiations did not address the issue. Nor did the MAI address tax policies, which can also create distortions in FDI flows. Taxation can affect the rate of return on an investment, and these rates are an important variable to which international investment responds.

Besides these broad omissions, the MAI would have allowed each of the signatory countries to stipulate numerous specific exceptions to the obligations it created. Indeed, so many exceptions had been lodged by the time the negotiations were terminated that, arguably, the agreement would have changed nothing. Furthermore, those reservations that were lodged applied only to national governments. State, provincial, and local governments had yet to weigh in with their reservations at the time the proceedings adjourned. Thus what the OECD countries were about to agree to do in principle, they apparently were unwilling to do in practice, at least in those cases where their current practices conflicted with the agreement's obligations. In addition, as chapter 2 details, certain issues arose in the course of the negotiations that might even have resulted in a *de*liberalization of policy toward international investment. This would have been an unfortunate step backward.

FDI and Its Benefits

To the extent the draft MAI failed to push the envelope of international investment liberalization, it can justifiably be called the dog that would not

---

3. To the author's knowledge, however, no one, not even the analytically oriented Secretariat of the OECD, has made a rigorous attempt to estimate the magnitude of the benefits that the MAI might have created. Such a task, admittedly, would be daunting, but the results would have been of great value to the negotiators and other participants in the debate over the agreement.

hunt. But that does not mean the negotiators were not after big game. Foreign direct investment is at the heart of the activity of those conspicuously investing organizations called "multinational corporations" (more or less equivalent terms include "multinational enterprises," "transnational corporations," and "global corporations"). Most FDI consists of equity investment by a firm in one country in a subsidiary firm in another country, with the intent of controlling that subsidiary; indeed it is the totality of a parent firm and its brood of foreign subsidiaries that constitutes a multinational corporation. And by any measure, multinational firms and the activities they control today account for a large share of economic activity worldwide.

According to estimates published by the United Nations, the book value of the worldwide stock of FDI at the end of 1995, when the MAI negotiations were launched, was over $2.8 trillion. As of this writing, the most recent estimate is for the end of 1998, at which time this stock had grown to more than $4.1 trillion, an increase of almost 45 percent in just three years. Impressive as those figures might sound, they are really only the tip of a much larger iceberg. Because FDI represents only the equity of investors in their investment, not their total assets, and because the investors in this instance are mostly large corporations whose foreign "investments" are affiliated firms, the combined asset values of these investments are vastly greater. Indeed, the United Nations estimates that the total asset value of these investments at the end of 1998 was more than $14.6 trillion, or more than one-and-a-half times US GDP. And even this figure does not include the asset value of the investor firms themselves. The United Nations does not estimate this figure, but it undoubtedly far exceeds the combined asset value of the overseas affiliates.[4]

FDI has indeed been increasing at a rapid rate in recent years. In 1985 the total stock of FDI worldwide, again as estimated by the United Nations, was only $685 billion. This stock therefore increased more than sixfold between 1985 and 1998, for a compound growth rate of almost 14 percent per year. By contrast, nominal world income (as measured by gross world product) and the total nominal value of world exports grew over the same period at compound rates of 6.8 percent and 8.1 percent, respectively. Changes in the stock of FDI correlate well with changes in the nominal value of output generated by foreign-controlled enterprises

---

4. Graham (1995) arrives at a crude estimate of the total asset value of foreign direct investors plus their investments of $25 trillion. Applying the same methodology to 1998 data yields an estimate of about $36.5 trillion, or more than total world GDP (about $30 trillion in 1997). Of course, asset value and GDP are quite different concepts—one is a stock, the other a single year's flow—but it is commonplace in other economic domains (e.g., analysis of international indebtedness) to measure stocks of various kinds against GDP. It would, however, be a gross error to infer from the above figures that multinational firms account for 100 percent of world GDP. A very rough guess is that about 15 percent of world GDP originates in these firms.

(i.e., when the former doubles, so, approximately, does the latter).[5] Thus, it is safe to conclude that the output of these enterprises has grown at a much faster rate over the past decade and a half than either world output or world trade.

Multinational firms are not without their detractors, however. Indeed, the antiglobal activists whose campaign against the MAI contributed to its downfall (as narrated in chapter 2) consistently depicted the multinational corporation as one of the chief "villains" in the MAI melodrama. Among the accusations they leveled against these firms were that they indiscriminately move activities from one country to another in pursuit of the cheapest possible labor, that in doing so they impoverish local citizens and damage the environment, and that they bring no offsetting benefit.

Later chapters of this book examine each of these accusations in detail. For now, suffice it to note that, according to most careful economic analysis, FDI does bring numerous benefits to those countries that welcome it. Developing countries in particular need savings from abroad to finance domestic capital formation, because their own domestic saving is typically insufficient. FDI is a channel by which those external savings can enter.

But beyond this immediate financial benefit, FDI typically brings with it a host of other benefits. One of the most important is technology transfer. Multinational firms, as has long been recognized, tend to be concentrated in sectors that are technologically intensive, and they perform a large proportion of the world's research and development. Through FDI, technologies created by these firms are transferred to their subsidiaries in countries around the world, giving rise to a number of tangible and intangible benefits.

The most direct benefit of FDI, however, is the following. The local subsidiary of a technologically sophisticated multinational produces, in the host country, goods that embody the latest and best technologies, in a facility that uses state-of-the-art production methods. The result can be lower prices and higher quality goods and services for consumers in these countries. But, perhaps more importantly (and it is documented in chapter 4), this technology transfer enables the foreign-controlled firm often to pay higher wages to its workers than do competing local firms. Another benefit, albeit an indirect one, is that the local subsidiary creates competition for domestically owned rivals. In many cases this competition inspires these rivals to improve their own products and processes. Generally, a less efficient producer is being replaced by a more efficient one,

---

5. This correlation deteriorates over long periods, however, because the FDI stock is measured on a historical cost basis (so that noncurrent portions of the total stock are not corrected for price inflation), whereas nominal output value is measured in current prices. However, over the 13 years from 1985 to 1998, world inflation was fairly low, and hence this error is not great. Also, the error tends to understate rather than overstate the growth in FDI and the imputed growth of output of foreign-controlled enterprises.

with positive benefits all around. Thus, for example, the case is strong that, during the 1980s, the entry by the three Japanese automakers into North America through direct investment induced the Big Three US automakers to upgrade their own operations. Substantial benefits flowed to Americans in the form of cars that were better and less costly than they might have been had Japanese direct investment in this sector never come on the scene.[6]

Another result of technology transfer is that, at the margin, the value of output per worker is enhanced. For reasons that chapter 4 develops in detail, this increased productivity should allow workers to be paid more than would otherwise be the case. And, indeed, empirical evidence (also reviewed in chapter 4) shows that a "wage premium" is associated with FDI. This finding contrasts quite sharply with the claim of many anticorporate activists that multinationals pay *lower* wages than their workers would receive in other employment. Looking at the broader picture, technological progress, furthered by both the creation of new technology and its diffusion into the world economy, is statistically associated with economic growth. That is, some large component of economic growth seems to be caused by technological progress. Thus, given that FDI is associated with technology transfer, which is a means of technology diffusion, it might be expected that FDI acts to increase economic growth in the countries that host it. And again statistical studies tend to bear this out (see chapter 4).

Most of the story relating technological advance to FDI suggests that the direction of causality is from the former to the latter: firms that create and apply new technologies achieve advantages over rivals that they then realize through FDI. But some theory and evidence also suggest that a firm with a multinational network of subsidiaries might be led to do more research and development than another firm whose operations are limited to one country. Thus causality may run in the other direction as well, from FDI to technological advance.[7]

One problem with all of this line of argument is that the benefits of FDI that theory predicts and research documents are difficult to quantify precisely. There are two reasons why this is so. The first is that it is simply intrinsically difficult from a statistical point of view to measure the benefits created by the advance and diffusion of technology. The second is that international data pertaining to FDI, and the activities of multinational corporations generally, leave much to be desired; the data needed to perform rigorous statistical testing are often sketchy, or missing altogether. One practical consequence for the MAI was that, even after the negotiations

---

6. The classic work showing benefits of this sort is Dunning (1958). For the North American experience, see Graham and Krugman (1995) and Emmott (1992).

7. The simple theory of why this is so is laid out in Graham (1985). For evidence, see Cantwell (1991a, 1991b).

had been going on for several years, the negotiators had little tangible evidence of how great the eventual benefits of an agreement might be. And without a good estimate of the benefits, it was difficult for negotiators to convince the political leaders to whom they reported to make those concessions that might have been needed to strike a final bargain to conclude the MAI. We return to the issue of the potential benefits from an MAI in chapter 7.

The MAI Negotiations Falter

Two years after the 1995 OECD ministerial meeting, the initial deadline for completion of the MAI came and went with no agreement in sight. The negotiators were granted a one-year extension, but at the end of that year the negotiations were still unfinished. A draft MAI had been written, but it was tentative and incomplete. Major substantive differences had developed among the negotiating parties, and their resolution was proving elusive. Yet ironically, thanks to the myriad exceptions that countries were lodging, this draft that was proving so contentious was becoming little more than a codification of existing law, policy, and practice among the negotiating countries. Moreover, some of the deepest disagreements were over provisions that had the potential not to liberalize investment policy but to move it in the opposite direction (these are discussed in chapter 2). Sadly, what had emerged after almost three years of MAI negotiations was a document that, despite its 200 pages, would have done little or nothing to change government policies that threatened to distort the flows and end uses of foreign investment.

Even more ironically, although the draft agreement thus did little more than codify the status quo, the MAI talks had become the focus of intense and emotional opposition outside the negotiating room. In particular, the MAI had become the *bête noire* of numerous nongovernmental organizations (NGOs) from around the world. Some of these groups were deeply worried about the agreement's potential impact on human rights, while others saw it as a profound threat to environmental protection and preservation. By late 1997, the OECD's Paris headquarters had become the site of frequent demonstrations and picketing by these groups.

Organized NGO opposition to the MAI began in Canada, when some of these groups became involved in a dispute with the government of Canada raised by the Ethyl Corporation, a US firm. The dispute was actually over a provision of NAFTA, not the MAI, but these NGOs soon concluded that the MAI posed a similar, and perhaps greater, menace. (The history and implications of this episode are discussed in chapter 2.) From that point opposition spread rapidly to the United States and Europe. During 1998, various NGOs created Web sites on the Internet to argue the case against the MAI. Anti-MAI rallies and demonstrations were organized in numerous locales. The movement grew to include at least 300 separate organizations. In late 1998, the largest grouping of US labor unions, the AFL-CIO, joined in opposing the MAI. Also in 1998, in what should have been seen as a foreshadowing of events to come, the city council of Seattle—host to the 1999 World Trade Organization (WTO) ministerial meeting—declared the city an "MAI-free zone."

The city council's action was more than a little ironic. For the NGOs' opposition to the MAI and the tactics they employed can be seen as a prologue to the activism these same groups displayed at the Seattle WTO ministerial. Their disruptive behavior ultimately proved embarrassing to the city, as the demonstrations flared out of control and the Seattle police used heavy-handed tactics to restore order.

It was largely through these demonstrations, combined with the natural affinity of the press for sensationalism, that the world at large was introduced to the cause of antiglobalism and the issue of international investment liberalization. But the Seattle protests were not the first of their kind. One year earlier in Paris and elsewhere, large numbers of activists had marched in the streets, shouting slogans and beating drums, in opposition to the MAI.

The phenomenon of large-scale, street-fighting opposition to a multilateral commercial agreement was something that the world had never seen before the anti-MAI demonstrations, and it poses an enigma. If, as argued above, the MAI was largely a status quo agreement that would have changed little if anything, why all the fuss? The short answer (the longer version deferred to chapters 3 and 5) is that, despite the fact that the MAI dog lacked teeth, some of the NGOs' grievances were legitimate. These included some of the issues they raised over the Ethyl Corporation case in Canada. But not all the NGOs' objections to the MAI were so well grounded: two in particular prove largely to be chimerical, as is argued in depth in chapters 2, 4, and 5.

One of these was the assertion that the MAI would intensify what some activists saw as a mass exodus of jobs from the industrial countries to the developing countries. This, of course, was a theme that Ross Perot had sounded in his 1992 run for the US presidency. The villain then was NAFTA, that great bunghole whose drainage of US jobs into Mexico would result in a "great sucking sound," in Perot's memorable phrase. Opponents of the MAI could not help but notice that the draft MAI incorporated many provisions similar to that of NAFTA's chapter 11, on investment. Thus, one rallying cry against the MAI was that the work in progress was a kind of "NAFTA on steroids."

Perot's focus, of course, was on the feared effects of NAFTA on US workers. But many of the anti-MAI activists were more concerned that the MAI, if it came into force, might hurt the interests of workers in developing countries as FDI flows to these countries increased. (This issue is examined in depth in chapter 4.) A frequently expressed concern was that multinational corporations would move to areas where labor standards were lax and where workers would be exploited. A parallel theme was that the MAI would enable large multinationals to transfer their particularly "dirty" operations to certain pollution havens—developing countries that lacked, or failed to adequately enforce, laws to protect the environment.

These criticisms of the MAI, unlike those surrounding the Ethyl case, can be dismissed with relative ease. The MAI was to have been, as noted at the outset, an agreement within the OECD, whose members are mostly industrial, not developing, countries.[8] It would not have been binding on nonmembers. It therefore would have done little or nothing to foster the transfer of jobs or of polluting activities by foreign investors to most developing countries. Concerns about net job loss in the industrial countries as a group, or about exploitation of workers in most developing countries, are therefore essentially a nonissue as far as the MAI was concerned.

Ironically in this light, the industrial countries seeking an MAI chose the OECD as the negotiating venue precisely in order to exclude the developing countries from the negotiating exercise. Why did they choose the OECD rather than, say, the World Trade Organization (WTO), where the developing countries would have had a role? Part of the reason was that OECD member countries alone account for by far the greater part of global stocks and flows of FDI, as well as of world GDP. However, a large and growing share of FDI flows in recent years has gone to developing countries that are not OECD members, mostly to a few large countries such as Brazil, China, and India. And FDI has been playing an increasingly significant role in these countries' development. Arguably, the greatest economic impact from liberalization of FDI policy would have come from exactly these countries.

In fact, the main reason for keeping these countries out of the MAI negotiations was the presumption that the OECD countries were "like-minded" on the subject of investment policy and already had in place relatively liberal investment policy regimes (see Lang 1998). It was thought that these countries, because they shared similar views on investment policy and similar policies, could quickly conclude a "high standards" agreement—that is, one in which relatively stringent rules would apply. In a negotiating forum such as the WTO, on the other hand, with its wider country representation, consensus would have been much more difficult to achieve, and any consensus would likely have been at a lower standard. In particular, the US and other OECD governments believed that a bloc of developing countries within the WTO would have prevented any high-standards agreement from ever coming into force.[9]

---

8. These less developed countries include Mexico, the Czech Republic, South Korea, and Turkey.

9. This perception may have been in error, however—a question taken up in chapter 6.

To be sure, had the MAI come into force, some developing countries might have joined it. Indeed, the draft agreement made provisions for non-OECD countries to accede to the agreement, and some had expressed an interest in doing so. Would the MAI's opponents' fears of massive job loss and rampant transfer of polluting activities to the developing world then have been realized? Probably not. The fact is that the agreement contained no provisions that would have significantly enhanced the ability of multinational firms to invest in developing countries. However, some developing nations might have been willing to sign on to the MAI and accept the obligations of doing so. Countries that indicated some interest in doing so did include Brazil (but only tentatively), Argentina and Chile (somewhat more strongly), Singapore (definitely, but Singapore has a higher per capita GNP than most OECD nations), and Hong Kong, if arrangements could have been made.

A second factor uniting opponents of the MAI was a perception that the agreement represented a major giveaway to big international business interests, at the expense of some of the opponents' own constituencies (such as organized labor). But if that is so, it is curious that the international business community did not trouble itself greatly to show its support of the MAI negotiations. The "corporate fat cats," as the antiglobalists called them, turned out to be another dog that did not bark.

The support of business interests has, in fact, been vital to the success of the multilateral trading system as a whole in the postwar era. In the mid-1990s, for example, business groups and associations worked hard to help bring the Uruguay Round of negotiations to a successful conclusion. They were also instrumental, in the United States, in securing the passage of NAFTA. These same business interests in the United States and other OECD member countries were, to be sure, generally supportive of the MAI negotiations. But rather than back the MAI wholeheartedly as they had the Uruguay Round and NAFTA, the business community tended to show indifference to the exercise once its limited scope became apparent. One international business executive told this author that the potential value of the MAI to his firm was positive, but too small to warrant much attention, precisely because it was largely a status quo agreement. But then the question becomes, Why did business groups not press harder for more aggressive provisions that would actually liberalize investment policy? This question is examined in chapter 2.

The Negotiations Fail

In the fall of 1998, faced with apparently irreconcilable disagreements among the negotiating parties and intense external opposition, the MAI negotiations came to an ignominious end. The momentum that was building for its speedy demise was perhaps best evidenced at a large rally held just outside the headquarters of the United Nations Conference on Trade and Development (UNCTAD) in Geneva in late September of that year. At the rally, in the presence of prominent rock bands and celebrity speakers, NGOs and other MAI opponents depicted the agreement as a monster that would impoverish workers in the developed and developing worlds alike. Their denunciations went largely unanswered.

Shortly thereafter, in mid-October, the government of France announced that it would no longer participate in the negotiations. Announcing the decision before the French National Assembly, Prime Minister Lionel Jospin cited irreconcilable differences between the French government and other negotiating parties (meaning mostly the United States) over a number of issues, most notably treatment of cultural industries.[10] However, the real reason for Jospin's decision seems to have been opposition to the whole idea of an MAI from within his rather fragile Socialist-Communist coalition government. This opposition came mainly from the far left and "green" factions of the coalition, with the strong backing of environmentally oriented NGOs and certain other constituencies.[11] The leftists and the greens (which in France, as elsewhere, overlap to a large degree) held common cause with NGOs worldwide that the MAI had the potential to do great harm to the environment, and that the agreement would make the interests of "international capital" sacrosanct.

The French pullout came at a time when the negotiations were already effectively in limbo. The talks were supposed to have been completed in time for the OECD ministers to sign the agreement at the OECD ministerial meeting scheduled for late May 1998. But the negotiations were still unfinished by the time of the meeting, forcing the OECD to announce, with some egg on its face, that the talks would necessarily have to continue into the fall. A six-month period of "reflection" was declared, during which time the negotiations were suspended, at the behest of the French government, to be restarted in October.

In fact, the negotiations had already suffered delays well before "la frappe de Jospin." They were originally due to be completed by the middle of 1997, at which time the OECD member countries would have had to decide individually whether to ratify the agreement.[12] However, this

---

10. A detailed explanation of French objections to the MAI is provided in Lalumière and Landau (1998).

11. One of these was the French copyright collective, which opposed the agreement on technical grounds, as explored in chapter 2.

12. Ratification procedures differ from country to country. In the United States, for example, the MAI might have been handled as a treaty or as an international trade agreement. In the first case, the president needed only the advice and consent of the Senate to make the agreement binding. An international trade agreement, on the other hand, would have required implementing legislation passed by the whole Congress. Obviously the US administration would have preferred the first option. But if the obligations of the agreement required changes in US law, the second option would have become a necessity.

deadline was not met, and at the OECD ministerial meeting held in May 1997 the negotiations were extended for another year. The reasons given for the delay were that, although there was consensus on the main provisions of the agreement, a considerable amount of detail remained to be worked out.[13]

When, a year later, the still unfinished negotiations were suspended until the last week of October, there was no repetition of the reassuring words about an imminent completion. Rather, by then it was clear to all that major unresolved differences separated the negotiating parties.

Less than two months after the French pullout, on 11 December 1998, an OECD deputy secretary general announced that, in effect, the negotiations would be terminated with no agreement in place or even in sight. It was stated that the problems encountered during the course of the negotiations had proved too numerous and intractable to allow a consensus to be reached.[14] Upon the announcement, representatives of NGOs camped out behind the OECD headquarters beat on drums.

An Economic Autopsy of the MAI

The remainder of this book is largely an autopsy of the failure of the MAI negotiations. The point of any autopsy is to determine why the victim died, and that is the subject of chapter 2. The question is framed as follows: Did the MAI die from internal causes (the inability of the negotiating parties to reach a consensus) or external ones (the opposition of NGOs and other constituencies)? In fact this question may have an easy answer: the dog died from both ailments, either one of which alone might have struck the fatal blow. But beyond this possible answer are some tough questions about the future of international policymaking in the investment arena. Therefore it is worth examining the details of this negotiation's failure, to inform future debate over what remains an important issue, namely, whether or not there should be multilateral rules on foreign investment.

Chapter 3 therefore goes on to examine the MAI itself in some detail. What is revealed is that the MAI contained some provisions that almost surely should be retained in any future agreement. In fact, the main failing of the MAI as drafted was not in what it would have done, but rather in what it would have failed to do.

Chapter 4 examines one set of arguments made by opponents of the MAI, namely, those pertaining to the effects of international investment on labor. As was noted earlier in this chapter, the MAI would not have applied to most developing countries. Yet most of the debate over the effects

---

13. See the OECD press release from the May 1997 meeting (OECD 1997).

14. Details are provided in chapter 4.

of FDI on labor has to do with developing countries. For this reason, and given that any future negotiation on investment will likely encompass these countries, the focus of chapter 4 is on the effects of direct investment on workers in developing and developed countries alike, when investment flows from the latter to the former.

Chapter 5 explores why a number of environmental groups also opposed the MAI. Environmentalists have raised some serious and important issues regarding globalization and world development. But they have often presented these issues in simplistic terms that ignore other compelling issues. Many of the world's people are desperately poor, and only economic growth can alleviate their misery. And in this international investment can play a positive and significant role. But, admittedly, growth puts additional stress on the natural environment. The "solution" proposed by many environmentalists to this problem comes down to advocacy of zero growth, but zero growth would leave much of the world in poverty. How then to trade off the need for poverty-alleviating growth with the need to prevent that growth from inflicting serious and irreparable environmental harm? This trade-off is, under the best of circumstances, highly difficult to resolve, but before it can be resolved it must be recognized. Many environmentalists, unfortunately, act as though no such trade-off exists.

Chapter 6 examines the interests of the developing countries themselves in multilateral rules on investment. What emerges from this analysis is that these countries themselves have not reached a consensus either as to whether such rules are in their interest, or, if they are, what those rules should actually be. However, it is clear that at least some developing countries would favor such rules, especially if they had the effect of drawing more direct investment into their economies.

Finally, chapter 7 looks at what might be the future of the trade and investment agenda at the WTO in light of the failure of the MAI and, more recently, the "battle in Seattle." Although the MAI itself is dead, this agenda is still alive, if not necessarily well. Where, if anywhere, it goes from here is still an open issue. This volume's main conclusion is that, given the current political opposition to a comprehensive agreement on investment, there is little hope that such an agreement can be struck at this time. Under these circumstances it might be better for negotiators in the investment area to focus their energy on, in effect, finishing the business that was left unfinished at the conclusion of the Uruguay Round. This outstanding business, which became part of the "built-in agenda" of the WTO, encompasses some of the same issues that the MAI would have covered, especially with respect to the General Agreement on Trade in Services (GATS).

In the meantime, as we have seen, FDI has burgeoned even in the absence of an investment agreement. This fact alone might seem to call into question the supposed benefits of a multilateral investment agreement in the OECD, the WTO, or elsewhere. To the extent that these benefits derive merely from the increase in investment flows, an investment agreement might be unnecessary, given that flows are expanding even without an agreement. But to the extent that realizing these benefits requires correcting the distortions that government policies create in investors' behavior, the case for an agreement may well remain valid. Either way, what seems to be called for is an effort to quantify the magnitudes and the distribution of the benefits (and the costs) associated with increased flows of FDI and the activities that accompany it. Without this analysis, the debate over whether multilateral investment rules are needed and, if so, what priorities they should address, is greatly hampered. The first order of business, therefore, should be to do the preparatory analytical work—work that in fact should have preceded the MAI negotiations themselves.

Indeed, only once this task of identifying the benefits of a multilateral investment agreement is complete should nations attempt to decide whether there now should be such an agreement. One of the very real problems that beset the MAI negotiations was that the negotiators had very little idea of what were the gains that might come from the exercise and, of the many subissues addressed by the negotiations, which of these, if addressed, had the potential to bring about the greatest gains. And, when opposition to the agreement materialized, the negotiators had no answer to allegations that the agreement had the potential to bring about harm. As will be demonstrated in the chapters that follow, many—but not all—of these allegations were in fact without much merit. But the negotiators were unable to present facts and analysis that might have allayed the fears of the opponents or, barring this, at least to demonstrate that the opponents were in fact on thin ice and that the potential benefits of an agreement outweighed the likely costs. In the future, negotiators can (and, indeed, will simply have to) do much better than they did in this exercise. This is a matter to which we return in the final chapter but, first, in the next five chapters, we examine the facts such as they can be established.

2

The MAI and the Politics of Failure: Who Killed the Dog?

Why did the MAI negotiations fail? This chapter explores two competing hypotheses. The first attributes their failure mainly to fundamental, substantive differences among the negotiating parties themselves that, in the end, proved irreconcilable. The second is that parties outside the negotiations (primarily a coalition of NGOs) were able to bring sufficient pressure to bear on certain of the negotiating parties to cause the negotiations to be terminated without conclusion. The first, "internal" hypothesis suggests that the MAI negotiations were doomed from the beginning. The second, "external" hypothesis implies, to the contrary, that the NGOs (and other opponents of globalization) were successful in derailing a train that otherwise would have reached its destination, albeit not without some long uphill climbs.

As noted in chapter 1, however, the two hypotheses are not that easily separable. Both internal and external factors clearly played major roles in the negotiations' failure, making it difficult to identify either as the fatal instrument. Certainly the negotiations were in deep difficulty well before the NGOs came on the scene. It is difficult to judge whether, if the external actors had never entered the picture, the internal differences were so deep and difficult as to put the negotiations on a one-way street to failure. Further complicating this issue, the business community—a constituency that supported the MAI effort—did not attempt to mount a serious countervailing effort to salvage the MAI once the NGOs did come on the scene. Had business leaders in the various OECD nations spoken out more loudly in favor of completing the negotiation, the outcome might have been different. But the fact is that the business community in all OECD nations was largely silent on the issue. This poses a serious issue. Many of the groups protesting the MAI believed that it would create new and unprecedented benefits for business—benefits that would come at the expense of the ordinary person. Either these groups seriously overestimated the potential of the MAI to do this (the position generally taken here) or the business community seriously underestimated the potential value of the MAI to their own interests.

These are not trivial issues, nor are they of interest only to historians of the negotiations. The NGOs have loudly claimed credit for bringing the MAI down, and a widely held perception that this indeed was the case helped fuel the spirited protests at the WTO meeting one year later, and again at the World Bank and International Monetary Fund meetings in April 2000. In the eyes of many, the NGOs' sacking of the MAI established them collectively as a power to be reckoned with in the international economic arena. If instead the MAI's demise was due to internal problems within the talks themselves, or to a failure of the business community to recognize its own stake in these negotiations and to act accordingly, the NGOs' perceived increased clout is based on a false premise.

Furthermore, if the MAI failed primarily because consensus on certain key issues was irretrievably beyond the negotiating parties' reach, that is something that any future negotiations on multilateral rules on investment must take into account, for the same difficulties are sure to reappear. If, on the other hand, the MAI failed primarily because the NGOs were able to make their weight felt, the implications for the future agenda are quite different.

Alas, when all is said and done, a definitive determination of the counterfactual—of whether, without the NGOs' active opposition, the MAI might have been salvageable—is probably impossible. True, the internal differences among the negotiating parties ran very deep, but profound differences have marked other multilateral negotiations (including the Uruguay Round) and yet were ultimately resolved. Thus, one might compare the MAI in its last few months to a ship that is taking on water and is in distress but has not yet foundered. The NGOs' torpedoes, in this analogy, sealed the ship's doom, but one will likely never know whether, were it not for the torpedoes, the ship might have eventually reached a safe harbor. Although it is not easy to provide a definitive explanation of why the MAI negotiations failed, it nonetheless is worthwhile to explore some of the factors behind the failure. What is argued here is that the preponderance of the evidence supports the case that the negotiations were indeed in very deep difficulty before the metaphorical torpedo was fired by the NGOs and that this torpedo thus was more a coup de grâce than a fatal blow in its own right. The "deep difficulty" arose from both internal problems among the negotiating parties, including a fundamental flaw in the way the negotiations were structured and lack of full support from the very constituency that they were intended to benefit, notably the business community.

What were some of the internal factors that contributed to sinking the MAI? Perhaps an important one is the fact that, to a very large extent, the impetus for the negotiations came not from the top leadership of the participating governments, but rather from their permanent bureaucracies. Most of the persons involved in the preparations for the talks were fairly junior and lacked experience with multilateral negotiations. Many were investment specialists in various ministries, with some experience in negotiating bilateral investment treaties or in working with the OECD Committee on International Investment and Multinational Enterprise. Often these specialists did not have easy access to higher-level officials inside their own governments.

By contrast, the impetus for most other multilateral economic negotiations of significance during the post-World War II era has come from the top political leaders of the countries involved. Indeed, in recent years the main impetus to multilateral trade negotiations has most often come from the political leaders of the United States. For example, both the Uruguay Round and the negotiations toward the North American Free Trade Agreement (NAFTA) were initiated under strong US leadership that derived ultimately from the commitment of the US president then in office. Well before the 1985 meeting of trade ministers that launched the Uruguay Round, President Ronald Reagan had consistently stated (including in his State of the Union addresses before Congress) that entering into such negotiations was a US priority. His successor George Bush did much the same in promoting NAFTA. Joining in this commitment were the political leaders of other countries, especially the European countries in the case of the Uruguay Round and Mexico in the case of NAFTA. The permanent professional staffs of their bureaucracies certainly played a major role both in defining the issues to be covered, and later in conducting the actual negotiations. But these bureaucrats operated under a mandate that came from the highest political levels of government.

In the case of the MAI, however, the political leaders of most participating countries played little if any part in launching the negotiations and gave them at most a somewhat distant blessing once they had begun. It is not clear that President Bill Clinton, for example, actively participated in the preparation for these negotiations.

This lack of commitment and participation on the part of top political leaders may have been critical to the outcome of the MAI negotiations. Their lack of involvement meant that, once it became apparent that issues were being raised over which the negotiating parties were in deep disagreement, the negotiators were unable to pass these issues upstairs to be resolved at the political level. Yet at the same time, no one at the negotiating table had authority to change the position of the government that he or she represented.

The fact that the MAI negotiations were conducted in relative obscurity by relatively low level bureaucrats led to another nagging problem: it laid the process open to the accusation that the negotiations were being held in secret. This charge was never quite true, as this chapter will document. The negotiations were indeed conducted out of the spotlight, but they were not held in the dark. It is also true that details of official negotiations are seldom made public (strategic leaks by one side or the other notwithstanding) until after the disagreements have been resolved, for the obvious reason that the publicity itself could hamper resolution. Nevertheless, the label of secrecy was one that the MAI's opponents made stick.

Much the same line of argumentation—that serious conflicts among governments can only be worked out at the highest levels—might be made about working-level officials involved in other negotiations that ultimately succeeded. For example, it is common practice to require official negotiators to advocate and hold to their government's preestablished position; they are not empowered to change that position. Where the positions of the various parties are reconcilable, these officials may be able on their own to achieve an outcome acceptable to all. But in any negotiation it may turn out that the parties' initial positions are not reconcilable. In both the Uruguay Round and the NAFTA negotiations, major disagreements led at some point to negotiating deadlock. Indeed, the Uruguay Round nearly foundered on several occasions because of such deadlocks, for example over agriculture. But in all these cases the deadlock was eventually broken by top political leaders determined to achieve the overall negotiating objective. Breaking the impasses required compromises whereby some of the negotiating parties had to change their positions, something that could be accomplished only at the highest political levels. By contrast, in the case of the MAI, when major disagreements became apparent, negotiators were unable to take the disputes upstairs for possible resolution. The top leaders simply were not engaged in the process.

The appearance of secrecy was also a consequence of the MAI being initiated at the bureaucratic rather than the political level. The discussions among government officials that led to the decision to start the negotiations were not publicly reported, as any decision made at the top surely would have been. Indeed, in the United States, where processes exist by which constituencies having an interest in multilateral economic issues can let their views be known to US negotiators (e.g., through the Advisory Committee on Trade Policy Negotiations of the US Trade Representative), few such constituencies even knew that the MAI negotiations were in the offing. Thus, when the launch of the negotiations was announced at the 1995 OECD ministerial meeting, there had been no public debate in the United States (or anywhere else) on the merits of entering into such an agreement. In contrast, for several years before the formal launch of the Uruguay Round in 1985, the pros and cons of a new round of trade talks were presented and debated at conferences and meetings throughout the

United States and other countries. Input was received from constituencies that would be affected by any agreement reached in the round, and in the end some of these constituencies (especially the US business community) were instrumental in ensuring that the US Congress ratified the final agreement.

Even the US business community was little informed of the negotiations at the OECD. One consequence was that this community subsequently did relatively little to support the effort. From the beginning, therefore, the MAI negotiations took place without the strong backing even of the constituency that presumably had the most to gain from their successful conclusion. In contrast, as detailed later in this chapter, by the time the negotiations had produced a draft text, constituencies opposed to the MAI had coalesced and organized themselves into a formidable force.

Perhaps an even more important contrast between the MAI and earlier negotiations is in the role played by the US Congress. In both the Uruguay Round and NAFTA, key members of Congress were involved in the decision by the US government to seek negotiations as well as in the negotiations themselves (from the sidelines, of course). This is of special importance because, under the US Constitution, the Congress, and not the executive branch, is ultimately in charge of policy pertaining to foreign commerce.

Although neither members of Congress nor their staffs negotiate international trade agreements on behalf of the US government, Congress must ratify the outcome of any such negotiation before it becomes binding. Since the early 1930s, Congress has delegated the negotiating function to the executive branch under various laws, but always on the condition that any change in US law necessitated by a new agreement be voted on by the Congress. Under the fast-track procedures whereby trade-negotiating authority was delegated to the executive branch during both the Uruguay Round and the earlier Tokyo Round of multilateral trade negotiations, key members of Congress were informed and consulted about the negotiations as they progressed.[1] Similar procedures were followed with respect to the NAFTA negotiations.

By contrast, officials in the executive branch established no process for consultation with Congress on the desirability of MAI negotiations before the negotiations got under way. Indeed, Congress was not even informed on the matter prior to the OECD ministerial declaration of 1995 (and even then, members of Congress or their staffs would have had to read the declaration itself to know that negotiations were about to begin). A number of legislators first learned of the negotiations from NGOs or other constituencies staunchly opposed to the MAI, and this tactical blunder was to haunt the US negotiators in the years that followed.

---

1. See Destler (1997a) for a description and analysis of the interactions between the executive branch and Congress during the negotiation of the Uruguay Round.

Although the muteness of the US Executive Branch (and of other OECD governments) led to charges of secrecy, these charges were not completely well founded. Certain nongovernmental advisory groups to the OECD were apprised of the discussions being held within the organization that led to the launch of the negotiations, and these groups continued to be kept well informed during the negotiations themselves. One of these groups, the Business-Industry Advisory Committee, represented business interests, and another, the Trade Union Advisory Committee, represented labor. Thus, although members of the US Congress were not directly informed through official channels about the start of negotiations, their relevant major constituencies, the US business and labor communities, were informed, at least in principle.[2] (Whether the two groups themselves were effective in informing their own memberships is another matter.) Also, the OECD Secretariat occasionally released statements regarding the MAI negotiations once they were under way. Thus, although the actual negotiating sessions were closed to the public (as are most intergovernmental meetings), they certainly were not held in secret. Rather, they simply remained rather obscure, or at least were so at the outset.

How did the negotiations come about at all? We turn to this issue next.

The MAI Is Conceived

Formal authorization to begin negotiating the MAI within the auspices of the OECD was provided, as already noted, by the OECD ministerial declaration of May 1995. Part of the background to this event, however, was the OECD's failure, four years earlier, to achieve a much less ambitious agreement pertaining to investment. This earlier effort would have created a binding National Treatment Instrument (NTI) that would have obliged each OECD member government to grant national treatment to the investors and investments of any other OECD country.[3] (A nonbinding version of this instrument was already in place.) The NTI negotiations were the responsibility of the OECD Committee on International Investment and Multinational Enterprise (CIIME), which meets on a regular basis. The US delegation to this committee is chaired by a deputy assistant secretary of state; in addition to this and other State Department officials, members of the professional staffs of the US Treasury and Commerce Departments often attend CIIME meetings.

The failure of the NTI talks resulted, in part at least, from an insistence by some European governments that a binding instrument cover law and

---

2. "We may not have told you, but we did tell your constituents" is not likely to be seen by congressmen as a defense—rather the opposite.

3. As noted in chapter 1, under a national treatment standard, a government must grant, in its laws and policies, treatment to foreign investors that is no less favorable than that granted to equivalent domestic investors. Chapter 3 provides a more detailed description.

policy at the level of subnational (provincial, state, and local) governments as well as that of national governments. The US representatives to the CIIME balked at this, because any agreement binding state governments would require legislation by Congress. The US delegation also anticipated that members of Congress would view such a binding of the states as a concession to the other governments at the table and would demand offsetting concessions from those governments. A more comprehensive agreement that included concessions that furthered US interests might be more palatable to Congress. In particular, the NTI would have granted national treatment to foreign investments on only a postestablishment basis, thus permitting certain countries to continue to screen (and perhaps block) new investment.[4] US officials believed that an instrument that granted, inter alia, preestablishment national treatment to foreign investors would be seen by Congress as in US interests.

Another factor that figured in the failure of the NTI talks was the insistence of some OECD countries that the agreement not cover "cultural" industries. This term loosely encompasses a group of activities that includes the publishing and motion picture industries and others whose output is regarded as an expression of national or regional culture. This complex issue was to surface again during the MAI negotiations themselves and is discussed later in this chapter.

Following the failure of the NTI discussions, the CIIME held a series of meetings to explore what might be a feasible and desirable agenda for the OECD (or other multilateral institutions) in the area of international investment. In the course of these meetings, European governments indicated a willingness to negotiate what was initially termed a "wider investment instrument," meaning one that went beyond the provisions of the NTI. Investors, mostly multinational firms, from a number of European countries had come to hold significant investments in the United States. Hence the immediate interest of most of these countries was to enter into an agreement with the United States that would grant national treatment at the state as well as the national level to these investments. However, during the discussions that ensued, officials from the US government agreed with their counterparts from individual European countries that the negotiations could usefully be extended to cover still other issues. Thus a consensus was reached to include, as issues for negotiation, such items as enterprise-to-state dispute settlement procedures, provisions for investor protection, limits on state interventions in the form of performance requirements and investment incentives going beyond existing disciplines in the WTO rules, and a number of other issues.

---

4. In fact, only two OECD nations, Canada and France, then had laws in place that allowed their governments to screen inward foreign investment. In practice, neither country used this authority routinely. Moreover, the United States itself had in place a law (the 1988 Exon-Florio amendment) that allowed the federal government to block acquisitions of US firms by foreign investors if it found that the acquisition would adversely affect national security.

How could the OECD expect to succeed in negotiating a wide investment agreement when it had just failed to conclude a narrow one encompassing some of the same issues? The reasoning of the CIIME, and of the US delegation to the CIIME, was that a wide instrument would have more to offer a broad range of constituencies than would a narrow one. Some of these constituencies might be willing to accept some provisions that they did not like in order to gain other provisions, in areas beyond the original scope of the talks, that they did like. This approach—of conducting negotiations across a broad range of issues so as to give each of a range of different constituencies something they liked—has in fact characterized all the major rounds of multilateral trade negotiations during the post–World War II era. But such an approach involves a considerable amount of give-and-take, and it implies that each negotiating party actually is empowered to "give." This in turn requires the engagement of the highest political officials, including those in the legislature. Thus, right from their inception, the MAI talks suffered from a potentially fatal flaw: their success would likely depend on a willingness to trade concessions across different domains, but the negotiators had no power to make such broad concessions and lacked access to more senior officials who did.

Some of the issues to be taken up in the wider investment instrument were in fact already covered in existing OECD instruments. In addition to the nonbinding NTI, there existed an OECD Code of Liberalization of Current Invisible Transactions[5] and a Code of Liberalization of Capital Movements. The feeling in the CIIME was that the new instrument would serve to modernize these existing instruments and perhaps to supersede them.

The preliminary discussions within the CIIME over the wider investment instrument took place over a period of about three years. Serious disagreements over some issues persisted (e.g., over the proposed exception for cultural industries) and, in fact, nearly derailed the consensus to begin the actual negotiations. Another disagreement that emerged was over whether the negotiations should take place at the OECD or in some other venue; this issue is discussed below. Despite these unresolved disagreements, some governments wanted to announce the onset of negotiations at the OECD ministerial meeting of 1994. However, lack of a full consensus forced a delay until the meeting of 1995.

When consensus was finally reached, it was agreed that "wider investment instrument" was not a proper sounding name for the anticipated end product of the talks. Thus the new, more ambitious agreement was at first dubbed the "Multilateral Investment Agreement." This name was hastily changed, however, at the request of the US government when wags pointed out that it abbreviated to MIA, commonly read within the

---

5. These are the nontrade components of the current account and consist mostly of interest payments and earnings on direct investment.

United States as "missing in action." Alas, as noted in chapter 1, the new name, "Multilateral Agreement on Investment," when written in French, would be abbreviated as AMI, the French word for "friend." (And in Italian, prophetically enough, "mai" means "never.") Later the opponents of the MAI in French-speaking countries would have a field day with this acronym, proclaiming that "With a 'friend' like this, you don't need any enemies." Perhaps a multilingual specialist in anagrams should have been consulted.

The 1995 OECD ministerial declaration (OECD 1995) specifically called for the following:

> The immediate start of negotiations . . . aimed at reaching a Multilateral Agreement on Investment by the Ministerial Meeting of 1997, which would:
> - provide a broad multilateral framework for international investment with high standards for the liberalisation of investment regimes and investment protection with effective dispute settlement procedures; [and]
> - be a free-standing international treaty open to all OECD Members and the European Communities, and to accession by non-OECD Member countries, which will be consulted as the negotiations progress.

These two negotiating guidelines reflected some differences in opinion with respect to the choice of the OECD as negotiating venue, as noted earlier. Officials of some OECD countries (and, especially, the Commission of the European Communities) had, in the preliminary discussions, indicated a preference for the World Trade Organization (WTO) over the OECD as the negotiating venue.

This preference was based on two grounds. First, some of the substantive issues that the MAI negotiations might cover intersected with the coverage of existing WTO instruments, especially the Agreement on Trade-Related Investment Measures (TRIMs) and the General Agreement on Trade in Services (GATS).[6] Second, the WTO's membership is much broader than that of the OECD. A number of countries in which international investment figures importantly are not OECD members but are WTO members (or, in some cases, candidates for WTO membership). Thus an agreement struck in the WTO would apply to more countries, including some to which such an agreement would be highly relevant, than an agreement struck in the OECD.

This second matter, however, was seen to cut in two directions. On one hand, it was seen as desirable to include as many countries as possible in the negotiations. On the other hand, it was believed that, within the WTO membership, some countries were unprepared to commit to the obligations envisaged under the MAI and might seek to block progress toward any agreement that imposed stringent standards on governments. This

---

6. Graham (1996) discusses in detail the issue of the negotiating venue for a multilateral agreement on investment and concludes that the WTO would be the optimal venue. On the overlap between MAI issues and existing WTO instruments see Sauvé (1997).

belief was perhaps most strongly held by officials of the US government (perhaps wrongly so; see chapter 5). At least some US business constituencies that backed the idea of an investment agreement shared this view.

Thus the US government and most other OECD governments felt that the way to a successful negotiation of a worldwide "high standards" agreement would be to first secure agreement among the like-minded nations of the OECD. Only after this had been accomplished would participation be offered to any other country willing to accept these standards. The clear expectation was that such an agreement would be relatively easy to achieve, and the negotiators' deadline reflected this expectation: the finished product was to be presented for approval at the OECD ministerial meeting scheduled for May 1997, only two years after the ministerial declaration launching the talks. Because the first full meeting of the negotiating group was not scheduled until September 1995, almost four months after the declaration was issued, the negotiating parties had only about 20 months to negotiate and conclude a major multilateral agreement.

The issue of venue in fact did not disappear even after the 1995 ministerial declaration. The European Commission continued to press for investment-related work to begin within the WTO, although it stressed that this work would be of an informal nature rather than a formal negotiation. However, following the January 1996 meeting of the MAI negotiating group at the OECD, the European members of the organization reaffirmed their commitment to the MAI process as the primary means by which a multilateral investment agreement would be achieved.

Even so, behind this commitment lay a certain amount of internal discord within Europe as well as dissension between the European Union and the United States. The European Commission, which does not have full authority over investment issues in the European Union, had in fact sought authority from its member countries to pursue a larger effort within the WTO, where the Commission, rather than the EU member governments, would sit at the negotiating table.[7] It was in the wake of these efforts by the Commission that the US government called upon the European national governments to reaffirm their commitment to the OECD negotiations.

In the end, a rather shaky consensus was reached between the European Union and the United States that the only mandate for actual negotiation on investment would reside in the OECD. However, it was also agreed that a WTO working group could be constituted that would, on a largely informal basis, lay the groundwork for future activity in the investment area in the WTO. Thus, at the December 1996 ministerial meeting of the WTO, a working group on trade and investment was established within

---

7. Although at the WTO the Commission leads the negotiations on behalf of the EU member countries, representatives of all the EU countries also monitor the proceedings.

the WTO. Subsequently, however, the work of the WTO group was effectively put on ice pending the outcome of the OECD negotiations.[8]

The first sign that the MAI was in serious trouble came at the OECD ministerial meeting of 1997, where it was announced that the MAI had not been completed on time and that a one-year extension was being granted. The ministerial declaration implied that the reason for the delay was that technical details of the agreement remained unfinished. There was no hint of major disagreement among the negotiating parties. But, in fact, time was being bought to resolve, if possible, some deep differences that had emerged.

Deep Internal Difficulties Emerge

The failure to complete the MAI negotiations by May 1997 was, of course, not due to technical details. During the negotiating sessions, major disagreements had emerged. As already noted, the negotiators could not resolve these disagreements on their own authority but lacked a mechanism by which to force these decisions to a higher political level. A more fundamental problem was that, with or without this mechanism, each of the major negotiating parties seems to have approached the exercise solely as a means to get other countries to give up laws or policies that discriminated against its own investors. In other words, if any large negotiation is a matter of give-and-take, the MAI negotiating parties seemed, almost from the beginning, prepared only to take, and to give nothing of substance in return. Each party took the position that its own policies and practices were either trivial in their discriminatory effect or justified on grounds that could not be altered. In other words, each party behaved as though an agreement could be struck that would leave its own policies and practices largely unaltered, if only the other parties could be made to see the errors of their demands or the need to change their own policies.

Even this would not have been a problem had all parties accepted that the relevant laws, policies, and practices of all other parties were in fact already consistent with the standards to be set by the new agreement. In that event, the MAI would have been nothing more than an exercise in codifying this existing law, policy, and practice, but at least such an agreement could serve as a starting point for real liberalization. To a great extent, the negotiating parties were willing to accept this outcome. They were prepared to negotiate an MAI that might have contained strong

---

8. However, speaking before the European Parliament following the withdrawal of France from the MAI negotiations in October 1998, EU Trade Commissioner Sir Leon Brittan noted that "I have always taken the view that the WTO is the best long-term home for this work for which the MAI has already provided valuable signposts." Sir Leon's perspective on this matter is of note because he is perhaps the highest-level official to have been actively and continuously involved in consideration of the issues surrounding the MAI.

obligations, but ones that were subject to such long lists of exceptions that nothing would really change (see chapter 3). It quickly became clear, however, that not all parties indeed did accept that nothing in the law, policy, and practice of other parties needed to change. Although the status quo was acceptable as a matter of consensus for most aspects of law and policy, on a subset of issues there were demands for change.

Nowhere was the perception stronger that the MAI could be achieved with little significant change in domestic law or policy than in the US delegation. Coming into the negotiations, the US negotiators apparently felt secure that US federal policies toward foreign investment were sufficiently liberal and nondiscriminatory that no other OECD members would see the need for significant change. The only major concession they believed they might have to make was to bind the US states to the national treatment and other provisions of the MAI. The US negotiators would quickly learn, however, that this was simply not the case. But as previously indicated, they were little prepared (and in fact unable) to negotiate anything that would require a change of US law or policy.[9]

The US negotiating position was also shaped by US experience in the negotiation of bilateral investment treaties (which had also shaped the US position in negotiating the investment chapter of NAFTA). In these treaties, the United States had demanded that US investors and their investments be given not simply nondiscriminatory treatment, but treatment that was "no less favorable" than that granted either to domestic investors or to foreign investors from other countries in similar circumstances. In practice, this amounted in some cases to treatment better than that accorded to domestic investors. Although such demands might make some sense in the context of a bilateral treaty with a country that pursued policies hostile to any type of private investment, they did not make sense in the context of a multilateral treaty. (A *reductio ad absurdum* outcome might be that investors everywhere would set up foreign subsidiaries to invest in their home countries, in order to receive the more favorable treatment accorded to foreign than to domestic investors.)[10] Arguably, the quest by the United States for language that might force a country to give foreign in-

---

9. There were a few relatively minor areas where US negotiators felt that the United States might be able to offer some liberalization of its policy. For example, it was hoped that Congress might be willing to repeal section 310(b) of the Communications Act of 1934 that effectively limited entry of foreign telecommunications services providers into the US market. But in the major piece of telecommunications legislation passed during the negotiations—the Telecommunications Act of 1996—Congress failed to do so. (Sidak 1997 provides comprehensive analyses of both laws and how they relate to foreign investment in US telecommunications.) Likewise, there was some hope that the United States might be able to offer some liberalization of restrictions on foreign participation in US research and development consortia.

10. There are cases where this has actually happened. For example, during the early and mid-1990s a number of Chinese firms—and even some state-owned enterprises—established subsidiaries in Hong Kong to invest in the mainland, to take advantage of preferences granted in the mainland to foreign investors.

vestors preferential treatment over domestic investors led to the MAI's language on expropriation that aroused the wrath of the environmental NGOs, as discussed below.

For their part, the European delegations also sought changes in US policy. An early example came in the area of taxation. In August 1995 the European-American Chamber of Commerce issued a report claiming that EU-owned firms operating in the United States faced more stringent auditing by US tax authorities than did US-owned firms in the same industries.[11] Had this been proved true, it could be argued that European-owned firms were receiving treatment less favorable than that accorded to their US-owned counterparts, contrary to the principle of national treatment. In one survey, 42 percent of European-owned firms indicated that US federal tax policies treated them differently from US-owned firms—this was a minority of respondents, to be sure, but an uncomfortably large one. The European Commission subsequently pushed for the inclusion of tax issues in the MAI, and at the meetings of the MAI negotiating group on 25-26 January 1996, an expert group was created to determine what tax-related issues should be included in the prospective agreement. However, a US government spokesperson indicated shortly thereafter that the United States "tends to be skeptical" about this issue, because it believes that tax treaties negotiated under OECD standards have worked well.[12] In the end, the MAI draft text contained very little relating to tax issues (see chapter 3).[13]

Allegedly discriminatory tax treatment of foreign-owned firms by the United States was, however, soon to become a relatively minor issue. On

---

11. See "Study Says EU-Owned Firms Face Tougher Tax Reviews in US," *Inside US Trade,* 25 August 1995. As the article noted, the assertion that foreign-owned companies faced tougher auditing by the Internal Revenue Service than domestically owned firms appears to be supported by a report to the Senate Finance Committee by the US General Accounting Office (GAO). The GAO found that, between 1990 and 1993, audits of foreign-owned firms increased 353 percent, whereas audits of domestically owned firms *decreased* 31 percent. This change in auditing practices came in the wake of accusations that foreign-owned firms in the United States had been avoiding US taxation through transfer price manipulation and other means; low tax payments by these firms in fact had been an issue in the 1992 US presidential campaign. For details, see Graham and Krugman (1995).

12. "OECD Investment Negotiators Form Group to Examine Tax Issues," *Inside US Trade,* 2 February 1986.

13. Intra-European differences also came into play on the tax issue. The European Commission has long sought greater authority over tax policy, with the ultimate objective of harmonizing tax policy within the European Union, something resisted by a number of EU member states. The Commission, according to officials interviewed by this author, saw the MAI negotiations as one means to advance this agenda. Some European countries were willing, in effect, to side with the United States to keep taxation largely out of the MAI. However, their willingness was not for substantive reasons—these countries were just as concerned about discriminatory US tax audits as was the Commission—rather they did not want to grant any additional authority to the Commission in this area, even implicitly.

12 March 1996, President Clinton signed into law the Cuban Liberty and Democratic Solidarity (Libertad) Act, better known as the Helms-Burton Act. Among other things, this law was designed to enable US nationals with claims to property expropriated by Cuba to bring suit in US courts against parties (including non-US-owned corporations) who "traffic" in such property. The law, intended to benefit the Cuban-American community, applied to any person of US nationality at the time the law entered into force, even if the expropriation had occurred before that person became a US national. Such a retroactive definition of expropriation is contrary to normal international standards. Normally, for such a seizure to be considered an expropriation under international law, the person who owns the seized property must be a national of a country other than the one whose government carries out the seizure, at the time the seizure takes place. The Helms-Burton law also allowed the denial of visas or entry into the United States of non-US persons (and their spouses and children) who traffic in such property.

The Clinton administration had opposed these provisions in the Helms-Burton Act until the Cuban government shot down an airplane registered in the United States from which Cuban-Americans based in Miami were distributing anti-Castro leaflets. The president signed the law, according to a statement issued to the OECD negotiating group by the US delegation, because he "recognized the need to take strong measures [after the airplane had been shot down]." The statement also noted that "the Government of Cuba's illegal shooting down of the aircraft greatly increased the bipartisan sentiment on Congress to pass this tough legislation."[14]

Mitigating somewhat the impact of the law was a provision that allowed the president to suspend the ability of US nationals to pursue lawsuits under the law. This the president did immediately upon the law's enactment. Also, the Secretary of State could waive the visa and entry restrictions for any of a number of reasons.

Reaction to the Helms-Burton Act was nonetheless rapid and severe. Already at a meeting of the MAI negotiating group on 14 March 1996—two days after President Clinton signed the measure into law—concerns were expressed about the law's compatibility with the proposed obligations the United States would undertake by signing the MAI. At this meeting the Canadian delegation announced that it would, at future meetings, introduce proposals to limit the extraterritorial application of national laws and to discipline "secondary boycotts." These proposals were clearly aimed at Helms-Burton. In addition, Canada suggested that it would propose disciplines to narrow the use of national security exemptions that might appear in the final MAI and to make any use of these exemptions subject to the agreement's dispute settlement procedures.

---

14. The text of the statement is reproduced in *Inside US Trade*, 26 March 1996.

Other national delegations expressed discomfiture with the Helms-Burton Act, leading the US delegation to issue its explanatory statement.

In fact, Canada's position on Helms-Burton reflected long-standing hostility on its part and that of other OECD countries to the propensity of the United States to assert extraterritorial jurisdiction with respect to its own law and policy. Almost all foreign countries, including such close allies of the United States as the United Kingdom, have objected to these assertions. These objections have often been voiced even when the affected countries were sympathetic to American objectives. The same was true in the case of Helms-Burton: citizens of a number of OECD countries have been victims of similar expropriations. The means of attaining the objective, however, were seen in this case as entirely objectionable.

Passage of the Helms-Burton Act placed a large cloud over the MAI negotiations that, according to some negotiators interviewed by this author, never fully dissipated. One very senior official from a European country, who played a major role in the negotiations, spoke to this author about Helms-Burton on condition of anonymity. According to this official, many delegations felt that the law was highly contrary to the spirit of the MAI, and that if the law were to stand as an accepted exception to MAI obligations, the agreement would be shown to be effectively toothless.[15] Sentiment against Helms-Burton was heightened by the fact that it had been passed by the United States—the same country that had led the early efforts to negotiate the MAI. Also, the United States had insisted upon the OECD as the negotiating venue because it was felt that an OECD negotiation promised an outcome embodying the highest possible standards. Helms-Burton seemed to many countries to fall far short of those standards.

Most delegations, according to this official, thus agreed with the position that the Canadian government took against the United States. In their view, the United States, "the leading proponent for an investment agreement with the highest possible standards, has taken actions, and has incorporated into its law further measures that strike at the very core of these negotiations."[16] The feeling was strong that, by insisting that the MAI would have to adapt to US law rather than the other way around, the United States was behaving hypocritically, because Helms-Burton was seen as highly discriminatory.

---

15. At the same time, this official acknowledged that Helms-Burton struck at a very real problem, namely, what to do when property that had been expropriated without compensation or due process of law was offered for sale to international investors. The objection to Helms-Burton was not that it addressed this problem, but rather that it did so in a manner that was unilateral and, in the eyes of non-Americans, discriminatory. For example, a US national, acting under the law, could sue a European company that bought property in Cuba that had been expropriated from that American. However, a European could not, under this law, sue an American who had bought property expropriated from the European in, say, one of the former Soviet bloc countries.

16. Quoted in *Inside US Trade*, 15 March 1996.

Acrimony between the United States and other OECD nations over Helms-Burton only increased in the months following the law's passage, culminating in a threat by the European Union to file a complaint that the law was inconsistent with US obligations under the agreements of the WTO. During the summer of 1996, US Under Secretary of Commerce Stuart Eizenstat was named Special Representative for the Promotion of Democracy in Cuba to try to work out the difficulties created between the United States and other countries by the provisions of Helms-Burton. In November of that year, over US objections, the WTO established a panel to hear the European Union's complaint against the United States. There followed an exchange of rather unusually strong language between the US government and the European Commission. Under Secretary Eizenstat expressed concerns that pursuit of the WTO case "should this result in a WTO panel attempting to define what are US national security interests—would strengthen the hand of those members of Congress who questioned whether the United States should even be a WTO member." EU Commissioner in charge of international trade Sir Leon Brittan responded that "it must not be possible for one country to evade [the WTO dispute procedures] simply by proclaiming that its national security is involved, however far-fetched such a claim might be."[17]

Subsequently, however, after the US government expressed a willingness to enter into direct talks with the European Commission on Helms-Burton, the European Union agreed to suspend its WTO complaint. On 11 April 1997, the Commission and the US government jointly announced an agreement whereby they would negotiate disciplines to deter EU investment in properties expropriated by the Cuban government. These negotiations were to be concluded by 15 October 1997. The European Union also expressed the hope that the disciplines thus worked out would be incorporated into the MAI. The October deadline was not met, however, largely because it became clear that a possible compromise between the two parties would not be accepted by key members of the US Congress.

Nonetheless, talks between the US government and the European Commission continued into 1998, during which time a number of proposals to resolve their differences failed to gain support from one side or the other. Meanwhile a new item was added to the agenda, namely, resolution of US-EU differences resulting from passage by Congress of the Iran-Libya Sanctions Act. That act called for sanctions against foreign companies that invest in the oil and gas industries of those two countries. Although the issues had not been fully resolved at the time of this writing, the European Union did allow its WTO case to expire, and in the meantime the United States continued to suspend enforcement of the relevant provisions of the Helms-Burton law. An understanding seemed to prevail that, if enforcement of these provisions were attempted, the European Union would reopen the WTO case.

17. Quoted in *Inside US Trade*, 14 February 1997.

Even as the European Union was expressing its outrage over what it felt was a major US violation of the spirit of the MAI, it was simultaneously defending what the United States saw as an unacceptable exception to the MAI. This was a blanket "carve-out" of regional economic integration organizations (REIOs) from the most-favored-nation (MFN) obligation proposed by the European Union. This carve-out would allow member states of REIOs (of which the European Union was one) to, in principle, grant more favorable treatment to each others' investors than to investors from nonmember signatories of the MAI. The US position—joined by a number of other non-EU governments—was that specific exemptions from MFN treatment might be permitted as listed exceptions but that a blanket carve-out was not acceptable. The least acceptable portion of this proposed general exemption was a provision that would allowed REIOs in the future to implement additional preferential policies toward each others' investors beyond those existing when the treaty is signed.

Underlying US concerns over the REIO carve-out was a fear by US officials that it implied a change in the internal policy of the European Union. Historically, consistent with Article 58 of the original Treaty of Rome, an affiliate of a foreign firm was treated as an EU firm if that affiliate was incorporated in an EU country. (In other words, such an affiliate was granted national treatment.) Thus the United States feared that the REIO carve-out in fact implied a major deliberalization of European policy toward foreign investment. In this regard, the US concern over the REIO carve-out was not much different from the European concern with Helms-Burton: in both cases, one side feared a major change in the other's law and policy in the direction of greater discrimination against foreign investors or their investments.

The issue of an MFN carve-out for REIOs had not been resolved at the time the MAI negotiations broke down. However, according to negotiators from both the United States and the European national governments, on this issue the two sides at least understood each other's point of view. These negotiators felt that a mutually satisfactory compromise would likely have been reached eventually, had the negotiations continued.[18]

A second issue on which the United States objected to proposals of certain other countries was that of a general exception for cultural industries. As already noted, this issue had emerged in the pre-MAI effort to negotiate a binding NTI and was an issue with a long and emotional history in multilateral trade negotiations. The governments of Canada and France sought a general exception for cultural industries from national treatment and other MAI obligations. They argued that the exception was necessary

---

18. This statement is based on interviews conducted by the author with officials of the US government and two European governments. The officials spoke on condition of anonymity. It is not clear exactly what the compromise might have been, but it almost surely would have preserved Article 58 of the original Treaty of Rome as this article has been interpreted throughout the existence of the European Union and its predecessor organizations.

to maintain national cultural autonomy in an era when the forces of globalization threatened to erase cultural expressions indigenous to a country or region. The position of the US government was that the exception was sought not so much for such lofty reasons as for the purpose of discriminating against foreign investors in these industries. In particular, the United States was concerned that the exception would allow governments to continue to favor certain local firms involved in magazine publishing, television broadcasting, and motion picture production.

The US government did indicate that it would accept exceptions for specified cultural activities from national treatment obligations as part of country-specific reservations to be lodged by all MAI signatory parties (see chapter 3). This was not acceptable to France, however, because specific reservations would not allow the introduction of new nonconforming measures in the future if these were deemed necessary to continue to protect French production of television programs and movies.[19]

Thus the dispute boiled down to whether cultural industries would be accorded a general exception in the MAI or would be subject to country-specific exceptions. On this the US position was that a general exception was unwarranted, difficult to execute, and easy to abuse (how, precisely, does one define a "cultural" industry?). The French, joined by Canada, countered that culture is too important to be relegated to a country-specific exception.

Closely related to the issue of cultural industries were issues pertaining to the protection of intellectual property rights (IPRs).[20] Under the MAI, intellectual property, when registered in a country where the rights holder is not a citizen of the country, would be treated as investment. Hence, within that country, the intellectual property in question would benefit from national treatment, most-favored-nation status, and similar national obligations under the agreement. However, in many countries, exceptions to national treatment and most-favored-nation treatment do exist with respect to IPRs, and these posed problems for the MAI.[21] For instance, in Europe there exist schemes by which fees are collected on the sale of blank video and audio tape, which are then used to compensate copyright holders for the private copying of their materials. The payments are administered through copyright collectives that enjoy, in effect, monopoly status in terms of the right to receive and distribute the proceeds from the collection of the fees. These schemes, however, fail to accord national treatment to foreign copyright holders. The fees are used to compensate national cre-

---

19. France has a long history of aversion to US movies. See Grantham (1998).

20. On this issue see Gervais and Nicholas-Gervais (1999).

21. These exceptions are nonetheless consistent with other international agreements pertaining to intellectual property protection, such as the Berne and Paris Conventions (on patents and copyrights, respectively) and the WTO Agreement on Trade-Related Aspects of Intellectual Property Rights.

ators of artistic works disproportionately,[22] and foreign copyright holders often are unrepresented in the governance of the collective, although their rights to their works might be administered by the collective.

Other governmental schemes extending financial support to creators of artistic products could also be, under the MAI as drafted, in violation of MAI obligations. In France, for example, the price of every movie ticket includes a fee that goes to finance French movie production. Under a strict standard of national treatment, fees collected on tickets for American-made films would have to be remitted to the American rights holders, something that certainly does not happen under the existing scheme. Similar arrangements exist in other European countries.

These issues could have been dealt with through IPR-specific derogations within the MAI, but this would have been tricky: a badly worded exception might open the way for claims for exceptions that were never intended. One factor that figured in this regard was that the MAI negotiators were not themselves experts in IPRs, and indeed, the implications of the draft MAI for existing IPR-related law and policy became apparent only after the draft was published.[23] At this point, in fact, on advice from IPR experts within their governments, the negotiators carved out of the draft agreement those obligations that might have created uncertainty with respect to existing obligations under the WTO Agreement on Trade-Related Intellectual Property Rights (TRIPs) or the World Intellectual Property Organization.

The issue of a general exception for cultural industries was cited by French Prime Minister Lionel Jospin in his October 1998 statement announcing that France would withdraw from the MAI negotiations (see chapter 1). Indeed, the French copyright collective had by then joined with NGOs and other constituents in protesting the MAI. However, negotiators interviewed by this author have indicated that, at the time of the French withdrawal, a compromise was in the offing on this issue. But the details of this potential compromise have not been revealed.

The issues posed by Helms-Burton, REIOs, and cultural exceptions created major conflicts among the MAI negotiating parties that had not been resolved when the negotiations were terminated in late 1998. These three sets of issues were not, however, the only major disagreements that

---

22. National treatment, according to Gervais and Nicholas-Gervais (1999), would seem to require that the fees be distributed in proportion to the volume of sales generated by each copyholder. But existing schemes do not do this. The position of the European Commission is that the appropriate standard is not national treatment (or most-favored-nation status) but one based on reciprocity. Because no such scheme exists in the United States, reciprocity would seem to justify exactly no payments to American rights holders.

23. Some of these issues could have been avoided had the MAI's definition of an investment not been exceedingly broad. It is not entirely clear, for example, why intellectual property should be seen, for purposes of the MAI, as an investment and hence subject to MAI obligations, when IPRs are already covered under WTO rules.

the negotiations had revealed. For example, at the final formal meeting of the negotiating group in the spring of 1998, the issue of country-specific exceptions to the MAI had only begun to be considered. One matter still unresolved at that time was whether countries would actually negotiate these exceptions. Indeed, no process was agreed upon under which exceptions might actually be scheduled. One solution would have been for each country simply to list all the exceptions that existed in its current law and policy. That is, each country would determine what elements of its law and policy were inconsistent with obligations that would be created by the MAI and list these as exceptions. But this would naturally lead countries to comb through their laws exhaustively and to list any law or policy that might conceivably conflict with the new obligations. The resulting lists would have been very long. Thus, the alternative would be to have the parties actually negotiate these exceptions, with a view to rolling back the number and extent of nonconforming measures, and thus actually liberalize policy. Early on in the negotiations, it had become clear that major problem areas existed in services in particular. Indeed, most of these problems had turned up in the GATS negotiations in the WTO.

Some European countries in particular insisted that they would not liberalize their services sectors beyond what they had done in the context of WTO, in part because they feared a "free-rider" problem emerging. Because the GATS imposed most-favored-nation obligations, service-sector liberalization granted to OECD nations in the context of MAI would have had to be extended automatically to all GATS members, even those that offered no reciprocal liberalization. The EU nations (and, eventually, other nations as well) found this prospect unacceptable. On the other hand, one reason why business interests, and US business interests in particular, did not enthusiastically embrace the MAI negotiations is that they had originally anticipated that progress in removing sector-specific investment obstacles in the services sector would be more rapid in the MAI than in the WTO. When this expectation was dashed, business interest in the negotiations receded.

Another unresolved matter pertaining to country-specific exceptions was whether or not, once the MAI came into force, country-specific lists of exceptions would be subject to standstill. "Standstill" is negotiating jargon meaning that, once the list has been finalized and the MAI is in effect, no additional exceptions may be added. At the beginning of the negotiations, the US negotiators had indicated that, if no rollback of existing nonconforming measures could be agreed on, at least a standstill should be achieved. However, by the time the negotiations were terminated, the US government was close to reversing its position on this issue, indicating that future exceptions pertaining to labor and environmental issues could not be ruled out.

Thus, when the MAI negotiations were terminated, there were major outstanding differences among the negotiating parties, some of which appeared close to irreconcilable. Were they of such magnitude as to cause a complete breakdown in the negotiating process? One cannot answer this question with certainty for the simple reason that the negotiations did not continue after May 1998. But for reasons discussed earlier, it is difficult to see how some of these differences might have been resolved, given the lack of high-level commitment to the goal of creating an MAI. In any case, the decision to terminate the negotiations was without question affected by "civil society" and, in particular, by the environmentally concerned NGOs.[24] We turn to this next.

The NGOs Enter the Stage

The history of NGO involvement in the world of multilateral commercial law, and in the negotiating processes by which this law is created, is very short. Indeed, before the 1990s, the world of the environmentally oriented NGOs and the world of international trade and investment agreements were essentially disjoint. They coexisted, but they did not touch or overlap to any significant degree.

That changed rather dramatically in 1991, when a dispute settlement panel of the General Agreement on Tariffs and Trade (GATT, the predecessor to the WTO) sided with the government of Mexico in a dispute with the United States. A provision of the Marine Mammal Protection Act of 1972 banned the importation of tuna from countries that did not require their fishermen to take steps to prevent the killing of marine mammals (mostly dolphins) in the catching of tuna. The United States had been enforcing this ban against Mexican fishermen. This enforcement in turn had come about when the Earth Island Institute, an environmentally oriented NGO, filed and won a lawsuit in a US federal court to force the Department of Commerce to enforce the law against Mexico. The GATT panel held that the US law violated GATT Article III on national treatment, and it threw out claims by the United States that the ban on tuna imports was consistent with GATT Article XX, parts b and c.[25] Environmentalists were outraged by the panel decision, which they saw as placing the goal of free

---

24. Included in this category would be those NGOs whose major mission is to protect and preserve wilderness areas, rare and endangered species, old-growth forests, and the like, as well as those primarily concerned with air and water pollution.

25. Article XX creates an allowable exception to Article III whereby a government can ban an import for health or safety reasons, or for a number of other reasons (including to prevent trade in products made from an endangered or protected species). The US reasoning was that the Mammal Protection Act established dolphins as a protected species. The GATT panel ruled that the US could in fact invoke Article XX to restrict imports made from dolphins (e.g., dolphin meat) but that tuna was not such a product. The fact that tuna fishing resulted in the deaths of dolphins was seen as beyond the reach of Article XX (a close call that was partially reversed in the later case on shrimp and turtles).

trade above that of saving the environment. But in fact the GATT decision did little to affect US policy. Rather, Mexico agreed to take steps to reduce the killing of marine mammals by its tuna fishermen. This agreement was reached during the course of negotiations toward the North American Free Trade Agreement (NAFTA).

This last matter notwithstanding, the tuna episode led some NGOs to become fervently involved in the debate over NAFTA. However, in both Canada and the United States, not all environmentally oriented NGOs were on the same side of this debate. Some supported NAFTA, arguing that the agreement would bring about higher incomes per capita in Mexico, which in turn would enable greater spending in that country on pollution abatement and other environmentally friendly investment. NAFTA supporters noted that Mexico already suffered from heavy pollution, and that some politically powerful groups in Mexico accorded a high priority to repairing the environmental damage already done, but that a general scarcity of resources was a major constraint on such action. NAFTA proponents also pointed out that one outcome of the negotiations was a joint commission that ultimately would have the authority to establish and enforce air quality standards in the Juarez-El Paso area. Other measures were being implemented under the agreement to deal with pollution elsewhere along the US-Mexico border.

Other environmental NGOs, however, took the position that, if NAFTA were passed, Mexico would become a haven for pollution-generating activities: firms would transfer operations there in order to avoid environmental laws and regulations in Canada and the United States. These groups pointed to the problems that existed along the US-Mexican border, arguing that efforts to correct these predated the NAFTA and had not been very effective. Some of the worst of the alleged environmental offenders were maquiladoras (product assembly operations near the border), most of which were owned ultimately by US-based firms.

In 1992, then-presidential candidate Bill Clinton took up the environmental side of NAFTA as a campaign issue, promising that, if elected, he would make it a priority to renegotiate NAFTA to make it more environmentally friendly. Following the election, his administration carried out this pledge by negotiating with Mexico and Canada an environmental sidebar to the agreement. The government of Mexico and, to a lesser degree, that of Canada resisted the sidebar. In Mexico there was sympathy for the notion that, with regard to certain border areas where environmental problems could be identified (for example, El Paso-Juarez, San Diego-Tijuana), a bilateral approach to solving these problems would be appropriate. Indeed, as already noted, efforts to deal with these problems were already in place. However, there was also considerable feeling in Mexico that NAFTA should not become a vehicle by which the United States forced its own views and approaches on the environment onto Mexico in cases where there was no issue of direct spillover into the United

States.[26] Thus, for example, Mexican authorities balked at the notion that NAFTA might be a vehicle by which air quality standards might be set for Mexico City.

In general, however, the environmental NGOs were unpersuaded by Mexico's arguments. They tended to see Mexico's desire for autonomy on internal environmental issues as a smokescreen for policies favoring pollution havens in the country. Most NGO spokespersons argued further that the substantive provisions of the environmental sidebar agreement were weak and its provisions for enforcement weaker still.

NGO opposition to NAFTA and, by extension, to the MAI stiffened substantially as a result of a dispute brought against the government of Canada by the Ethyl Corporation, a US firm, under the investor-to-state dispute settlement procedures of NAFTA chapter 11. This dispute and its outcome were in fact pivotal to NGO involvement in the MAI, and it is important to understand the dispute in some detail.

The dispute arose in response to a bill passed by the Canadian parliament in the spring of 1997. This bill effectively banned the use of the gasoline additive methylcyclopentadienyl manganese tricarbonyl (MMT) by prohibiting interprovincial trade of this substance.[27] The bill had been initiated by the Canadian environmental ministry, whose motivations were complex. First, the ministry sought to support Canadian manufacturers in the automotive industry, who believed that MMT could damage the ability of sensors in certain advanced automotive emission systems to function properly. The manufacturers sought to implement a North American standard for such systems, but this effort was impaired by the fact that MMT was generally not used as an additive in the United States; hence Canadian use might require redesign of these systems. Second, the ministry sought to protect the health of Canadians, because there was some evidence that MMT could pose a health risk when its by-products were released into the atmosphere. Third, the ministry sought to protect both producers and consumers from the added engineering costs that might be required to modify emissions monitoring devices (Soloway 1999).

Also figuring in the case were the interests of Canadian producers of ethanol, an additive that could, albeit imperfectly, substitute for MMT.[28]

---

26. See the discussion of this issue in Hufbauer and Schott (1992), chapter 7.

27. Soloway (1999) provides an exhaustive treatment of the MMT case. It should be noted that the Ethyl Corporation had announced prior to the passage of the Canadian bill that, if the bill went into force, it would be challenged under the NAFTA procedures.

28. Soloway (1999) argues that the ethanol producers in Canada tended to serve as the "bootlegger" faction of a "bootlegger-Baptist" coalition against Ethyl. In such a coalition, two quite disparate constituencies form an alliance over a public policy issue, where the interest of one constituency (the "bootlegger") is largely commercially driven and the other (the "Baptist") is largely driven by matters of principle or ideology. Chapter 7 of this volume will argue that the whole issue of multinational rules on investment has in fact been captured by just such a "bootlegger-Baptist" coalition.

The ethanol producers promoted their product as an environmentally friendly alternative to MMT that did not pose a health hazard. Whether or not the use of ethanol as a substitute for MMT would on balance be good for health or environmental reasons is not actually clear: scientific evidence suggests that ethanol itself is a pollutant. Thus, the ethanol promoters probably are best seen simply as a special interest group who sought to use environmental and health concerns to benefit their commercial interests.

In any case, the Canadian bill did not ban the use of MMT outright on health or environmental grounds, because the scientific evidence against MMT was, in fact, rather thin. This evidence certainly did not give MMT a clean bill of health—some credible evidence did exist that MMT, when used as a gasoline additive, posed health risks. But this evidence was not conclusive enough to qualify MMT for a ban under the Canadian Environmental Protection Act, either for reasons of public health or for the potential of MMT to befoul automotive emissions control systems.

Thus, for the Canadian government, the ban on interprovincial trade of MMT was an indirect way of banning the suspicious chemical altogther when direct measures to do so were unavailable. The Ethyl Corporation could in principle have manufactured MMT in each of the Canadian provinces and sold it within the province of manufacture. In practice, however, this would have been prohibitively expensive, and therefore the ban on interprovincial trade of MMT effectively created a ban on the use of the substance in Canada. This set up the legal challenges that followed.

In fact, there were four such challenges. The first of these was pursued by Ethyl in Canadian domestic courts, where the company argued that the interprovincial trade ban on MMT was unconstitutional because it created a federal intrusion into matters reserved for the provincial governments.[29] Second, the government of Alberta, backed by several other provincial governments, brought a complaint under Canada's Agreement on Internal Trade (AIT). Alberta maintained that the MMT ban constituted a restriction on interprovincial trade that was illegal under provisions of the AIT that mirror GATT Articles I and III (on most-favored-nation status and national treatment). Third, as already noted, the Ethyl Corporation brought a complaint under NAFTA chapter 11, arguing that the ban violated that chapter's national treatment provisions and was tantamount to an expropriation, which would require compensation by the government. (It was mostly this last element that the NGOs seized upon, as detailed below.) Fourth, Ethyl appealed to the US government to initiate a complaint under the state-to-state dispute settlement procedures of NAFTA, alleging a number of non-chapter 11 violations.

---

29. As chapter 1 noted, under proposals made by this author (in Graham 1996), Ethyl would not have been allowed to invoke investor-to-state dispute resolution proceedings until domestic alternatives within Canada had been exhausted. If the dispute were not resolved to Ethyl's satisfaction in these proceedings, Ethyl could then show cause that the result of the domestic proceedings was likely in violation of Canada's obligations under NAFTA.

The fourth challenge was never pursued, because the US government decided not to respond to Ethyl's request. The first, domestic case never went to trial, because the MMT ban was repealed before the trial opened. With respect to the remaining two challenges, on 12 June 1998 the government of Alberta won its case asserting that the MMT ban violated the AIT. Following this, on 20 July 1998 the Canadian government agreed to a monetary settlement of Ethyl's NAFTA case before the case went to formal dispute settlement procedures.[30]

The outcome of Ethyl's NAFTA challenge provided much fuel to the fire of those NGOs that opposed NAFTA. Although the case had not been formally ruled in Ethyl's favor, the NGOs saw the settlement as a tacit admission by the Canadian government that it was unlikely to prevail. If, these NGOs claimed, Ethyl could use NAFTA to effectively strike down this particular environmental law, then no environmentally motivated law or regulation in the United States, Canada, or Mexico was safe from challenge under the agreement.

Meanwhile, in May 1997, a draft text of the MAI dated January of that year had been placed on the Internet by Multinational Monitor, an NGO. The text contained provisions very similar to those under which Ethyl was pursuing its NAFTA chapter 11 complaint against Canada; in particular, the MAI contained provisions to establish investor-to-state dispute settlement procedures and to establish standards for investor protection that were very close to those of NAFTA. The posting of this document sounded an alarm that spread almost immediately throughout the worldwide community of NGOs. If, as the NGOs feared, NAFTA chapter 11 could be used to challenge laws that effectively banned the use of a potentially toxic substance, then the MAI, if it came into effect, could be used to challenge any such law or regulation in any country that signed the agreement.

Thus, among the NGO community, the MAI came to be known as "NAFTA on steroids." The antienvironmental "muscle" they perceived to exist in NAFTA would be dramatically pumped up if the MAI were to come into force. (In fact, this muscle had yet to be demonstrated—at the time, Ethyl's NAFTA case had not yet been settled in Ethyl's favor.) The "NAFTA on steroids" argument proliferated in the months that followed, mostly on the Internet but also in handbills and posters. The tone of the NGOs' campaign at times crossed over into hyperbole. For example, in Geneva in 1998 this author saw numerous posters placed by anti-MAI activists. These posters depicted the MAI as a Godzilla-like monster wearing an Uncle Sam top hat and presiding at a ball, where serpents variously identified as the OECD and other international organizations danced with other serpents bearing the logos of major multinational firms. The posters epitomized the mixing of environmental and antibusiness themes that characterized much of the NGO opposition to the MAI.

---

30. The AIT panel report can be found at http://www.ec.gc.ca/press/mmt98_n_e.htm.

Despite this flurry of anti-MAI activity during the second half of 1997, the MAI negotiators at first seemed unaware of the intensity of the storm that was gathering. Indeed, the first hint that the NGOs were mounting an activist opposition to the MAI reached official circles only in February 1998, when US Trade Representative (USTR) Charlene Barshefsky received a letter cosigned by the heads of nine NGOs stating that their groups would oppose the MAI. Most of these groups were advocates of environmental protection and/or preservation of wilderness and wildlife.[31] These groups' initial lack of familiarity with international economic policymaking was reflected in the fact that the letter was addressed to the USTR, when in fact the State Department was the lead US agency for MAI negotiations.[32] In a later letter, these groups addressed their concerns both to the Secretary of State and to the USTR.

What followed might have been a series of dress rehearsals for the large-scale demonstrations that took place in Seattle at the time of the WTO ministerial meeting there in November 1999. Beginning in the summer of 1998, representatives of some NGOs posted themselves regularly near the OECD's offices in Paris, where they beat on drums and chanted anti-MAI mantras. In the meantime, the US organization Public Citizen Trade Watch, founded by Ralph Nader, became the coordinator of anti-MAI activity in the United States. This organization held a number of rallies against the MAI in Washington during 1998, circulating leaflets calling for a "large and rowdy crowd" to assemble on Capitol Hill. The leaflets for one such rally announced a special guest appearance by "the Corporate Fat Cat." An academic colloquium on the MAI was held at the Cornell University Law School in March 1998 and was attended by this author. The colloquium was open to the public. Most of the attendees proved to be activists who had come to demonstrate against the MAI. The Deputy US Trade Representative, the keynote speaker, was greeted by a phalanx of demonstrators bearing anti-MAI signs, at least one of which suggested that to ratify the MAI would bring on the apocalypse.

Rowdiness was very evident at the June 1998 ministerial meeting of the WTO in Geneva, where persons calling themselves representatives of the NGOs organized demonstrations that turned into little less than street riots. The posters and flyers of the demonstrators were directed as much at the MAI as at the WTO. Anti-WTO and anti-MAI slogans were spray-

---

31. These were the World Wildlife Fund, the Center for International Environmental Law, the Friends of the Earth, the Community Nutrition Institute, the Defenders of Wildlife, the Institute for Agriculture and Trade Policy, the Sierra Club, Greenpeace, and the National Wildlife Federation.

32. The State Department is the lead US government agency on all matters pertaining to the OECD, whereas the USTR is the lead agency for most trade issues, including trade negotiations conducted within the WTO (see chapter 4.) The NGOs' earlier interactions with the USTR on international trade issues, specifically the Uruguay Round and NAFTA, perhaps understandably led them to assume that the USTR also was in charge of the MAI negotiations.

painted on buildings throughout the city indiscriminately. The personal automobile of the ambassador to the WTO from Jamaica was overturned and burned. A Swiss television documentary captured some of the details of these events.

Although the campaign mounted against the MAI clearly suffered from excesses, some of the NGOs' objections were not without substance. Indeed, Ethyl's NAFTA case against Canada raised some deep and troubling issues and arguably revealed some serious flaws in both NAFTA and the MAI. At the root of these issues is how governments should deal with "takings," that is, the seizure of property by governments from private citizens for a public purpose.

In the MAI, and in NAFTA, the takings issue centers around provisions in both documents pertaining to investor protection and investor-to-state dispute settlement procedures.[33] Perhaps the first thing to be said on this issue is that, in every nation of the world, governments have the right under certain circumstances to seize private property. However, the second thing to be said is that, in established democracies at least, these circumstances are usually precisely defined, and the government must meet certain obligations when it exercises its right of seizure. The exact circumstances in which seizure is permitted, and the exact obligations that the government must then meet, vary from country to country. But in much of the world, a number of general standards apply to the seizure of *tangible* property. For example, in general the seizure must be for a public purpose, be conducted under due process of law, be nondiscriminatory, and be followed by prompt, adequate, and effective compensation of the property owner.[34] And, indeed, the investor protection provisions of both the MAI and NAFTA contain language that establishes these standards; chapter 3 reviews these provisions in some detail.

US law and, indeed, the law of most countries are thus quite clear about seizure of tangible property, for example where the government takes title to land in order to build a road. The original owner might have no choice in the matter of the land being seized, but he or she is entitled to compensation. This kind of government taking is termed a "physical taking." But in other situations the law is not always so clear. For example, what if the government enacts a law or promulgates a regulation that has a legitimate public purpose but also has the effect of reducing the value of a privately owned asset, such as an ordinance that forbids loud noise late at night that in turn forces the owner of a bar to shut at midnight so that

---

33. What follows is based on Graham (1999a), which provides a somewhat more detailed examination of the issues, including extensive bibliographical citations.

34. The Fifth Amendment to the US Constitution, for example, provides that "No person shall be . . . deprived of life, liberty, or property, without due process of law; nor shall private property be taken for public use, without just compensation." But the requirement of compensation has not always existed in American law.

some of the clientele choose to go to another bar in a less restrictive neighborhood? Such a reduction in value of an asset as the result of a government regulation is termed a "regulatory taking." Whether regulatory takings have the same standing in law as physical takings is an issue with a long history.

There was, in fact, a time in US history when many laws or regulations that led to regulatory takings might have been struck down by US courts as violations of the Fifth Amendment. Indeed, the first US law to create an income tax was struck down by the US Supreme Court in 1895 on these grounds. The creation of a federal income tax thus required a constitutional amendment, which was not passed until almost twenty years later, in 1913. During the first two decades or so of the twentieth century, the so-called Lochner era,[35] a number of laws passed by Congress and signed by the president to regulate industries (including to establish standards for workplace safety) were struck down by US courts as creating unconstitutional takings. Certain laws to protect public health, safety, and morality were excepted, but these exceptions were quite narrow and generally did not extend to laws regulating the safety of the workplace or the quality of the environment.[36] After a landmark case in 1922, US courts began to find that most laws designed to promulgate standards pertaining to public health and safety were in fact constitutional.[37] However, there survived a rather imprecise "rule of diminished value," which left open the possibility that certain regulations could be ruled, in effect, overzealous and thus creating a taking subject to the Fifth Amendment.

Today the boundary between a regulatory taking that is subject to the Fifth Amendment and one that is not remains somewhat murky in US law.

---

35. After the landmark case Lochner vs. New York, 198 US 45 (1905).

36. The prevailing standard was the "noxious use doctrine," also termed the "harm doctrine." Under this standard, a regulation affecting use of a private property was held not to be a taking if the property, unregulated, created a situation that was injurious to the health, morals, or safety of the community. In implementing the harm doctrine, courts applied two tests. The first was a "means/end" test to determine whether the regulation actually prevented the harm it addressed. The second was a "cause/effect" test to determine whether the regulated party actually caused the harm. Although in principle the harm doctrine, and the two tests applied toward it, seem quite reasonable, in practice early in this century they often were employed very narrowly or stringently, so that regulation that today would be generally accepted as in the public interest was in fact struck down. For example, the courts generally accepted zoning laws requiring factories that produced noxious emissions to be located only in certain districts, but they might not have accepted laws requiring these same factories to install devices to reduce those emissions.

37. The case was Pennsylvania Coal Company vs. Mahon, US 393 (1922). In this case, Justice Oliver Wendell Holmes articulated the doctrine that the government can regulate the use of private property to prevent public harm unless the regulation "goes too far" in reducing the value of the property. This opinion did not actually reverse the noxious use doctrine of the Lochner era, but rather softened it somewhat, so that courts might accept a less stringent standard as to what constitutes noxious use or harm.

One school of legal thought holds that regulatory taking under at least some circumstances should be treated equivalently to a physical taking (see Epstein 1985). A 1992 Supreme Court ruling (in Lucas vs. South Carolina Coastal Council) that a state prohibition on development on beachfront property created a requirement that owners of such property be compensated for the resulting diminution of the value of the land tilts somewhat in this direction. This ruling was, in fact, met with consternation and ire on the part of environmentalists (McUsic 1996). However, legal scholars have largely interpreted this ruling as applying to land use only and not to regulation of other types of assets. They note that US law has long applied somewhat different standards regarding taking of land than regarding taking of any other asset, possibly because Congress seemed most clearly to have land in mind in framing the Fifth Amendment.

US law is, in fact, among the most friendly toward property holders on the matter of takings. In most countries' law, regulatory takings are for all practical purposes exempt from requirements for compensation, even when such requirements might apply to physical takings by the government.

What the NGOs brought to light is that NAFTA (and the MAI, had it come into force) could be interpreted as creating a new doctrine toward regulatory takings. This doctrine would be much more friendly to owners of assets whose value might be diminished by regulation than is any national law in effect in the OECD countries. Article IV.2.1 of the draft MAI states that:

> A Contracting Party shall not expropriate or nationalize directly or indirectly an investment in its territory of an investor of another Contracting Party or take any measure or measures having equivalent effect (hereinafter referred to as "expropriation") except:
> a. for a purpose which is in the public interest,
> b. on a nondiscriminatory basis,
> c. in accordance with due process of law, [and]
> d. accompanied by payment of prompt, adequate, and effective compensation.

The phrase "measures having an equivalent effect" could reasonably be interpreted to encompass regulatory takings. Thus these previsions do not seem to preclude that a regulatory taking could be treated as an expropriation and, hence, be subject to the requirement for compensation. This was a key point argued by the Ethyl Corporation in its NAFTA case. Under this interpretation, NAFTA and the MAI would both seem to grant to international investors a privileged position, in that these investors could seek compensation for regulatory takings through a venue not available to domestic investors under like circumstances. Furthermore, the rules under which international investors could press such claims for compensation would be highly favorable to them, and more favorable than those under which domestic investors might press similar claims (in other venues).

It is difficult to explain how the negotiators overlooked this problem. (Or perhaps some of them did not overlook it: as noted earlier, US negotiators had no objection to any provision that would create better treatment for US investors in a foreign country than was accorded to domestic investors in that country. Indeed, the US negotiators were eager for other countries to accept such provisions.) But clearly such an asymmetry has no place in a multilateral agreement. As already noted, such an asymmetry could lead to perverse responses by domestic investors. Such investors might decide to set up operations in foreign countries and use these to make investments in their own home country, simply in order to claim the better treatment accorded to foreigners. Quite a lot of domestic law might be circumvented in this manner—a point that the NGOs seem to have missed.

However, it must be remembered that this interpretation of MAI Article IV.2.1 (and the equivalent language in NAFTA) is not the only possible interpretation. Unfortunately, no tribunal has yet had the chance to rule on the matter, or at least none had by the time the NGOs rallied against the MAI. In particular, the Ethyl Corporation's case never got heard by a NAFTA tribunal. But contrary to the NGOs' claim, the fact that the Canadian government settled the case does not necessarily signal that it believed it would have lost that part of the case based on Ethyl's claim that the interprovincial trade ban was equivalent in effect to an expropriation. Indeed (and this is a point never made in NGO literature), this claim might have been the weakest link in Ethyl's NAFTA dispute with Canada. A counterargument can be easily made, based on NAFTA Article 1114:

> Nothing in this Chapter [i.e., chapter 11] shall be construed to prevent a Party from adopting, maintaining or enforcing any measure otherwise consistent with this Chapter that it considers appropriate to ensure that investment activity in its territory is undertaken in a manner sensitive to environmental concerns.

It is thus quite possible that the tribunal might have ruled out Ethyl's claim of expropriation on grounds that the interprovincial ban, being motivated primarily by environmental concerns, was subject to an immunity created by Article 1114.

If this was so, why did Canada agree to settle the case before it went to the tribunal? Doesn't this prove the NGOs' contention that Canada expected to lose, and hence that the above interpretation of MAI IV.2.1 would likely have been locked in through the NAFTA precedent? The answer is no. Even if the tribunal had found that the ban on interprovincial trade of MMT was not an expropriation, the government of Canada might still have lost the case for other reasons. For example, as Ethyl also argued, the ban could have been interpreted as a de facto performance requirement to force the MMT additive to be manufactured in every province; this would have violated NAFTA provisions banning local content requirements on international investors. Such a finding arguably would not have been subject to Article 1114 because, had MMT been manufactured and used in each province, the environmental risk would have been the same as if interprovincial trade in the chemical had been allowed. Had the government lost the case on these grounds, it would have weakened the NGOs' claim that the case established a presumption that takings created by environmental regulations could be treated under NAFTA and the MAI as expropriations. Perhaps less likely, the court might have found that the main purpose of the MMT ban was to favor the Canadian ethanol industry, and that the ban was therefore inconsistent with NAFTA, which requires national treatment for investors from another NAFTA country.

Some have argued that it is unfortunate that the case never reached the tribunal, because an opportunity to rule on the scope of the expropriation language was thereby lost.[38] As matters stand, whether the investor protection provisions of NAFTA (or the MAI) would apply to regulatory takings is unresolved.

Further, if governments would prefer that these provisions (in NAFTA or the MAI) not be interpreted as applying to regulatory takings, they can act to remove the ambiguity in the current language. Indeed, MAI negotiators interviewed by this author said that, had the negotiations resumed in the fall of 1998, removal or revision of the offending language would have been considered. Also, the MMT case has led the NAFTA countries to actively consider how best to remove regulatory takings from the coverage of the investor protection provisions. But at the time of this writing, no action had been taken.

According to the negotiators, the language in question was never intended to cover regulatory takings by governments that might result from laws or regulations to protect the environment or public health or safety. Hence it was never anticipated that the investor protection provisions would be used by a private investor, through NAFTA's enterprise-to-state dispute settlement procedures, to sue for compensation for such a regulatory taking. Many agreements entered into by human beings do, of course, lead to unanticipated and undesirable outcomes. When this happens, a reasonable response is for the relevant parties to alter the agreement so as to avoid such outcomes in the future.

However, for the MAI the solution is not as simple as striking the words "measures having equivalent effect" from the draft Article IV. That language was included because the negotiators wanted the agreement's expropriation provisions to cover "expropriation via the back door." It was meant to cover any measure that a country might have taken for ostensibly legitimate reasons but whose real intent (or consequence) was to force the exit of an unwanted, foreign-controlled enterprise from a local market. For example, during the 1950s, populist regimes in some developing countries had used price regulation to prevent foreign-controlled firms

---

38. Soloway (1999).

from raising prices in response to inflation, in effect forcing these firms to sell their output below cost. The firm then had to choose either to stay in the market and subsidize its customers, or to exit the market, which usually meant selling its assets for less than their market value. It was not unreasonable for the negotiators to seek to curtail such practices. One solution, therefore, might have been to have insert a provision like the following:

> Article IV.2.1 will not apply to any measure taken to protect public health or safety; to ensure the preservation of a species of plant or animal; or to safeguard the physical environment, provided that the measure is applied in a manner that does not discriminate against any individual or class of investment or investor in order to achieve a benefit for some other individual or class of investment or investor.

This would require that, if a case that involved a regulatory taking were brought under investor-to-state dispute settlement procedures, the disputant (the investor) would have to demonstrate that the relevant measure was discriminatory. The dispute settlement tribunal would have to decide whether this condition was met.

Thus, to the extent that the investor protection provisions of the MAI, when coupled with the agreement's investor-to-state dispute settlement procedures, actually did pose a threat to environmental protection laws, as the NGOs claimed, this was a problem for which solutions could have been found. It was not necessary to reject the MAI entirely to fix this particular problem. Unfortunately, although the NGOs did succeed in identifying (or at least in publicizing) what is arguably a major flaw in both the MAI and NAFTA, they also greatly exaggerated its likely impact. Indeed, the more radical NGOs tended to generalize this one correctable flaw into a characterization of the whole MAI as something close to evil incarnate. One unfortunate consequence is that these organizations missed a very real opportunity to play a constructive role in correcting the flaw. Instead, they—or at least a dominant subset of them—chose to use the opportunity to try to bring the whole exercise down. It can be argued, of course, that in this they were highly successful. But it remains to be seen whether, in sealing the agreement's fate, the NGOs did a service to the causes they espouse. It may be that, by acting as they did, they performed a major disservice to their own long-run missions.

To see why this is so, consider the following. The NAFTA investor-to-state dispute settlement procedures have been in place now for five years, yet corporate interests have brought challenges against only a handful of environmental laws or regulations under these procedures.[39] There appear to have been about five to seven such cases to date, the exact number de-

---

39. In addition to the Ethyl case in Canada, a case brought against Mexico by the Metalclad Corporation of the United States had environmental implications. Metalclad alleged that delays in approval of its purchase of a hazardous waste site in the state of San Luís Potosí constituted an expropriation. The delays originated at the state level, not at the Mexican federal

pending on which cases one classifies as involving environmental and public health issues. Moreover, of the few challenges that have been brought, none have been resolved against the environmentalists' interests. Certainly, then, the wholesale gutting of environmental regulation that some predicted simply has not happened. Some environmentalists claim that the Ethyl Corporation's challenge of Canada's effective ban on MMT demonstrated that NAFTA does pose a threat to environmental law. But, as we have seen, the ban in question was on interprovincial trade in MMT, not on its manufacture or use. And the Canadian government took this route because the case for an outright ban on environmental or health grounds was too weak to permit a ban under Canada's existing health and environmental laws. Thus, if Ethyl had won its NAFTA case, it would have created an unfortunate precedent, but it would hardly have been a shattering blow to the cause of environmentalism. These facts should be contrasted with the claims of some NGOs. These groups assert that, if the MAI had come into force with provisions similar to those of NAFTA, it would have resulted in a crushing reversal of virtually all progress made over the past several decades to implement laws and regulations to protect the environment. That claim is, to put it mildly, overblown. And, as noted above, to the extent that the MAI poses a danger to environmental law, the danger could be easily eliminated, and the negotiators were prepared to try to correct the danger, had the MAI negotiations continued.

Perhaps recognizing that, by any reasonable standard, the substantive problems that the environmental NGOs might have had with the MAI were ones that could be fixed, the OECD did invite representatives of NGOs to meetings held at the OECD headquarters. The invited NGOs effectively divided into three groups. One group refused to participate at all, indicating that the only acceptable outcome was for investment negotiations at the OECD to cease entirely. Another group did send representatives, but once inside the OECD these representatives saw their mission solely as one of delivering the message, "Death to the MAI!" A third group sent representatives who sought to work with the OECD Secretariat to propose changes to the MAI to make it environmentally friendly. However, this third group was rather a small one.

These meetings were, in fact, the first ever at which the environmental NGOs were asked to participate directly in the process of negotiating a multilateral commercial agreement. An opportunity for constructive exchange was thus created whereby the NGOs could have offered valuable

---

level. One issue was whether the state of San Luís Potosí would create an expropriation by forbidding hazardous waste processing on its territory. This case was decided in favor of Mexico. For an environmentalist perspective on this and other NAFTA cases, see Van Dyke, Porter, and Sewall (1999) and Swenarchuk (1999). Recently, however, the number of NAFTA chapter 11 cases has grown; hence, the environmentalist position might yet be proved correct, but only if the tribunals hearing the cases start deciding in favor of firms on regulatory takings issues.

substantive input. To be sure, at the end of the day this exchange might have failed to give the environmentalists much satisfaction. But had this been the outcome, they could have walked out, held a press conference to air their grievances, and the world would have noted that they had tried and failed.

More likely, however, is that the outcome would have been much more favorable to the NGOs. The MAI negotiators in 1998 were in a genuine quandary over what to do about the regulatory takings issue raised by the Ethyl case, and their sense was that this indeed was a problem that needed fixing. By refusing to engage the OECD and the negotiators in a constructive dialogue, the NGOs in effect walked away from a wide-open opportunity to achieve something that they could have claimed as a major substantive victory as opposed to the major PR victory that they did claim. They could have rightly claimed that an important multilateral negotiation had, under their advice, removed from proposed new rules provisions that had the potential to cause environmental damage. Had this been the outcome, the resulting "MAI precedent" might have reverberated all of the way to Geneva: henceforth, multilateral trade agreements would have had to be concluded in a way that addressed environmental concerns. Instead, however, the NGOs largely chose to remain outside the negotiating process or, if they did come into the negotiating room, to use the opportunity merely to shout.

Did their shouting bring down the MAI? Many NGOs seemed to think so, and encouraged by their perceived victory, they planned the demonstrations that took place in Seattle in November 1999. One of the rallying points was a site on the Internet on which was posted a "Call to Reject any Proposal for Moving the MAI or an Investment Agreement to the WTO."[40] The statement was signed by over 300 NGOs and begins as follows:

> The Multilateral Agreement on Investment in the OECD has run into problems because of strong public protests in many OECD countries as well as objections from developing-country groups and governments. Objections from the public include that the MAI would grant new unprecedented rights for corporations (whilst removing the authority of states to place obligations or regulations on them), threaten national sovereignty and the viability of domestic firms and farms, remove conditions for development in the South and magnify environmental and social problems. Since there is no sign that the OECD governments are willing to consider a basic change in the premises and framework of the MAI, we call for the termination of the negotiations and the treaty in the OECD.

The statement goes on to note that "some OECD governments, including the European Union" were seeking to move the MAI process to the WTO. It opposes this move and asserts further that "promises to include environmental and social concerns are likely only to be an eyewash to co-opt the public to accept the basic tenets of the MAI." An MAI-like agree-

---

40. See http://www.tradewatch.org/MAI.htm.

ment at the WTO, according to the statement, would have "disastrous effects" on the developmental prospects of poorer countries and would force countries to change domestic laws and policies "even if these were to cause job losses, closure of local enterprises and farms, financial instability, balance of payments deficits, and environmental degradation."

The Cavalry That Did Not Arrive

One of the key questions raised by the history of the MAI (see chapter 1) is why the international business community did not support the negotiation more strongly than it did. If, as its opponents claim, the MAI amounted to a munificent feast for the "corporate fat cats," why did these interests fail to mount a countercampaign to keep the feast from being spirited off the table?

The US business community did, in fact, initially support the MAI undertaking with greater enthusiasm than did business groups in Europe or Japan. According to several spokespersons for US business groups, the main reason they and their foreign counterparts did not do more was that "there was not much 'there' there." In their eyes, the prospective MAI was no feast, but rather at most a modest picnic.

In an initial round of enthusiasm, a number of business groups, including the US Council for International Business, polled their members to determine what objectives they would like the MAI negotiations to achieve. The overwhelming response was "up-front liberalization," for example, removal of existing investment barriers in the European Union. As already noted, these were to be found predominantly in the services sector—hardly one noted for its environmental depredations.

The nonchalance of the business community supports the notion that, at the end of the day, the MAI as drafted would have done little to change anything. And the disagreements among the negotiating parties largely centered on proposals that would have taken investment liberalization several steps backward. The case could be made that the furor of the NGOs was largely a tempest in a teapot.

Was this really the case? The next chapter attempts to glean some insight into the substance of the MAI through a close look at the document itself, as it stood at the time the negotiations were terminated.

3

Dissecting the MAI

This chapter provides a brief but comprehensive examination of the MAI itself, based on the negotiating text dated 24 April 1998. This was the last draft completed before the negotiations collapsed in the autumn of 1998, and, in fact, no further negotiations took place following publication of this draft. Thus one is faced at the outset with the problem of evaluating a draft that was neither agreed to by all parties nor even completely finished. And although most of the main provisions of the agreement were in place, much of the language was bracketed, meaning that consensus had not been reached on that language. Some of the bracketed language represents major unresolved conflicts, but most of it reflects minor differences over wording. The upshot is that the April text is sufficiently complete to provide a fair idea of where the MAI was headed, even if some of its main provisions and a number of its details might later have changed, some substantially.

This chapter also identifies some deficiencies in the MAI as it stood at the time of the talks' collapse. The main ones in the core text were failures to address investment incentives and taxation. (Chapters 1 and 2 have already discussed some reasons why these were omitted.) This chapter also argues why some discipline on investment incentives would have been appropriate and examines why the negotiating parties failed to achieve this objective.

A third major deficiency was that the MAI failed to achieve significant liberalization of current policy toward direct investment in the OECD countries. This is largely the result of the large number of exceptions that would have been registered in annexes to the main text. Thus, although the MAI draft was close to 200 pages in length and contained many provisions covering a wide range of issues, at the end of the day it would have changed little in the investment policies of the signatory countries. Any evaluation of the MAI's potential effectiveness must, of course, be based on a simple criterion: would these provisions have served to remove or significantly reduce distortions created by governments that diminish the total value of goods and services that international investment makes possible (see chapter 1)? Granted, it is very difficult to quantify this lost value of goods and services, or the extent to which an international agreement such as the MAI might have been able to prevent this loss. Nonetheless, it is clear that the MAI, as it was drafted and had all extant national exceptions to core principles been allowed, would have been inadequate to reduce these distortions and losses to any significant degree.

The main reason this was so was, again, simply that the MAI would have achieved virtually no change in current government policy or practice on the part of any of the signatory countries. However, this statement must be qualified. Although the MAI itself would not have forced significant, immediate changes in national policy, such changes might have resulted from decisions handed down under the application of the agreement's investor-to-state dispute settlement procedures. Unfortunately, as we saw in chapter 2, experience to date with similar provisions in NAFTA has not been wholly reassuring. The dispute settlement provisions have so far been used in many cases to attack regulatory takings, including those created under regulations designed to protect health and the environment.

Although some such regulations might produce economic distortions, it can be argued that such distortions are the price one pays for a cleaner and healthier environment (see chapter 5). And as argued in chapter 2, the Ethyl Corporation's complaint against Canada—the NAFTA case to date with the clearest environmental implications—was settled without resort to a tribunal finding and did not establish an antienvironmental precedent. Another case with environmental implications, Metalclad's complaint against Mexico, also described in chapter 2, was decided in Mexico's (and the environmentalist movement's) favor. Nonetheless, the investor-to-state dispute settlement procedures represent the one element that the MAI would have created having the potential to force changes in countries' law and policy. What outcomes would have resulted from application of these procedures remains unknown.

But this in itself poses a problem. One of the worst fears of the MAI's opponents was that countries that signed the MAI might be yielding elements of their sovereignty to some unknown tribunal unaccountable to anyone. This fear might have been overblown, but it did bolster opposition to the agreement.

Also figuring importantly in the MAI's failure to achieve real liberalization was the fact that it would have been a stand-alone instrument. That is, it would not have been linked (in a formal legalistic sense) to existing agreements in the WTO or elsewhere. This creates the problem in the services sectors already alluded to in chapter 1: any concessions granted in the MAI in sectors covered by the WTO's General Agreement on Trade in Services (GATS) would, under GATS obligations, have to be granted on a most-favored-nation basis to all WTO members. Thus, liberalizing measures to which the OECD countries might have been able to agree among themselves could not be realized unless these countries were willing, in effect, to extend them almost universally.

The draft MAI did incorporate certain core provisions on which, for the most part, the negotiating parties had achieved consensus. These would have established clear principles acting in the direction of investment liberalization, by removing laws and policies that discriminate against foreign investors. These included provisions pertaining to national treatment, most-favored-nation status, and investor protection, which are discussed in detail below. Most of these provisions were, in fact, borrowed from existing legal instruments, such as NAFTA and various bilateral investment treaties.[1] Even so, some of the language in these provisions was bracketed, again indicating that no consensus existed.

Had the draft MAI's core principles been applied without exception, they would have served to eliminate most remaining barriers to investment within the OECD, and hence would have generated some benefits. Their value would have been enhanced had they been extended to developing countries, where barriers and discriminatory policies are more widespread. Thus, even though the MAI, by virtue of the exceptions, would have done little to liberalize current policy, it nonetheless might have contributed to future liberalization by establishing a set of strong principles on which certain countries had agreed and on which future negotiations to liberalize further would be based. In other words, the MAI arguably set the stage for future policy changes, even if it did not immediately lead to such changes.[2] Also, had countries not party to the MAI negotiations subsequently joined the agreement, they might have been required, as a condition of accession, to change their policies that did not conform to MAI obligations. Whether any of this would have actually happened is, of course, a matter of conjecture. Nonetheless, the case can be made that, even if the MAI had achieved little in the way of "up-front" liberalization, it would have created a long-run dynamic process by which substantial liberalization could have been achieved over time.

However, whether such a dynamic would have come about is speculative and the fact remains that the MAI was largely status quo preserving. Given this, it is perhaps surprising that the MAI became such a lightning

---

1. On this matter see Dymond (1999).

2. However, as is stressed in both chapter 1 and chapter 7, significant investment liberalization has taken place worldwide over the past decade or so even without the MAI. At most, the MAI would have helped this process along.

rod for interest groups opposed to economic globalization. As we saw in chapter 2, these groups mounted their intensive campaign to defeat the MAI only after the release of the April 1998 draft. This campaign was never effectively countered by any pro-MAI constituency, presumably because no such constituency could identify any tangible benefit to itself from the MAI as drafted that was worth fighting for.

The objective of this chapter's examination of the April 1998 draft is to describe in some detail what purpose each provision was meant to accomplish and to evaluate whether it would have achieved that purpose. Where appropriate, this evaluation itself is embedded in a discussion of whether the purpose addressed a desirable end. Again, however, the draft MAI was a very lengthy document, and perforce the evaluation presented here is rather lengthy as well. The reader who is not interested in the details of the MAI provisions might therefore wish to skip the remainder of this chapter and proceed to chapter 4.

The Structure of the MAI

The MAI as drafted is what international economic policymakers call a top-down, free-standing agreement.[3] "Top-down" means that its obligations are binding on all signatory countries in all sectors, except where explicitly stated otherwise. By contrast, a "bottom-up" agreement would be one whose provisions apply only to certain specifically enumerated sectors and activities.[4] Exceptions in the draft MAI are of two types: "general exceptions," which would apply to all countries (and, in some instances, to all sectors) and country-specific "reservations." In the draft, the general exceptions are included in the main text with the core provisions. Separate from these are the country-specific reservations, which themselves come in two varieties, list A (those that may be negotiated away) and list B (those that are nonnegotiable). At the time that negotiations were suspended, not all countries had submitted detailed lists, but all had submitted indicative lists outlining the sort of exceptions that would be sought.

The entire MAI thus consists of the core provisions and the list of separate, country-specific and sector-specific reservations. Although, unlike the core provisions, this list has not been published, persons involved with

---

3. For expositional convenience, the rest of this chapter describes the draft MAI's provisions in the present tense rather than the conditional, having duly noted that the agreement never actually came into force.

4. Thus, for example, the WTO General Agreement on Trade in Services (GATS) is a bottom-up agreement, whereas the General Agreement on Trade and Tariffs (GATT) is top-down. In terminology also sometimes used in diplomatic contexts, a top-down agreement adopts a negative-list approach, that is, the agreement covers all but a list of sanctioned exceptions. A "bottom-up" agreement, conversely, takes a positive-list approach, with obligations applying only to what is explicitly listed.

the negotiations have indicated that, when complete, it would have codified essentially without modification all existing provisions of the OECD countries' laws that were not in conformity with the core provisions.[5]

The term "free-standing" means that the MAI would not have been part of the WTO framework but rather would have operated outside this framework. As noted earlier, this aspect of the MAI could have caused problems of consistency between countries' MAI obligations and their WTO obligations. If an MAI signatory wished to avoid this problem in a given sector, it might have registered that sector as an exception to the MAI. This would have been risky, however. If the exception were later challenged under the WTO's dispute settlement mechanism, the panel empowered to resolve the dispute might not have recognized the exception. This problem of potential inconsistencies between MAI and WTO obligations was one that had not been addressed at the time the MAI negotiations ended.

Goals, Scope, and Application

The draft MAI is organized into 12 articles:

I.   General Provisions
II.   Scope and Application
III.   Treatment of Investors and Investments
IV.   Investment Protection
V.   Dispute Settlement
VI.   Exceptions and Safeguards
VII.   Financial Services
VIII.   Taxation
IX.   Reservations
X.   Relationship to Other International Agreements
XI.   Implementation and Operation
XII.   Final Provisions

This text discusses only the eight articles that would have created new substantive rules. Four articles (VII, VIII, X, and XI) tied the MAI to other international agreements without adding new provisions.

Article I consists mostly of a preamble outlining the basic goals of the agreement. These goals include "to strengthen ties of friendship and to promote greater economic co-operation" among the participating countries, to further recognition that "international investment has assumed great importance in the world economy and has considerably contributed to the development of their countries," to seek "agreement upon the treat-

5. See Dymond (1999); see also Henderson (1999).

ment to be accorded to investors and their investments [that] will contribute to the efficient utilization of economic resources, the creation of employment opportunities, and the improvement of living standards," and to ensure that "fair, transparent, and predictable investment regimes complement and benefit the world trading system." The article further affirms that the signatories (which the draft refers to as the contracting parties) wish "to establish a broad multilateral framework for international investment with high standards for the liberalization of investment regimes and investment protection and with effective dispute settlement procedures." Also mentioned among the goals is a renewal of the signatories' commitment to the Copenhagen Declaration of the World Summit on Social Development and to observance of internationally recognized core labor standards.

Even this preamble contains bracketed language, however. Examples include references to environmental protection and conservation, to a reaffirmation of the 1992 Rio Declaration on Environment, and to the "development of world-wide rules on foreign direct investment in the framework of the world trading system as embodied in the World Trade Organization."

The preamble's provisions pertaining to the environment and labor, incidentally, constitute the only language in the draft MAI on these issues apart from Article III. (As discussed below, provisions in that article bind governments to not lower standards on labor or the environment as a means of attracting investment). Nothing in the preamble, however, represents a binding obligation on any signatory—the preamble is simply a statement of goals. One issue that remained unresolved when the MAI negotiations were terminated was whether or not to add language to create binding obligations pertaining to these goals. As chapter 2 noted, any such obligations would have reduced the likelihood of non-OECD countries signing the MAI; they would also have generated opposition within the business communities of the OECD countries themselves. Indeed, the OECD Business-Industry Advisory Committee (BIAC), the official liaison between the OECD and the business community, had advised against inclusion of such obligations. But at the same time, certain negotiating parties, including most fervently the United States, favored their inclusion.

Finally, the preamble also indicates that the MAI shall be free-standing (as defined above) and open to accession by all countries, not just OECD members.

Article II, on the scope and application of the agreement, defines the terms "investor" and "investment" for purposes of the agreement and lays out its geographic scope. At the outset of the negotiations, in response to pressure from the business community, the goal was established to define very broadly the types of investors and investments that would be covered. Thus, "investor" includes both natural persons having "the nationality of, or . . . permanently residing in, a Contracting Party in accordance with its applicable law" and "legal person[s] or any other entity constituted or organized under the applicable law of a Contracting Party." The first category covers investors who are living human beings, whereas the second includes all types of business enterprises, whether for profit or not, and whether privately owned or state owned. An "investment" includes "every kind of asset owned or controlled, directly or indirectly, by an investor." Thus the scope of the MAI would have extended quite broadly, to portfolio investment as well as to direct investment. Intangible investments such as intellectual property would also have fallen under the scope of the agreement. This provision was sought by the business community as a means to create additional ammunition over and above that already created in the WTO Agreement on Trade-Related Intellectual Property Rights (TRIPs) against unauthorized use of intellectual property. Also covered are "nonequity" alternatives to direct investment such as long-term management contracts, under which a firm holds managerial control over, but not equity in, another business firm outside its home country. In all, the article defines eight categories of assets to be covered by the agreement.

Whether the agreement should have been so wide in scope is open to question. Without a doubt, the principal intent of the participating countries (and of their business communities) was for the agreement to apply primarily to direct investment: business operations in one country owned by and under the direct managerial control of investors in another. Most of the MAI's core provisions are indeed written primarily to apply to this type of investment, and their application to other forms of investment can pose certain problems. Some of the most important of these are illustrated later in this chapter and in chapter 6. Chapter 7 presents a case for narrowing this scope in any future multilateral investment agreement.

The geographic scope of the agreement essentially extends to all territory under the sovereign control of the signatory countries, including maritime areas beyond the "territorial sea" as defined in the 1982 United Nations Convention on the Law of the Sea. Elsewhere in the agreement (and discussed later in this chapter) are provisions for resolving disputes between signatories, as well as those between private investors and signatories, arising under the agreement. The draft MAI implicitly discourages application of one country's law and policy into territory under the sovereign control of another (so-called extraterritoriality), in favor of recourse to these dispute settlement procedures. Issues of extraterritoriality, especially those arising from the US Helms-Burton legislation, led to much difficulty in the negotiations, as narrated in chapter 2.

Obligations of Host Countries

Article III of the draft MAI, titled "Treatment of Investors and Investments," covers the obligations of signatory governments toward investors and their investments. Not all of these obligations are of equal importance, of course. However, these and the provisions on dispute settlement are, collectively, the most important parts of the whole agreement, and the parts most worth salvaging in any future investment negotiations, because they establish two key principles. The first is that governments should not, within their territories, discriminate in favor of domestically controlled enterprises against enterprises controlled by investors in a signatory country. And the second is that governments should not favor enterprises controlled by investors from one foreign country over enterprises controlled by investors from a signatory country. These principles of nondiscrimination are a critical tool for removing the government-imposed distortions that limit the efficient worldwide allocation of investment. Without these principles in place, the world economy will fail to achieve the maximum output from the limited investment resources available.

Binding international obligations of this kind can in effect "save governments from themselves," by giving them reasons to deny preferential treatment of investments controlled by politically powerful domestic constituencies (or by foreign investors with ties to local politicians). These preferences often have the effect of creating local monopolies or oligopolies and stifling the benefits that accrue from open competition among rival sellers of comparable goods and services. Such preferences might be very good for the domestic group that receives them. They might even be good for a politically well-connected foreign multinational that seeks to preserve a local monopoly against incursion by other multinationals. But rarely are they good for a country or its citizens as a whole.

The list of obligations in Article III is lengthy, but five of them appear essential to achieve the agreement's overall objectives. These five core obligations pertain to national treatment, most-favored-nation treatment, transparency, performance requirements, and investment incentives (on which there was no agreement at the time the negotiations were terminated). The rest of this section first examines each of these core obligations in detail, and then turns to an examination of other, arguably less important obligations.

National Treatment and Most-Favored-Nation Treatment

Two obligations of the MAI—the national treatment obligation and the most-favored-nation obligation—constitute the agreement's main provisions against discriminatory treatment of foreign investors and their investments. The national treatment clause reads as follows:

> Each Contracting Party shall accord to investors of another Contracting Party and to their investments, treatment no less favorable than the treatment it accords [in like circumstances] to its own investors and their investments with respect to the establishment, acquisition, expansion, operation, management, maintenance, use, enjoyment, and sale or other disposition of investments.

This clause is meant to ensure that neither foreign investors nor their investments are subject to discriminatory treatment from governments, in the sense that the foreign investors or investments are treated less favorably than domestic investors or investments.

One element of the draft MAI that distinguishes it from most other efforts to codify rules for investment is that the national treatment clause applies on a preestablishment as well as a postestablishment basis. Most bilateral investment treaties call only for the latter. Thus the MAI, in principle, rules out laws and policies designed to discourage new entry by foreign investors if these laws and policies do not apply equally to new entry by domestic investors. Had this principle been implemented without exception, it alone would have been a major liberalization. Even among OECD countries, national governments do have in place laws and policies that discriminate against foreign entry. However, these almost surely would have been preserved in the form of reservations had the MAI come into force.

The clause establishing most-favored-nation treatment reads as follows:

> Each Contracting Party shall accord to investors of another Contracting Party and to their investments, treatment no less favorable than the treatment it accords [in like circumstances] to investors of any other Contracting Party or of a non-Contracting Party, with respect to the establishment, acquisition, expansion, operation, management, maintenance, use, enjoyment, and sale or other disposition of investments.

This clause is meant to ensure that investors of one country (whether an MAI signatory or not) and their investments do not receive more favorable treatment than that granted to any MAI signatory. A third clause requires that signatory countries grant investors and investments of all MAI signatories the more favorable of national treatment or most-favored-nation treatment.

One issue not fully resolved when the negotiations broke down was whether or not there should be an exception to the most-favored-nation clause for regional economic integration organizations (REIOs). The issue was whether or not preferences granted within the European Union could be continued without the EU members having to extend these to non-member MAI signatories on a most-favored-nation basis. The United States, on behalf of itself and most of the other non-EU countries in the OECD, argued that such preferences should, as a matter of principle, not be allowed. The United States stuck to this position in spite of the fact that certain preferences created by NAFTA might have been covered under the REIO exception, to the benefit of investors of the United States and their investments. Apparently, the United States was prepared to give these benefits up. The United States seems to have been mainly concerned not over preferences currently in effect in the European Union, but rather over new preferences that might be created in the future, especially regarding investment in countries that are candidates for future EU accession. Of major concern was that the European Union might conclude agreements with former Soviet bloc countries that would give EU investors preferential claims on assets being privatized in these countries. Separate provisions of the MAI, discussed below, pertain to privatizations that attempt to provide nonpreferential and nondiscriminatory treatment for foreign investors as potential acquirers of privatized assets. Thus a major US concern was that a REIO clause would create special exemptions from these provisions.

Transparency

The basic requirement of the draft MAI's transparency clause is that all signatory countries publish "or otherwise make publicly available" all laws, regulations, and other policies applicable to foreign investors. Also, each signatory is required to "promptly respond to specific questions and provide, upon request, information" to other signatory governments with respect to such laws, regulations, and policies. However, neither these requirements nor any other provision of the MAI prevent a signatory government from requiring foreign investors or their investments to provide "routine information concerning that investment solely for information or statistical purposes." Governments can protect the confidentiality of information thus given. That is, information that must be provided to other signatory governments would not include information provided by foreign investors and their investments that is protected by assurances of confidentiality.

The transparency requirement is very important for the simple reason that, without it, governments might pursue unannounced or unpublicized policies that are highly discriminatory. This would clearly undermine the benefits that would ensue from the pursuit of those nondiscriminatory policies that are announced.

Performance Requirements

The draft MAI's provisions on performance requirements are among its most important elements, and it is important to understand what the agreement would and would not do in this matter. Performance requirements are obligations placed on foreign investors or (more commonly) their investments to do certain things in pursuit of national objectives. Often these objectives pertain to industrial policy. The objectives can be economic in nature, but may be social or political. Analysts, especially economists, have long objected to such requirements, largely on grounds that they can distort economic decisions and render the outcomes suboptimal. For example, a government might require that a local subsidiary of a multinational firm export some minimum percentage of its output. Such a requirement might help that government meet a national goal of export expansion, but it might also cause the exports of some other country to be displaced. The net result would be an overall reduction of economic efficiency, under the presumption that the second country can produce and export those goods or services at lower cost than the first country. Thus, it is argued, such a performance requirement can have effects not unlike those of a trade restriction or export subsidy, and hence should be subject to the same level of international discipline.

A recent study (Moran 1998) stresses that the effects of most performance requirements imposed on multinationals by developing countries are so perverse as to actually retard development in the country imposing them. Thus, whereas most analysis of performance requirements highlights the adverse effects on countries other than the one imposing the requirement, the latter is not immune. Those performance requirements especially likely to have negative effects on host countries include local content requirements, requirements for joint ventures or other forms of local equity participation, and requirements that would force technology transfer. Moran does note, however, that export performance requirements have in some cases benefited the country imposing them. (Mexico's export requirements placed on local subsidiaries of major automobile firms are an example.)

The negative aspects of performance requirements were explicitly recognized during the Uruguay Round of multilateral trade negotiations. One of the products of those negotiations was a new Agreement on Trade-Related Investment Measures (TRIMs), which has been administered by the World Trade Organization since 1995. The TRIMs agreement, however, covers only two types of performance requirements: local content requirements and trade balancing requirements (these are defined below). Local content requirements had already been declared inconsistent with Article III of the General Agreement on Tariffs and Trade (GATT) by a GATT disputes settlement panel during the 1980s. Certain of the parties that had negotiated the TRIMs agreement (including the European Union, Japan, and the United States) had sought a wider coverage than was actually agreed to, and the clause on performance requirements in the draft MAI reflects their earlier position.

The draft MAI bans signatory governments from imposing a number of types of performance requirements as conditions of entry or of continued presence of a foreign investor or investment. This list significantly expands the TRIMs obligations. However, the qualification "as conditions of entry or of continued presence" is important. As is discussed below, the same performance requirements in other circumstances, such as when linked to investment incentives, would not necessarily be banned. Indeed, performance requirements are most commonly used in OECD countries under just such circumstances.

The requirements to be banned as conditions of entry (or expansion, operation, maintenance, use, enjoyment, sale, or other disposition) of an investment were those that require a foreign investor:[6]

- to export a certain percentage or level of goods or services (export performance requirements);

- to achieve a certain percentage or level of domestic content in their output (local content requirements);

- to purchase, use, or accord a preference to goods or services produced or provided in the territory of a signatory country or from persons in its territory (a variant on local content requirements);

- "to relate in any way the volume or value of imports to the volume or value of exports or to the amount of foreign exchange inflows associated with such investment" (trade balancing requirements);

- "to restrict sales of goods or services in its territory that such investment produces or provides by relating such sales to the volume or value of its exports or foreign exchange earnings" (a variant on trade balancing requirements);

- "to transfer technology, a production process or other proprietary knowledge to a natural or a legal person in [the host country's][7] territory, except when the requirement is imposed or the commitment or undertaking is enforced by a court, administrative tribunal, or competition authority to remedy an alleged violation of competition laws [or to act in a manner not inconsistent with (relevant articles) of the TRIPs Agreement]" (technology transfer requirements);

- to "locate its headquarters for a specific region of the world or the world market in the territory of that Contracting Party";

- to "supply one or more of the goods that it produces or the services that it provides to a specific region or the world market exclusively from the territory of that Contracting Party";

- to "achieve a given level or value of production, investment, sales, employment, or research and development in its territory" (another variant on local content requirements);

- "to hire a given level of [local personnel] [nationals]";

- "to establish a joint venture" (presumably with local partners, although this is not specified); or

- "to achieve a minimum level of local equity participation."

---

6. "Foreign investor" includes subsidiaries under the investor's control.

7. The alternative bracketed phrases indicate that the choice of wording remained undecided in the draft.

All the items in the list except the first are types of performance requirements identified by Moran (1998) as potentially harmful to economic development. The apparent redundancy in the language banning local content requirements was considered necessary because, in implementing the TRIMs agreement, which also bans local content requirements, much confusion has arisen over what exactly constitutes such a requirement. Some of this confusion has resulted from the efforts of certain governments to preserve local content requirements by, in essence, disguising their true nature. The negotiators of the MAI thus felt it necessary to supplement the blanket ban on local content requirements by specifically banning those variants that have been subject to controversy in the TRIMs agreement.

Investment Incentives

At the time of the MAI negotiations, no OECD country generally imposed performance requirements on foreign direct investors as a condition of entry or continued presence. But some OECD countries have often made performance requirements conditions of receipt of investment incentives. Investment incentives are subsidies and subsidy-like measures granted to investors who agree to place their investments in the territory of the government granting the incentive. In addition to these OECD countries, many Asian countries, including some in Southeast Asia as well as China, have offered these incentives.

As already noted, the MAI draft did not effectively establish disciplines over investment incentives. But considerable theoretical analysis and empirical evidence indicates that such incentives can result in foreign investments going to locations where they are less efficient than they could have been. Investment incentives may, in addition, waste the resources of the governments that offer them, in the sense that any benefits derived locally therefrom may be fully offset (or more than offset) by the costs.

These propositions can be illustrated by the following example, which is based on an actual case as described by a senior government official of the country (an Asian nation) that offered the incentive. The official claimed that the incentive created benefits for this country. In fact, a dissection of the official's own arguments shows that the incentive reduced world welfare, and may have failed even to bring net local benefits.

What happened was as follows. A large multinational firm was considering investing in one of two countries in order to expand output of one of its products. In one of the countries (that of the official who is the source of the example, which we will call country A), the firm had no existing facilities for this product and would have had to build a new one from scratch. In the other country (country B), however, the firm already owned a production facility and could have simply expanded that facility. The product in question embodied a rather sophisticated technology, and officials of country A believed that, if the firm could be enticed to locate the new facility in their territory, the country would capture some external benefits in the form of technology transfer.

Management of the firm represented to officials of country A that to expand the facility in country B was in fact the more economic alternative. However, management also indicated that they would consider building a new facility in country A instead if given some sort of financial incentive to do so. In response, country A did offer a large package of incentives, and the production facility ended up being located there. Officials of this country therefore proclaimed its granting of investment incentives to be a major success.

But who were the real winners and losers in this episode? Let us first assume that the firm told the truth when it said that, incentives aside, it was more economical to locate facilities in country B than in country A. It follows that location of the investment in country B reduced world economic efficiency. It simply would have been less costly (that is, would have required fewer economic resources, and, hence, from a world perspective, efficiency-enhancing) had the firm located the investment in country B.

In the actual case, the firm did not disclose the reasons why it saw country B as the lower-cost location. However, a reasonable conjecture is that expansion of the existing facility would have enabled the realization of scale economies, or economies in logistics, that could not be realized by a new facility in country A. Thus the incentives represented, in effect, a transfer payment by the taxpayers of country A to subsidize the inefficient location of the facility in that country. One wonders whether the officials of country A would have won praise from their country's taxpayers if they had presented their "triumph" in this light.

But it gets worse for the hapless officials of country A. What if the firm in fact was bluffing about country A's locational disadvantage? What if country A had been the preferred choice all along, and the firm had claimed to prefer country B simply as a ruse, to induce country A's officials to offer an incentive package? This is not a far-fetched hypothesis. Country A was known to be rather profligate in its use of investment incentives, and executives of the firm were surely aware of this. If indeed the firm was bluffing, then the outcome of the story was that taxpayers in country A were suckered into paying the firm to do what it would have done without the incentives. In other words, all the benefits of the investment in country A might have been attained at no cost to the country. If this were true, rather than proclaiming success, the officials who granted the incentives should have hung their heads in shame.

In their defense, however, the officials might have pointed to the external benefits generated by the investment and noted that, given uncertainty about the firm's true situation, it was economically rational to grant incentives up to the amount of these externalities. If the officials had no way of differentiating bluff from truth, the granting of incentives served as a kind of insurance policy, ensuring that country A would realize at least some of the potential benefits. This possibility arguably exonerates these officials from wasting the taxpayers' money. But it does not exonerate them from the charge that their actions contributed to lost welfare globally. Indeed, even if the firm was not bluffing, the net result of the offering of incentives was that potential external benefits were created in country A at the expense of country B. In other words, the incentive created a "beggar-thy-neighbor" effect as well as a reduction in world economic welfare.

One argument for international rules to abolish or constrain the use of investment incentives is that, in cases like that just described, firms would have a reduced incentive, or none, to bluff about their locational preferences for new investments when dealing with host-country governments. An even stronger argument is that investment incentives necessarily result in either a loss of world welfare or an unnecessary transfer from taxpayers to foreign investors. If an investment would have gone to a particular location even without incentives, then incentives impose a cost on local taxpayers without creating any offsetting gain. But if the incentive results in placement of an investment in a nonoptimal location, it creates global welfare losses accompanied by beggar-thy-neighbor effects.

Why, then, does there seem to be so little willingness on the part of officials to end investment incentives? One reason is that, as we have seen, such incentives can create external benefits for the country offering them. The incentives may reduce global welfare, but the costs are felt elsewhere. And officials, after all, are accountable to their own citizens, not to those of foreign lands. The value of incentives as an insurance policy also accounts for countries' reluctance to give them up.

This propensity to offer incentives is magnified if governments believe that other governments are offering incentives for the same investment. Indeed, if multiple governments are seeking the same investment, the likely result is that they will bid against each other. The price paid by the winning government will then likely be significantly higher than if only one government were in the bidding. The reason is that each government believes, to a point, that if it can outbid other governments, the investment will generate net benefits even after accounting for all the costs of the bid. But without question, all governments would be better off if none of them bid for the investment and the "winner" were determined by its intrinsic locational advantage.

The situation just described is a familiar one in economics, where it is known as a "prisoner's dilemma." In a prisoner's dilemma, each party has an incentive to bid if it believes that other parties will also bid, but also, and perversely, each party has an incentive to bid if it knows that *no* other parties will bid. Yet if all parties bid, all are made worse off than if no one bids. Hence the best outcome for all is for all parties to agree that no one will bid. But this outcome is difficult to achieve, because each party believes that if it cheats on the agreement (and no one else does), it will come out ahead. Thus each party faces an incentive to cheat. Further, each party knows that all other parties face the same perverse incentive. Thus the likely outcome is that all parties will cheat. Indeed, because each party also knows that, if other parties cheat, it should cheat as well, each party's best move is to cheat from the outset. The consequence is that, even if all parties understand that their mutual interest lies in no one bidding, the actual outcome will be that all bid.

It is well established in the economic literature based on game theory that there is only one way to achieve the optimal solution in a prisoner's dilemma. That is for the parties both to agree among themselves not to bid *and* to devise a means to punish those that might cheat on the agreement (see, e.g., Friedman 1986, chapter 3). Indeed, it has been suggested in the theoretical literature that the whole WTO framework constitutes such an agreement, where sanctions applied through the dispute settlement process serve as punishment for any party that cheats on a WTO obligation. Similarly, it can be argued that multilateral rules like those of the WTO, together with an effective dispute resolution mechanism, are the only available and potentially effective means of limiting the efficiency- and welfare-reducing properties of investment incentives.

In the meantime, however, governments persist in granting such incentives. Indeed, there is evidence that their use rose substantially over the course of the 1990s.[8] Hence there would appear to be a strong prima facie case for some sort of ban or restriction on these incentives as part of a multilateral investment agreement.

This case is magnified greatly when such incentives are linked to performance requirements. In effect, this linkage serves to compensate investors for making suboptimal investment decisions. Thus, for example, a given site for the manufacture of a product might be uneconomic, in the sense that the delivered cost of the output is greater than could be achieved at another location. But a firm might be willing to locate production at the inferior site if it is offered enough of a subsidy to do so. In such a case, production at the inferior site imposes a cost on society at large: resources are used wastefully, and total output is less than what it could otherwise be. Of course, the main burden is borne by those whose taxes fund the subsidy.

Another problem with linking performance requirements to incentives is that these arrangements tend to be highly nontransparent: often they result from covert understandings between the agencies that grant the subsidies and the firms that do the investing. Thus, information about the

---

8. E.g., for Europe see European Union (1997). Among the major users of investment incentives are the US states, but information about the magnitudes and costs of these incentives are not published.

true extent of the practice is scant. However, it is clear that the investment subsidies granted by US states often do come with strings attached, as do investment incentives offered by national and regional investment promotion boards in Europe.[9]

Despite the clear distortions caused by linking investment incentives and performance requirements, the MAI negotiators were unable to agree on what to do about the problem. Bracketed language in the draft text would have committed the MAI signatories to future negotiations "to further avoid and minimize such distorting effects and to avoid undue competition between Contracting Parties in order to attract or retain investments." But it seems that certain OECD member governments preferred not to address the issue in the MAI at all. The main reason has to do with the federal structure of several of these governments, including those of Canada, Germany, and the United States. In all of these countries, investment incentives are handed out primarily by subnational governments: the state governments in the United States, the provincial governments in Canada, and the governments of the *länder* in Germany. In some (e.g., Canada), the problem is that, legally, the federal government might not be able to bind the subnational governments to a multilateral discipline on incentives, because it has no power over their spending policies. In others (e.g., the United States), the federal government clearly has this power but may be unwilling to use it for political reasons.[10]

The omission of investment incentives from the MAI is arguably the agreement's most blatant deficiency in terms of its ability to alter the practices of governments that might have adverse effects on the outcome of investment decisions. It probably is the most intractable as well, given that the problem has the nature of a prisoner's dilemma. (As one negotiator [who wishes to remain anonymous] put it, the failure of the MAI to create disciplines on investment incentives "was a triumph of realpolitik over economics.") As argued above, the only way to solve such a problem is for the parties to reach a consensus to bind themselves to mutually agreed upon disciplines, but for reasons just cited, no such consensus existed at the time the MAI negotiations were terminated.[11]

In addition to these four core obligations (or five, if one counts the empty obligation on investment incentives), Article III created other obligations that would apply to governments in their treatment of investors and investments. Many of the provisions establishing these obligations, however, were either not finished or not agreed upon when the negotiations broke down. Each of these is treated briefly in what follows.

---

9. Some of the best documentation of this practice is provided in reports prepared by governments of other countries. See, e.g., MITI (2000).

10. On the legal powers of the US federal government in this domain, see Enrich (1996).

11. Arriving at such a consensus would require a strong commitment to the desired outcome on the part of the top leadership of the negotiating countries. However, as chapter 2 revealed, such a commitment was almost totally lacking with respect to the MAI.

Temporary Entry, Stay, and Work of Investors and Key Personnel

The MAI negotiators originally intended to greatly simplify visa and other official requirements for nonnational personnel who might be assigned to work in an investment (usually a controlled subsidiary) of a foreign investor in an executive or technical capacity on a temporary basis. Provisions toward this goal would have qualified as promoting nondiscrimination in the sense that they would have ended preferences in employment for nationals of the country in which an investment is located. This goal was sought mostly by the business community.

The actual provisions in the draft MAI fell somewhat short of this goal. However, they did require that "Each Contracting Party shall grant temporary entry, stay, and authorization to work" to a natural person of another contracting party who is either an investor seeking to establish an investment or an employee of an enterprise covered by the agreement. The spouse and children of such a person must also be granted temporary entry and stay, and signatory governments are encouraged (but not required) to grant these spouses permission to work. Another provision allows investors to employ persons of any nationality to work in an investment, provided those persons have met national requirements.

According to some persons familiar with the negotiations, the negotiators' original intent was to make it easier than it typically is under existing law for foreign investors to employ in their subsidiaries persons who are not nationals of the host country. However, the existing text seems to do little more than ensure that signatory governments cannot require foreign investors to discriminate in their employment practices in favor of local nationals.

Nationality Requirements for Executives, Managers, and Directors

The draft MAI bans requirements relating to the nationality of executives, managers, and members of boards of directors of a foreign subsidiary whose parent firm is in an MAI signatory. Such requirements might include the stipulation that citizens of the host country be appointed to such positions in these subsidiaries.

Employment Requirements

The draft MAI requires signatory countries to allow investors of other signatories and their investments to employ any person of any nationality, providing that person holds a "valid permit of sejour and work" and the employment is compatible with that permit. It should be noted that this obligation and the one governing executives, managers, and directors are ones that all member countries of the OECD could meet with no change in existing law or policy. Members of the business community had sought a stronger provision that would have eased requirements for work permits. The extant, status quo-preserving language does not, of course, meet this goal. The language was retained in part at the behest of the business community in order that the issue might be revisited at some later time.

Privatization

The draft MAI imposes an obligation on signatories to accord both national treatment and most-favored-nation treatment to foreign investors seeking to purchase publicly owned assets being privatized. The same obligations would also apply to transactions after the initial sale. These obligations, however, do not disallow governments from executing voucher schemes that limit the purchase of such assets in an initial privatization to domestic residents, provided that this right is granted only to natural persons and that there are no restrictions on subsequent sales of the assets covered by the vouchers. Also, the MAI imposes no obligation on a signatory actually to privatize anything. The MAI negotiators sought to have the agreement cover special share arrangements (i.e., arrangements whereby managers, employees, or local residents are granted special treatment with respect to acquisition of shares in an enterprise to be privatized). However, four alternative drafts of such language were under consideration at the time the negotiations were terminated. These ranged from one draft that would ban most such arrangements to one that would permit them unless they were explicitly discriminatory or in violation of most-favored-nation provisions. (An example would be if the arrangement disallowed subsequent sale of the shares to a national of a signatory.)

Entities with Delegated Government Authority

Other provisions of the draft require that any entity to which a signatory government has granted regulatory, administrative, or other government authority act in a manner not inconsistent with MAI obligations. Among other things, the provision was a useful clarification that the obligation to provide national treatment extended to governmental and quasi-governmental regulatory agencies.

Monopolies, State Enterprises, and Concessions

The MAI draft contains the following bracketed provision: "Nothing in this Agreement shall be construed to prevent a Contracting Party from maintaining, designating, or eliminating a monopoly." An accompanying provision (not in brackets except as indicated) states that "Each Contracting Party shall [endeavor to] accord non-discriminatory treatment when designating a monopoly." The bracketed phrase would, of course, render this provision largely unenforceable. The MAI was meant to contain language precisely defining what constitutes a "monopoly" or a "designated monopoly," but as of the time that the negotiations were terminated, such language was not agreed upon, and several alternative definitions had been put forth.

A further provision requires that any designated privately or publicly owned monopoly:

1. not act in a manner inconsistent with MAI obligations with respect to any governmental, regulatory, or administrative authority delegated to it;

2. provide nondiscriminatory treatment to investors or investments of investors of another contracting party in the sale of monopoly goods or services;

3. provide nondiscriminatory treatment to these investors or investments in its purchases of monopoly goods or services (but this provision does not apply to procurement of goods or services by a government agency where these are for government purposes and are not for resale or for use in the production of a good or service for commercial sale);

4. not abuse its monopoly position;[12] and

5. act solely in accordance with commercial considerations in its sale or purchase of monopoly goods or services, except to comply with "terms of its designation that are not inconsistent with (the obligations just listed)."

Disputes arising over the application of these five obligations are not subject to the investor-to-state dispute settlement procedures but are subject to the state-to-state procedures.

If an activity is demonopolized, the relevant signatory is allowed to list a reservation regarding that activity at the time. Officially designated monopolies must also be notified to the MAI within 60 days of the agreement's entry into force, and any monopolies designated after the entry into force must be notified within 60 days, as must any elimination of designated monopolies and related new reservations.

State enterprises under the draft MAI would be subject to unfinished provisions for anticircumvention. "Anticircumvention" in this instance

---

12. Three alternative drafts to restrict such abuse are proposed, one of which is a "zero option" imposing no such obligation.

means that a government may not use a state enterprise to get around its MAI obligations. Rather, such enterprises would be bound by these obligations.

With respect to concessions (i.e., the transfer of any operation from public to private hands without transfer of ownership, for example, transfer of the right to mine on public land), two provisions would have applied. First, any such concessions must be transparent. "Transparent" here means that all relevant rules and procedures must be written in one of the two official languages of the OECD (French and English) and publicly available. It also means that publication must occur sufficiently in advance to enable candidates "to engage and, in so far as it remains compatible with an efficient operation of the mechanism of attribution of concessions, to accomplish the formalities required by qualifying evaluations." This latter (rather cumbersome) requirement was clearly intended to bolster nondiscrimination by disallowing procedures that de facto discriminate in favor of local persons over foreign investors. However, this requirement clearly would have been difficult to enforce. Second, the requirement for transparency does not apply to very small concessions (a threshold requirement was to have been established but was never decided) or to concessions associated with a designated monopoly.

Not Lowering Standards

Rather late in the negotiations, a provision was added to the draft MAI aimed at preventing other provisions from leading to an undesirable reduction in health, safety, labor, or environmental standards. This provision was inserted in response to pressure from nongovernmental organizations that believed that the MAI might have the effect of lowering such standards (see chapter 1). However, no specific language had been agreed to at the time that negotiations ceased. One version would obligate governments not to lower health, safety, and environmental standards and not to relax core domestic labor standards as a means to encourage investment. Another version would merely assert that it was "inappropriate" to lower or relax these standards.

As in other areas where language was not agreed upon, the main issue was whether or not the provision might be enforceable, in the sense that it could be the basis for bringing a dispute to the agreement's investor-to-state or state-to-state dispute settlement procedures. At the final negotiating sessions in the spring of 1998, certain negotiators, especially those of the United States, were leaning toward the obligatory language. Indeed, one of the US negotiators had made public statements suggesting that the United States might seek provisions pertaining to labor and the environment that went beyond this provision. But no action in this direction was actually taken.

Investment Protection Provisions

Article IV of the draft MAI deals with investment protection. One of the goals of the MAI, as articulated by the OECD Secretariat in a series of meetings held at the beginning of the negotiations, was to achieve very high levels of investment protection. Thus Article IV was accorded high priority during the negotiations, and this part of the draft agreement is largely devoid of bracketed or contested language. However, public reaction against the investment protection provisions as drafted was widespread and vocal. As detailed in chapter 2, critics of the MAI, especially the environmentally oriented NGOs, complained that these provisions, in conjunction with the MAI's investor-to-state dispute settlement procedures (and, arguably, an overly broad definition of what constitutes "investment") would have damaging repercussions. They could, the NGOs claimed, enable foreign firms to sue governments on an unprecedented scale for actions formerly considered within their sovereign rights but that might have adversely affected foreign investors' interests.

One issue that remains something of a mystery, especially in light of the opposition that the investment protection provisions created, is why the draft MAI should have contained the investment protection provisions it did. After all, the agreement was meant mostly to cover investment among the OECD countries, and these countries have a solid record of not expropriating each other's investments except in rare circumstances, and even then under due process of law and with compensation. In other words, there seemed to be little or no need for these provisions, at least unless and until the agreement was expanded to include developing countries, some of which have a history of expropriating foreign investments without due process or compensation.

These investment protection provisions of the draft MAI consist of six parts. The first part is on general treatment. This would have obligated MAI signatories to accord to investors of other signatories "fair and equitable treatment and full and constant protection and security . . . [no] less favorable than that required by international law."

The second part contained the article's core provision. It pertained to expropriation and compensation, the treatment of which is at the heart of the regulatory takings issue, discussed in the next chapter. This provision itself is in four subparts. The first is the one already quoted in chapter 2: "A Contracting Party shall not expropriate or nationalize directly or indirectly an investment in its territory of another Contracting Party or take any measure or measures having equivalent effect . . . except:

a. for a purpose which is in the public interest,
b. on a nondiscriminatory basis,
c. in accordance with due process of law, and

d. accompanied by payment of prompt, adequate, and effective com-
      pensation. . . ."

The remaining three subparts provide that such compensation is to be paid without delay, must be for the fair market value of the expropriated investment, and must be fully realizable and transferable. A further sub-provision stipulates that "due process of law" includes the right of appeal for investors who feel that the compensation they receive for an expro-priated property is less than the fair market value.

The third provision of the investor protection provisions deals with pro-tection from strife. This provision essentially calls for national treatment in the event that investors suffer losses from war, civil disturbance, or sim-ilar disruptions. The negotiators meant this provision to be interpreted to mean that any such losses would be compensated only to the extent that the government chooses to compensate any party for losses due to strife. Because under most circumstances such loss is not subject to compensa-tion, foreign investors would not normally be entitled to compensation. However, one subprovision explicitly states that if an investor of a signa-tory suffers loss as the result of requisition by another signatory's armed forces or destruction of assets by these armed forces, where this destruc-tion is "not required by the necessity of the situation," the investor is en-titled to have the loss treated as though it were an expropriation.

A fourth provision obliges signatories to allow investors of another sig-natory to transfer payments into and out of its territory freely and with-out delay. An illustrative list of payments that are allowed is provided, al-though it is noted that the list is not exhaustive. Thus, types of payments not on the list might nonetheless be subject to the same obligation. Signa-tories are obligated to ensure that such payments be made in a freely con-vertible currency at spot exchange rates. An important exception pertains to investors' freedom to transfer funds, however: signatories may restrict transfers in circumstances consistent with GATT provisions pertaining to balance of payments crises.

The remaining three provisions of the investor protection section are largely technical in nature. The first of these deals with information trans-fer and data processing. Signatories are not allowed to take measures to prevent the transfer outside their territory of information necessary for the conduct of business or related to the purchase or sale of an enterprise. They may, however, impose record-keeping and reporting requirements and take measures to protect privacy "including the protection of per-sonal data, intellectual and industrial property, and the confidentiality of individual records and accounts."

The second of these provisions has to do with subrogation of claims. Here the basic obligation is that signatories must recognize claims that might arise out of assignment of a claim to a party other than the party originally holding the claim.

The third of these provisions is bracketed in the draft MAI. The basic obligation under this provision is that the investor protection provisions shall apply to investments existing at the time the MAI enters into force as well as to investments that might be established or acquired thereafter. What is left unresolved is whether the agreement would apply to "events which occurred, or to claims that had been settled, prior to its entry into force."

Dispute Settlement Procedures

Article V of the MAI establishes a set of dispute settlement procedures. Further, because the MAI was to have been a free-standing agreement and not part of the WTO, these dispute settlement procedures were to be independent and different from those of the WTO. Indeed, because the draft MAI imposes obligations on countries pertaining to international investors, which are not governments, and because only governments have standing (that is, the right to bring complaints) in the WTO's dispute settlement procedures, these procedures would not be adequate to the requirements of the MAI. The reason is that investors (e.g., large international firms) can have interests that diverge from those of their home-country governments. Indeed, disputes might arise between an investor and a host country in which the investor's home-country government would prefer an outcome entirely contrary to that sought by the investor. For example, the home-country government might not have wanted the investor to make the investment at all.

Thus the draft MAI provides for two distinct dispute settlement mechanisms. The first is a set of state-to-state procedures, intended to resolve disputes between governments. The second is a set of investor-to-state procedures, meant to resolve disputes between investors and governments. Both sets of procedures are modeled more closely on existing procedures of NAFTA than on those of the WTO.

In the MAI draft, the state-to-state dispute settlement procedures appear before the investor-to-state procedures. However, the negotiators envisaged that the former would normally be invoked only in the event of some failure in the execution of the latter. For example, the state-to-state procedures might be invoked if a signatory country should fail to abide by the outcome of proceedings under the investor-to-state procedures. For this reason it makes more sense to discuss the dispute settlement procedures in reverse order from that in which they appear in the text.

The draft MAI's investor-to-state dispute resolution procedures are similar but not identical to those of NAFTA. In both procedures, in the event of a dispute over interpretation or application of the agreement, investors are first urged to settle the dispute through consultation and negotiation with the appropriate authorities of the government against which the complaint is lodged. Failing this, under the MAI, an investor may submit the dispute to any of the following for resolution:[13]

- a competent court or administrative tribunal of the signatory country against which the dispute is brought;

- any procedure agreed to by both disputants; or

- arbitration in accordance with the MAI under the Convention on the Settlement of Investment Disputes between States and Nationals of other States (the ICSID convention), the Additional Facility Rules of the Centre for Settlement of Investment Disputes (the ICSID Additional Facility), the arbitration rules of the United Nations Commission on International Trade Law (UNCITRAL), or the arbitration rules of the International Chamber of Commerce (ICC).[14]

The ICSID Additional Facility is part of the World Bank Group, and UNCITRAL, as its name suggests, is part of the United Nations.

Under the draft MAI, each signatory would give its "unconditional consent to the submission of a dispute to international arbitration. . . ." However, a signatory could condition this consent on the investor (or investment) that is party to the dispute waiving its right "to initiate any other dispute settlement procedure with respect to the same dispute and withdraw from any such procedure in progress before its conclusion." (This condition is termed "limitation of consent.")

Under the arbitration procedures, a three-person tribunal would be formed to arbitrate the dispute. The parties to the dispute would each appoint one member of the tribunal, and the third, who would preside, would be appointed jointly by the disputants. A roster of persons qualified to be arbiters would be maintained by the MAI signatories, and under most circumstances arbiters would be drawn from this roster. However, if resolution of a dispute required special expertise not possessed by any person on the roster acceptable to the disputants, other persons possessing this expertise could be named to the tribunal.

If two or more disputes submitted for arbitration involving the same signatory have a question of law or fact in common, a tribunal may be established for "consolidated consideration" of all or part of these disputes. Because this tribunal might hear the complaint of more than one investor, the investors must decide jointly whom to appoint to the tribunal and under which set of rules the arbitration shall proceed. If no such agree-

13. In NAFTA, only a party that is strictly an investor of another signatory may institute arbitration procedures against a signatory. Under the MAI, an investment of such an investor (i.e., a subsidiary) may also initiate these procedures. In other words, the standing of enterprises with respect to the enterprise-to-state procedures extends further than in NAFTA.

14. Here the only difference between the MAI and NAFTA is the addition of the ICC option.

ment were reached within a specified time, the proceedings would be conducted under UNCITRAL rules. The tribunal would "assume jurisdiction over all or part of the disputes and the other arbitral proceedings shall be stayed or adjourned, as appropriate if, after considering the views of the parties, it decides that to do so would best serve the fair and efficient resolution of the disputes and that the disputes fall within the scope [of these provisions]." An investor could pull out of the procedure but, in doing so, would forfeit its rights to have the same dispute arbitrated later. The dispute could be resolved by other means, however.

In arbitrating a dispute, the tribunal could call upon expert advice. Third parties (signatories that are not disputants but have an interest in the case are entitled to make their positions known to the tribunal. All decisions of the tribunal must be decided in accordance with the MAI; that is, the MAI is the "applicable law." The tribunal "may recommend an interim measure of protection to preserve the rights of a disputing Contracting Party or to ensure that the tribunal's jurisdiction is made fully effective." A disputant may seek interim relief not involving monetary damages, and this is not deemed to be a submission of the dispute for resolution under which the signatory's limitation of consent (see above) could be invoked. The tribunal could determine that, if a signatory has failed to comply with its obligations under the MAI, a pecuniary award may be granted to the disputing investor. Members of a tribunal and parties to the dispute must protect the confidentiality of information revealed in the course of the proceedings, and this confidentiality must also be preserved in the draft of the final award.

The final award by an arbitral tribunal could consist of any combination of the following:

- a declaration that the signatory in a dispute has failed to comply with its obligations under the MAI;

- pecuniary compensation, including interest accruing from the time that the loss or damage was incurred;

- "restitution in kind in appropriate cases, providing that the Contracting Party may pay pecuniary compensation in lieu thereof where restitution is not practicable"; and

- "with the agreement of the parties to the dispute, any other form of relief."

The state-to-state dispute settlement procedures would be invoked in disputes between or among MAI signatories as to whether an action taken by one signatory is in conformance with its MAI obligations. This could include instances where a signatory has violated an obligation but claimed a national security or public order exception (see below). But as suggested above, if a signatory should fail to abide by the outcome of an arbitral award granted to an investor under the investor-to-state procedures, or if investor-to-state dispute settlement procedures are terminated without resolution by the tribunal arbitrating the investor's claim, state-to-state procedures might also be invoked. In such instances, presumably, the investor's home government would act on its behalf.

The state-to-state procedures laid out in the draft MAI mirror other dispute settlement procedures (including those of the WTO) in that a period of consultation is required prior to invoking the arbitration mechanism. Any MAI signatory may request that another signatory enter into consultations over a dispute regarding interpretation or application of the agreement. The request must be in writing and must "provide sufficient information to understand the basis for the request." The requested signatory must then actually enter into consultations within 30 days. If after 60 days from the date of the request the parties have failed to resolve the dispute, they may seek multilateral consultations with other signatories not involved in the dispute, which then must make a (nonbinding) recommendation within 60 days. Likewise, the disputing parties may, in the event of failure to resolve their dispute through consultations, "have recourse to good offices or to mediation or conciliation under such rules and procedures as they may agree."

However, the draft provides that, should all of these procedures fail to resolve the dispute, arbitration may be invoked. Under this procedure, a tribunal would be established that could then "decide disputes in accordance with this Agreement, interpreted and applied in accordance with the applicable rules of international law." The tribunal could, in the event that it decides that a signatory is indeed in contravention of its obligations, take remedial action, including recommending interim remedial action pending a final decision. The final remedial action might include:

- a declaration that an action of a signatory is in contravention of its MAI obligations;

- a recommendation that a signatory bring its actions into conformity with its MAI obligations;

- pecuniary compensation to the investor for any losses that might be incurred by the investor of the contracting party that requested the arbitration; or

- any other form of relief to which the signatory against whom the dispute is directed might agree.

Other provisions allow the decision of a tribunal to be nullified (e.g., if the tribunal has exceeded its powers or was not properly constituted). However, still other provisions are designed to encourage compliance with a remedial action (e.g., a signatory can be effectively suspended from participation in the agreement in the event of noncompliance, and other limited sanctions can be taken).

The investor-to-state dispute settlement procedures were, as chapter 2 described in some detail, an aspect of the draft agreement to which NGOs objected strenuously. The NGOs claimed that private companies might use the procedures to sue governments for losses claimed by the companies to result from application of environmental and other regulations. Whether this would actually have happened is, of course, an untested issue, but experience with similar provisions in NAFTA would seem to buttress the NGOs' case. Indeed, it could be argued that the dynamic created by these procedures would have been the major means by which the MAI would have had an impact. A series of cases in which panels found violations of core provisions of the MAI not covered by the exceptions might, for instance, have a significant impact on the investment policies of countries that practiced de facto discrimination against foreign investors in favor of incumbent domestic firms.

Exceptions, Safeguards, and Reservations

Article VI of the draft MAI allows a number of general exceptions to the agreement's obligations. In addition, certain temporary safeguards are allowed. The latter are exceptions that may be applied only on a temporary basis, whereas the former are subject to no time limit. And, of course, there would have existed lists of country-specific exceptions to obligations (reservations).

Reservations are covered under Article IX. This article requires that reservations be negotiated at the time of a country's accession to the MAI. In contrast, exceptions apply to all countries, and safeguards are available to all countries, automatically at the time of accession.

General exceptions are allowed for national security and for maintenance of the public order. These exceptions do not apply to the investor protection obligations, however. The national security exception essentially allows a signatory to take measures considered necessary for the "protection of its essential security interests . . . in time of war, or armed conflict, or other emergency in international relations" or "relating to nonproliferation of weapons of mass destruction, or relating to the production of arms and ammunition," even if these would otherwise violate MAI obligations. Also, a signatory is exempt from furnishing or providing access to information where such revelation would be considered contrary to its national security interests. Likewise, signatories may take actions in pursuance of obligations under the UN Charter without violating MAI obligations.

The general exception for public order states that, "subject to the requirement that such measures are not applied in a manner which would constitute a means of arbitrary or unjustifiable discrimination between

Contracting Parties," signatories may take any measure necessary for the maintenance of public order without violating MAI obligations. The ambiguity of this exception is apparent: how, after all, does one define whether a measure ostensibly taken to protect public order is in fact a "means of arbitrary or unjustifiable discrimination"?

Actions or measures taken pursuant to these general exceptions are subject to a notification requirement. This requirement was instituted so that, if one signatory believed that another signatory had taken such actions or measures solely for economic reasons, or that the actions or measures were "not in proportion to the interest being protected," it could initiate state-to-state dispute settlement procedures.

Safeguards in the draft MAI are designed to allow signatories to apply measures inconsistent with MAI obligations regarding transfers, national treatment, or certain other obligations in the event of a balance of payments crisis or other monetary crisis. Such measures must be consistent with the Articles of Agreement of the International Monetary Fund and must "not exceed those necessary to deal with [the crisis]." They must also be reviewed no less frequently than every six months and terminated when circumstances allow. Provisions are also made for determining whether measures invoked by a signatory are in fact consistent with the allowed safeguard. A bracketed provision, however, would disallow the use of this safeguard to delay compensation in the event of an expropriation.

The most important exceptions in the MAI, as already noted, would have been the country-specific reservations. The lists of reservations as submitted were not made public, but reportedly they incorporated virtually all existing laws and policies of the negotiating countries that were inconsistent with obligations established in the draft MAI. However, acceptance of a country's proposed reservations would have been a matter of negotiation, and one reason completion of the MAI was repeatedly delayed was that negotiations over reservations were never really begun in earnest, let alone completed. Whether these negotiations would have resulted in actual liberalization of investment regimes among the negotiating parties is thus unknowable.

As noted earlier, accession to the MAI would have been open to any country (or regional economic integration organization or autonomous customs area) that "possesses full autonomy in the conduct of matters covered by (the MAI) [and] is willing and able to undertake its obligations on terms agreed between it and the Contracting Parties. . . ." The last phrase would include negotiations involving the proposed reservations that would be lodged by the acceding country. Of course, no such negotiations have ever been undertaken, since the MAI has never come into force. One can reasonably conjecture, however, that the main difficulty facing a non-OECD country seeking accession to the MAI would have been in the negotiation of reservations.

The Mouse That Might Have Roared?

If one were to try to characterize the MAI in a single phrase, it might well be "the mouse that might have roared." The agreement was a mouse in the sense that it did virtually nothing to liberalize the international investment policies of the countries that negotiated it, or to remove distortions that reduce the economic value of an investment. But it would have created a new dispute settlement procedure as well as a number of provisions that, applied without reservation, would doubtless have led to liberalization eventually. Given time, the possibility of future rollback of countries' reservations, and the likelihood of disputes being resolved in ways that would force liberalization, there is some probability that the mouse might indeed have roared.

But the draft agreement also contained some very zealous investor and investment protection provisions and established a very broad definition of investment. These might have opened the door to investors to use the agreement's dispute settlement procedures to sue governments for policies and practices that really had very little to do with international investment. Thus, if the MAI was the mouse that might have roared, its roar might not have been an altogether constructive one. In fact, certain interests saw the potential for an undesirable roar as so great that they combined to kill the MAI in its nest. But had the MAI survived, whether its roar might ever have been actually heard is another matter, on which one can only conjecture.

4

Globalization, Foreign Direct Investment, and Labor

In the United States, opposition to globalization is centered in the organized labor movement and in certain environmentally oriented nongovernmental organizations. This chapter deals with the former. The concerns of the latter are discussed in chapter 5.

Leaders of the labor movement sometimes talk of globalism and its effects on people in the world's poor countries in terms that border on the apocalyptic. For example, writing in a recent issue of *Foreign Affairs,* Jay Mazur, president of the Union of Needletrades, Industrial, and Textile Workers (UNITE), states:

> Millions of workers are losing out in a global economy that disrupts traditional economies and weakens the ability of their governments to assist them. They are left to fend for themselves within failed states against destitution, famine, and plagues. They are forced to migrate, to offer their labor at wages below subsistence, sacrifice their children, and cash in on their natural environments and often their personal health—all in a desperate struggle to survive. (Mazur 2000, 82)

Much of this chapter is devoted to examining whether or not the causal link that Mazur implies between globalization and the undeniable miseries that one sees in many developing countries is borne out by the evidence. But if US union leaders like Mazur are concerned about the effects of globalization on workers everywhere (and in this they are joined by a number of human rights-oriented NGOs), they are especially concerned, and understandably so, about the effects of globalization generally—and of outward US direct investment specifically—on the members of their own unions. Therefore this chapter examines the evidence on the effects of globalization and of FDI on workers in the United States and other developed countries as well.

Here the concerns regarding direct investment center around two issues. The first has to do with the "export" of US jobs. It is alleged that, when US firms make direct investments overseas, the output of these ventures substitutes for output of domestic plants operated by these same firms, and thus reduces job opportunities in the United States. The second is that this direct investment abroad suppresses wages at home in the affected industries. A more subtle version of this argument is that wages of US workers are bid downward as employers threaten to move production offshore.

In fact, US labor leaders' concern about the effects of globalization on the wages and working conditions of workers in foreign countries is linked to their concerns about its effects at home. US labor unions fear that US direct investment in countries where average wages are low by US standards not only further impoverishes workers in those countries, especially where collective bargaining rights are lacking, but lowers wages and reduces employment opportunities in the United States as well.

On the face of it, the proposition that the establishment of US-owned operations in developing countries would act to reduce wages in those countries seems counter to basic economic reasoning. After all, the entry of a new employer into a labor market should tend to *increase* the demand for labor and, all else being equal, that should drive up the price of labor. Therefore wages should rise, not fall.

But the unions' position is more subtle than this. The unions are mostly concerned that workers in these countries lack collective bargaining rights of the sort that unionized workers have fought for and won in the United States. Lacking these rights, the unions believe, workers in developing countries lack the power to translate the increased demand for their labor into higher wages and better working conditions. Worse still, US-based and other multinational firms, they allege, actively work to suppress the organization of labor unions in developing countries, among other means by supporting governments in those countries that deny workers the right to unionize. If workers in these countries had these rights, and if they had union representation, US unions maintain, their wages would be higher than they are. Thus, with respect to the plight of workers in these countries, direct investment is seen as the source of the problem, or at least an aggravating factor.

These are serious concerns. Is there empirical evidence to support them? This chapter will argue that the empirical evidence does *not* support the contention that outward US investment creates or contributes to low wages or, in most cases, creates or contributes to poor working conditions in developing countries. Nor does the evidence support the contention that outward US FDI causes a net loss of job opportunities in the United States or even the destruction of jobs in high-paying industries. Indeed, the evidence largely suggests that the effects of FDI are the opposite of what organized labor in the United States claims they are. US direct investors in the manufacturing sectors of developing countries tend to pay significantly *higher* wages than do domestically based employers there. In addition, outward US FDI, if anything, tends in the aggregate to create rather than destroy US job opportunities in high-wage, export-oriented industries. Although outward investment doubtless has the effect of destroying some jobs at home, it creates others, and the jobs thus gained tend to pay higher wages than the jobs lost. Thus, in the aggregate, outward direct investment helps rather than hurts US workers.

However, it must be acknowledged that some US workers are indeed hurt by US outward direct investment—by no means will all workers who lose their jobs because of FDI be rehired at one of the higher-paying jobs that FDI creates. Nor is the evidence presented here meant to deny that working conditions are often miserable in the world's poorer countries, or that some workers there are being prevented from forming independent unions, capable of bargaining for higher wages or better working conditions on their behalf.

Nor is it easy to dismiss the claim that the bargaining position of some workers in the United States (and other advanced countries) may be weakened by FDI. Whether or not this translates into reduced wages in some industries is likewise a matter not easily resolved. As this chapter will argue, considerations such as the particular skills of the affected workers and the structure of the market for the goods they produce are likely to matter greatly in determining whether and how FDI affects their bargaining power.

This chapter is organized in five sections. The first addresses the issue of the relationship between the activity of multinational firms and the wages earned in the countries, especially developing countries, that host their operations. The second section addresses what might be termed the "sweatshop" issue: whether international trade and investment foster unacceptable working conditions in developing countries. The third section explores whether the activity of multinational firms has an adverse effect on labor in the home countries of those firms, including job loss or reduced wages. The fourth section examines the specific issue of whether multinationals' activity acts to reduce the bargaining position of unionized workers in their home countries. The final section draws some conclusions from the findings of the previous four.[1]

---

1. For an overview of the issues discussed in this chapter, see Moran (1999).

Direct Investment and Wages in Developing Countries

Let us start with the following bold assertion: Whatever effects direct investment has on the home country (e.g., the United States), this investment, if it flows into activities that are internationally competitive, will in principle be in the economic interests of workers in the host country. Whether, thus qualified, the proposition is actually true is an empirical matter, to which we will turn shortly. But first, let us examine this assertion on the basis of what amount to first principles.

Let us first examine the "if" clause. If the condition it stipulates is not met—that is, if foreign investment flows into activities in the host country that are *not* internationally competitive—then its effects on workers there might not be positive at all. Sad to say, a significant portion of the FDI that has gone to developing countries in the past has been invested in activities that were not internationally competitive. Often in the past, the governments of developing countries have been eager to substitute local production for imports, on the now outmoded theory that the key to development lay in building self-sufficiency in domestic industry. And all too often, governments have offered inducements to foreign-controlled firms to get them to set up shop in their countries and produce these import substitutes. Among these inducements have been various forms of trade protection, often at levels that made imports prohibitively costly, thus enabling the foreign producer to become a monopoly supplier. In some cases the foreign firm has even been subsidized or (what amounts to the same thing) granted exemptions from local taxes. Encarnation and Wells (1986), in a detailed analysis of 50 foreign investment projects in a large (but unnamed) developing country during the 1970s and early 1980s, conclude that about 40 percent of these were uncompetitive. Earlier studies reported similar findings.

Why are foreign investments under these circumstances not in the interests of workers? Such investments do create jobs, after all, sometimes even jobs at (by local standards) attractive wages.[2] However, the operations associated with these jobs absorb scarce resources and thus penalize other, often more promising sectors with the potential to create better

---

2. There are, as always, exceptions. Some foreign-controlled operations start out uncompetitive but become competitive as they evolve. Indeed, part of the intellectual justification for import substitution has been based on so-called infant-industry arguments: the notion that internationally competitive operations can be created through import substitution, but that these operations will initially be uncompetitive, and must be protected, until they accumulate operating experience. In practice, however, import substitution policies premised on infant-industry arguments have resulted in the creation of numerous facilities that have little or no hope of ever becoming competitive. Evidence is reviewed in Meier (1987).

employment opportunities. Trade liberalization will destroy these jobs, and hence the very existence of these operations can create political pressures against liberalization. But as is now widely recognized, trade liberalization is often the key to economic reform that has the potential to put the developing country on a more dynamic growth path than import substitution policies could ever have hoped to achieve. Thus, in many cases, citizens of these countries—including workers—would have been better off if FDI of the import substitution variety had never entered the country.

In recent decades, economic reform in many developing countries has led to the replacement of import substitution policies by more open trade policies, and the result is that foreign direct investors must now seek projects that are, or have strong potential to become, internationally competitive. Alas, no empirical study of recent prospects along the lines of Encarnation and Wells has been conducted. However, Louis Wells, coauthor of the study cited above, recently revisited the country on which the study was based. In correspondence to this author, he asserts, "it is almost certain that declining protection [in this country, which has undergone policy reform] has meant that an increasing percentage of foreign investment projects are 'good'."

To be sure, many of the policies that foster uncompetitive FDI remain in place, even in countries that have experienced some policy reform (Moran 1998 and 2000). Indeed, one potential benefit of a multilateral agreement on investment, if it were extended to developing countries, would be to help push along the process of dismantling such counterproductive policies. But given that much policy reform has taken place, and that more seems likely to come, in what follows we assume that FDI takes place in projects that are internationally competitive.

We begin by exploring some simple yet powerful theoretical reasons why direct investment in competitive endeavors in any country, and especially developing countries, should bring benefits. Most recent FDI in developing countries has been "greenfield" investment, that is, investment in the form of new plant and equipment, rather than acquisitions of ongoing operations of existing companies.[3] And new investment—whether by domestic residents or by foreigners—in developing countries that practice open international trade policies contributes, in most instances at least, positively to economic growth, which in turn increases

---

3. In contrast, much US outward FDI in more developed countries, especially in Europe, has been in the form of acquisitions of existing firms or their subsidiaries. There may be a trend afoot toward more such acquisitions in some developing countries, for example as a result of "fire sales" of assets in East Asia in the wake of that region's recent crisis, and as a result of privatizations in Latin America. But the available data do not indicate that acquisition has yet become the dominant mode of FDI in developing countries.

the demand for labor. Empirical studies confirm this.[4] In the case of FDI, the additional demand for labor comes not only from the investors themselves but also from local firms that supply inputs to the foreign-controlled firms. And it is certainly true in labor markets, as in any market, that increased demand causes the price—in this case, wages, which are the price of labor—to rise.

This statement, too, has to be qualified, however. Empirical evidence suggests (see below) that foreign direct investors tend to demand relatively skilled rather than unskilled labor. Thus it is plausible that the gains from FDI for workers are largely captured by a subset of workers who hold the needed skills. As we shall see, some evidence does exist that wage differentials between skilled and unskilled labor have widened in those developing countries most affected by globalization. But with some exceptions, the main reason (at least in those countries where the phenomenon has been studied) seems to be that the wages of the former have risen, rather than that those of the latter have fallen.

This argument notwithstanding, some US labor leaders have made statements suggesting that direct investment actually tends to reduce wages in developing countries. We say "suggesting" because their statements are not always models of clarity. For example, these leaders sometimes assert that globalization creates income inequality. This may or may not be true, but rising inequality may or may not lower wages. If inequality results from a rapid but uneven growth of income in response to globalization, higher-paid workers will benefit more than lower-paid workers, but all receive higher, not lower-wages. Writing in the *Washington Post* on 30 January 2000, AFL-CIO President John J. Sweeney states that, "If the global system continues to generate growing inequality, environmental destruction, and a race to the bottom for working people, then it will create an increasingly volatile reaction that will make Seattle look tame." Which kind of inequality is he talking about? Does a "race for the bottom for working people" mean that workers will suffer from declining real wages as a result of globalization? Or simply that the gap between rich and poor will widen, with everyone gaining, but the rich gaining more? The grim scenario of social upheaval that he depicts seems to imply the former, but he does not say so explicitly, possibly because the empirical evidence supports more the latter, which weakens Sweeney's case.

---

4. However, Borzenstein et al. (1998) also find that this positive relationship between FDI and growth of the host economy is subject to a "human capital constraint." The workforce of the host country must have achieved a certain minimal educational level before inward FDI can create growth. This only makes sense: without a threshold level of education, workers might not be able to use the technology brought in by the foreign firm. Also, in some instances new investment has been found *not* to contribute positively to growth: de Gregorio (1992) suggests that there are circumstances where the relationship is neutral. It is nonetheless difficult to envisage circumstances where the relationship would be negative.

It is also true that increased demand for labor created by foreign direct investors could be offset by reduced demand for labor by locally controlled enterprises, if the former drive the latter out of business or force them to curtail their operations. (There have been cases where this has happened; see, for example, Langdon 1975.) Also, if the foreign firm is more efficient than the domestic rival, and thus able to generate the same output with fewer workers, the job gains created by the former's entry might not fully offset the job loss resulting from the latter's exit. Under these circumstances, whether there is a net gain or a net loss in demand for labor may depend on how much economic growth the foreign investment generates. For if the foreign-controlled firm is more efficient than the local firm it replaces, and if that greater efficiency leads to lower prices for its products, demand for those products will rise. Then the foreign firm will be able to expand its output, and it will seek to hire additional workers.[5]

Also, to the extent that FDI accelerates overall economic growth, new job opportunities will be created outside the sectors in which this investment occurs. Empirical evidence suggests that this growth effect might in fact swamp any displacement effect in those countries meeting a "human capital threshold" (see note 4)—those whose workers possess the skills and levels of educational attainment that multinational firms require. (Alas, this might not hold for the poorest countries, where these preconditions are not met.)

In countries where the human capital threshold is met, FDI in principle does not place upward pressure only on domestic wages generally. Foreign-controlled firms are also likely to compensate workers in these economies better than do locally controlled firms. In other words, workers employed by foreign-controlled firms can expect to benefit from a "wage premium." Empirical evidence for such a wage premium is presented below.[6] For the moment, let's explore why in principle such a wage premium might prevail.

The main reason centers around explanations for why FDI occurs at all. A rather large body of literature has accumulated to explain the occurrence of FDI and the multinational spread of firms and their consequences.[7] The key point for this discussion to emerge from this literature

---

5. The aggregate effect of an increase in the average efficiency of enterprises in an economy is measured econometrically as an increase in total factor productivity. The evidence suggests that, in economies with rapid rates of growth of total factor productivity, unemployment rates tend to be low, not high. This can happen because those workers who lose jobs because of efficiency gains (which, in isolation, cause jobs to be shed) are reemployed as economic growth results in new jobs being created.

6. Much of the recent work on FDI and compensation has focused on Mexico, in response to the debate over the North American Free Trade Agreement. This work is summarized later in this chapter.

7. Comprehensive, if somewhat dated, reviews of the relevant literature are contained in Dunning (1993) and Caves (1995).

is that, for a firm to succeed as a multinational, it must possess some attribute or attributes that give it advantages over local rivals in foreign markets. These attributes may include superior product or process technologies, superior management skills, access to markets not possessed by local rivals, or some other "ownership advantage."[8] It has also been argued that, to succeed as a multinational, a firm must be able to achieve some sort of economy by working these advantages internally, that is, in operations controlled by the parent firm within the foreign market.[9] A firm doing business abroad does, after all, have alternatives to setting up its own local operations there: it can simply export goods produced at home, or it can license the use of its ownership advantage to independent local firms in the foreign market. If it cannot achieve any economies through the internal working of its advantages, the firm will choose to serve overseas markets through one of these cheaper, simpler alternatives to local operations.

One implication is that, to be competitive as a multinational, a firm must be prepared actually to use its ownership advantage in its overseas operations. This typically implies transfer of technology to the firm's overseas subsidiaries and, in many cases, transfer of technology to suppliers and distributors as well. To the extent that this technology transfer occurs, the effect will be to raise the productivity of the foreign subsidiary above that of its rivals. The productivity rise enables the subsidiary to pay wages in excess of those prevailing in the local economy. Furthermore, to the extent that technology is transferred to local firms that act as suppliers or distributors to the subsidiary, these firms can pay a wage premium as well. However, the productivity rise does not automatically ensure that a wage premium is paid by either the subsidiary or its suppliers or distributors. Indeed, if these firms were to be "price takers" in the local labor market, there would be no wage premium.

Empirical evidence, to be presented shortly, does indicate however that there is indeed a wage premium associated with foreign ownership. Such a premium most likely is caused by foreign firms bidding for relatively scarce skilled labor, such that workers with needed skills are paid a premium over what they would have been paid had the foreign direct investment not occurred. However, it remains that a precondition for such a premium is that technology transfer does occur. And that such transfer actually does occur is very well documented.[10] A consequence of this technology transfer should be that local affiliates of multinationals are more productive than their domestically owned rivals, and empirical research has consistently found this to be so. One recent study (Aitken and Harrison 1999), for ex-

---

8. The classic work on this is Hymer (1976). See also Dunning (1988).

9. The classic work on this is Buckley and Casson (1976).

10. The evidence is summarized by Caves (1999).

ample, find that local affiliates of multinationals in Venezuela are more productive than domestically controlled firms, even after allowance is made for factors affecting productivity other than ownership. There is also some evidence, however, that the widespread use in developing countries of certain policies toward inward FDI, most notably local content requirements, joint venture requirements, and mandatory technology transfer requirements, actually reduce the incentives of multinational firms to transfer their best technologies to local affiliates (Moran 1998).

Technology transfer from multinational firms to local firms is termed technological spillover. This, as noted, results in an enhancement of productivity of these local firms. Some additional spillover happens as a result of technological "catch-up" effects, as local rivals of the multinational firm upgrade their own technological and managerial capabilities in an effort to remain competitive. It has been demonstrated empirically that the activity of multinationals does result in technological spillovers, including technological catch-up, under some circumstances but not others.[11] Several factors have been found to affect the extent of spillovers. One is the specific type of FDI and the circumstances under which it takes place; for example, manufacturing for export is more likely to create spillovers than manufacturing for import substitution. Another set of factors is the characteristics of the foreign company making the investment, including its strategy. Others include the absorptive capacity of the local economy, the nature of markets in the local economy for inputs used by the foreign-owned company, and the policies of the host-country government.

Where technology transfers and spillovers do occur, the aggregate effect is to increase productivity of both labor and capital. Although these increases are important in their own right, the main point to be made here is that the resultant gains in labor productivity should, in theory at least, enable affiliates of multinational firms and certain local firms to pay higher real wages than generally prevail. Indeed, theory argues that wages must equal the marginal product of labor, which is another way of saying that wages are determined by labor productivity.[12] (Appendix A lays out the elementary theory.)

Thus, to the extent that FDI does in fact result in technology transfer and technological spillover, theory predicts that the consequences could include higher wages paid not only by foreign-controlled operations in

---

11. The classic work on this is Dunning (1958), who found significant spillovers resulting from US direct investment in the United Kingdom during the 1950s. Later work pertaining to developing countries includes Blomström and Persson (1983), who found such effects in Mexico. Recent literature bearing on the evidence for spillovers is summarized by Caves (1999), who finds that the evidence is mostly positive.

12. Or at least this is so if markets for labor and for end products are competitive. The situation where entry into these markets is restricted is discussed later.

the host country, but also by local firms affected by these operations.[13] These wage differentials could, in principle, occur even if FDI does not create a net increase in the local demand for labor.[14]

A major question posed by US labor unions is, Does this happen in practice? Do increases in the productivity of labor really translate into higher wages for workers, as theory says they should? Answering this empirical question requires addressing two issues. One of these is whether in fact foreign-controlled enterprises in developing countries pay a premium over the generally prevailing wage rate. We defer this question for now to address a more basic question first, namely, Do wage differences across countries in general reflect productivity differentials? One way to test this is to determine whether, when productivity in developing countries rises more quickly than in the United States, real wages in these countries also rise relative to wages in the United States.

In the real world there are cases where this would appear not to be so. For example, Mexico during the early 1980s suffered a major drop in real wages, at a time when measured labor productivity in Mexico was rising faster than it was in the United States.[15] However, such counterexamples are relatively rare. The empirical evidence shows that, in most developing countries most of the time, there is a positive correlation between rising relative productivity (that is, a faster rise in productivity than in the United States) and rising relative wages (that is, a faster rise in wages than in the United States).[16] Major exceptions to this finding are just that—exceptions—and most of them can be explained. In Mexico, for example, the steep decline in real wages occurred following the debt crisis there during the early 1980s. That crisis was the result of too much public spending by the Mexican government, financed by international borrowing, and it caused the Mexican peso to suffer a very sharp depreciation, which lowered the average wage as measured in dollars.

One indicator of whether rising relative productivity is correlated with rising relative real wages is the index of unit labor costs at purchasing

---

13. Strictly speaking, for an economy in full equilibrium, this wage differential should disappear. If foreign-controlled firms face no constraints on their ability to substitute labor for capital, they will add labor up to the point where diminishing marginal returns cause the marginal product of labor to fall to the prevailing wage rate. However, it is almost surely true that the nature of the technology employed by the foreign firm typically constrains the extent to which labor can substitute for capital. Given such a constraint, and given its higher labor productivity, the foreign-controlled firm might seek to hire workers selectively, paying a premium for workers with skills or innate characteristics (e.g., those who are intelligent and hence easy to train) needed for particular tasks. Such a premium could last indefinitely.

14. But the existence of a wage premium does not negate the concern of unions that, in the absence of collective bargaining rights and union representation, workers employed by US-controlled firms would be better compensated than they currently are. We return to this issue below.

15. Golub (1999); Golub's findings are summarized later in this chapter.

16. Golub (1999).

power parity. This quantity reflects corrections in labor costs for both productivity changes and deviations of exchange rates from levels that would hold real prices constant. Golub (1999) examines changes in this index for seven developing countries and finds that, for five of them (India, Korea, Malaysia, the Philippines, and Thailand), it rose from 1970 through 1993. This indicates that real wages in these countries have actually risen faster than productivity growth would suggest. In two other countries (Mexico and Indonesia), however, Golub found that this index had fallen. Golub also found a strong correlation, on a cross-sectional basis (that is, comparing a number of countries at a single point in time), between productivity growth and growth in real wages.[17]

These findings support the theoretical proposition that, for an economy as a whole, the relationship between productivity increases and wage changes in developing countries is generally positive. But as stated above, theory also indicates that the greater productivity of foreign-controlled enterprises in developing countries should enable these firms to pay a wage premium over and above the wages prevailing in the broader economy.[18] But does empirical evidence show that they do so?

To begin to answer this question, table 4.1 presents data on compensation paid by the overseas affiliates of US firms, broken down by industry and by income category of the host country. (The table uses the three income categories defined by the World Bank; details of this categorization are presented below.) The table also shows compensation paid by US parent firms to their employees in the United States and US domestic average compensation, broken down by the same industries. The data pertain to 1996, the latest year for which all of the data were available as of this writing.

As the table shows, the employees of foreign affiliates of US firms in the high-income economies—who constitute the majority of non-US employers of US firms—typically are compensated at least as well as, or even somewhat better than, the employees of parent firms in the United States. This result varies somewhat from industry to industry. In the petroleum, wholesale trade, and services industries, for example, overseas workers in the high-income countries are slightly better compensated on average than their counterparts at home, whereas in the manufacturing and finance sectors the reverse is true. Within the manufacturing sector, domestic employees are

---

17. Regressing a wage index (the dependent variable) against a productivity index (the independent variable) for 49 countries, where the index is expressed such that its value for the United States is one, the regression coefficient is 1.30 and the R^2 statistic (which measures "goodness of fit") is about 0.7, using unadjusted data. This indicates a positive relationship (rises in productivity are associated with rises in real wages) that explains about 70 percent of the variation in the data. When the data are adjusted (e.g., using purchasing power parity rates), the regression coefficient comes closer to unity and the R^2 statistic improves.

18. These economywide findings do not exclude the possibility that some MNCs (and some countries) have high productivity but pay low wages.

Table 4.1 Annual compensation per worker by foreign affiliates and parent companies of US multinational corporations, by industry, 1996 (thousands of dollars)

Industry	Affiliates — All countries	Affiliates — Income category of host country — High	Affiliates — Income category of host country — Middle	Affiliates — Income category of host country — Low	Parent companies	US average
All	34.5	45.9	19.3	10.1	44.9	34.9
Petroleum	49.7	72.8	30.7	25.4	64.8	65.8
Manufacturing	32.9	45.0	14.1	4.9	51.8	45.1
Food and kindred products	29.2	45.6	13.8	5.9	33.4	36.8
Chemicals and allied products	42.9	56.6	21.7	5.7	64.2	51.7
Primary and fabricated metals	32.8	38.6	18.0	13.8	45.6	46.3
Industrial machinery and equipment	41.1	50.2	n.a.	5.1	53.7	49.7
Electronic and electric equipment	19.0	32.0	8.8	3.6	49.5	48.8
Transportation equipment	38.1	47.2	n.a.	n.a.	66.1	63.2
Other	32.7	43.0	15.9	n.a.	45.2	37.9
Wholesale trade	50.1	56.0	25.0	11.8	38.4	44.1
Finance, insurance, and real estate[a]	57.4	65.3	24.8	27.3	68.2	52.9
Services	39.2	42.4	19.7	25.8	33.2	30.8
Other	19.6	22.3	13.1	5.1	32.8	25.8

n.a. = indicates that data were available for fewer than half the countries in the income category.

a. Excludes deposit institutions.

Sources: Affiliate figures calculated by the author from data from Bureau of Economic Analysis (1999); US data from Bureau of Labor Statistics (2000).

less well compensated than overseas employees in the food and kindred products industry, whereas the reverse is true in other industries. Overall, however, the difference in compensation between domestic employees and overseas employees in the high-income countries is only about 5 percent.

However, what concerns the critics is, of course, not the wages paid by affiliates of US multinationals in the affluent countries but the wages paid by these affiliates in poorer countries. Table 4.1 also indicates that compensation by affiliates of US firms in middle- and low-income countries is much lower than compensation by their parent firms in the United States. On average, compensation in the middle-income countries is only 37 percent of that in the United States, and in the low-income countries this ratio drops to 18 percent. These data confirm that compensation of workers by US multinationals in low-wage countries is indeed low by US standards.

But the question we are asking is whether these wages are high or low by *local* standards. The most direct test is simply to look at compensation per worker in foreign-controlled companies as a ratio to economywide compensation in each of the same three country income groups. If this ratio is approximately one for any group of countries, it would be reasonable to conclude that compensation by US-controlled firms in that group of companies is determined solely by prevailing local wages. If instead this ratio turns out to be lower than one for any group, it would suggest that US-controlled firms pay lower than the prevailing wage in these countries. But, of course, if this ratio were found to be greater than one, it would suggest that workers employed by US-controlled firms in these countries are, by local standards, relatively well off—that there is indeed a wage premium.

One practical problem with comparing average compensation in foreign-controlled firms with an average economywide compensation, as suggested in the previous paragraph, is that within an economy, average compensation in one sector can be quite different than in another sector. Thus, the comparison just suggested could be affected by "selection bias." This would occur if, say, foreign-controlled firms were concentrated in those sectors in which workers were compensated at rates above those prevailing in other sectors where foreign direct investment did not occur. In this instance, even if foreign-controlled firms compensated their workers at rates no higher than their domestically owned rivals, the compensation of the former would be at rates above average economywide compensation. Hence, such comparisons are more meaningful if they pertain to a common sector. In what follows, comparisons are limited to within the manufacturing sector, which accounts for the largest sectoral share of US direct investment abroad.

Accordingly, table 4.2 shows compensation per worker by US-controlled firms relative to manufacturing wages in each of the three income groups. The figures are adjusted to take out the possible distortions caused by including expatriate employee compensation. (Especially in the low-income countries, one might expect expatriates, who mostly would be in managerial or skilled technical positions, to be paid much more than domestic residents.)

In the high-income countries, compensation per worker in the foreign affiliates is 1.4 times average manufacturing compensation. In the middle-income countries this ratio is substantially higher, at 1.8. And in the low-income countries this ratio is 2.0. Thus, adjusted compensation per employee in the overseas affiliates of US manufacturing firms, measured as a ratio to average local manufacturing wages, is well above one, and higher in developing than in developed countries. Of course, as the table also shows, compensation is significantly higher in absolute terms in the high-income countries than in the middle- or low-income countries. Thus, relative to employees in high-income countries, employees in low- and middle-income countries fare less well. But relative to other workers in their own countries, the employees of overseas affiliates do much better in the lower-income countries than in higher-income countries.

This conclusion is consistent with results recently reported in the academic literature that workers employed by foreign investors in develop-

Table 4.2 Average compensation paid by foreign affiliates and average domestic manufacturing wage, by host-country income, 1994

	All countries	Income category of host country		
		High	Middle	Low
Average compensation paid by affiliates[a] (thousands of dollars)	15.1	32.4	9.5	3.4
Average domestic manufacturing wage[b] (thousands of dollars)	9.9	22.6	5.4	1.7
Ratio[c]	1.5	1.4	1.8	2.0

a. Total compensation paid by foreign affiliates of US firms (less an estimate of compensation paid to US citizens employed by these affiliates) divided by the number of non-US citizens employed by these affiliates. Compensation to US citizens is estimated from base data from the Internal Revenue Service for 1987, extrapolated to 1994 using average growth in compensation for all US workers.

b. Hourly wage rate published by the International Labour Organization (ILO) times average working hours per year for 1990-94 as published by the World Bank.

c. Ratio of the average compensation paid by affiliates to the average domestic manufacturing wage.

Sources: Author's calculations based on data from Bureau of Economic Analysis (1997), ILO (2000), Internal Revenue Service (1998), and World Bank (1997).

ing countries tend to be paid high wages relative to workers employed by domestic investors in those countries. For example, Feenstra and Hanson (1997) show that wages are higher along the US-Mexico border, where the maquiladora operations of US firms are concentrated, than in other regions of Mexico. Aitken, Harrison, and Lipsey (1996) show that direct investors pay higher wages in Mexico and Venezuela than do local firms, even after controlling for industry and other factors that might affect wage premiums. There in fact seems to be a wage premium associated with foreign investment even in advanced countries. For example, Bora and Wooden (1998) demonstrate that wages paid by foreign-controlled firms even in high-income Australia exceed those paid by domestic enterprises, after controlling for other variables that might affect wage levels, such as the amount of physical capital per worker and the amount of human capital (i.e., educational attainment of the workers).[19] Rosen (1999)

19. Such a wage premium indeed exists in the United States (Graham and Krugman 1995). However, Aitken et al. (1996) show that, in the United States at least, this premium is associated with certain industries, not with foreign versus domestic ownership. That is, although foreign-controlled enterprises in the United States do pay higher than average wages, they concentrate their activities in sectors where higher than average wages are the norm. Compared with US-controlled firms operating in the same sectors, the foreign-controlled firms do not pay higher wages. By contrast, Feenstra and Hanson (1997) show that wage premiums in Mexico have arisen within sectors following inflow of FDI, suggesting that the wage premium there is not due to sectoral selection bias.

argues that firms with foreign investors in China are able to (and do) pay their workers more than do state-owned enterprises, precisely because the former are significantly more productive.

In short, are local workers employed by affiliates of US firms in lower-income countries underpaid? By US standards, they are. But US standards are irrelevant in developing countries—very few workers are paid at US levels in these countries. The key point is that, by local standards, these workers typically fare quite well.

The bottom line would seem to be that FDI in developing countries benefits labor in these countries, or at least benefits those workers employed by local affiliates of foreign firms, in the sense that these workers earn more than workers employed in these nations. How much benefit accrues to these workers, however, seems to depend upon a number of factors, including the type of activity in which they are employed. Also, there appears to be little to no evidence that FDI makes workers not employed by foreign-owned firms worse off. The closest such evidence is that of Hanson and Harrison (1999), which indicates that the least-skilled Mexican workers might not be gaining from trade liberalization.[20] Even this result does not suggest that liberalization actually makes these workers worse off; rather, they do not receive the gains that other, more skilled workers receive. Furthermore, other work by Feenstra and Hanson (1997) shows that less-skilled workers are generally not associated with direct investment in Mexico; foreign investors tend to demand skilled, not unskilled, labor in their operations. The case seems to be strong, then, that as nongainers from trade (and perhaps investment) liberalization, the least-skilled workers suffer more, not because they are thrust onto a down escalator, but because they are unable to get onto the up escalator.[21] Thus, the very bottom line seems to be that FDI in developing countries brings benefits that are captured primarily by workers possessing some threshold of skills. Very little FDI flows to areas or sectors where wages, and hence skills, are low. This point is demonstrated in the next section.

Before that, however, one more important point should be made. We have demonstrated here two facts that bear on the wages paid by multinational firms in low-income countries. First, these firms pay higher wages than prevail locally, and the wage premium paid by these firms persists even after certain other factors (such as industry composition) are

---

20. However, this result might be idiosyncratic to Mexico. A recent paper by Dollar and Kray (2000) concludes that the lowest income quintile of the population in other developing countries—a group that is likely to contain the least-skilled workers—generally benefits from greater openness of the economy.

21. However, as noted earlier, Mexican unit labor costs have fallen relative to US unit labor costs over the past 25 years. Thus, Mexico as a whole has been on the down escalator, largely because of the real depreciation of the peso. It is not clear to what extent this phenomenon is related to trade or investment liberalization, but clearly a number of other developing countries that have also undergone liberalization have *not* experienced this phenomenon.

accounted for. Second, these firms tend to transfer technology to their overseas locations, raising the productivity of labor in these firms above that in their local rivals.

But we have not yet resolved whether the wage premium accurately reflects the greater productivity of the local operations of multinational firms in developing countries. A position taken by some in the US labor unions is that wages paid by the local affiliates of multinational corporations are low in the sense that the marginal product of the worker exceeds the wage paid, when the marginal product is valued at world prices. In this view, the multinationals, rather than paying what they "should" pay the workers in their foreign affiliates, are making handsome profits in overseas markets from their labor. For example, suppose the wages paid by the local affiliates of multinationals in the world's poorest nations are indeed (as table 4.2 suggests) twice the average manufacturing sector wage prevailing there, but that the marginal product of these workers is four times that of the average manufacturing worker. Then the case could be made that local affiliates are paying half what they should be paying.[22]

Whether the wage premium fails to fully reflect the productivity differential thus measured is an issue that the empirical literature does not resolve fully. (Importantly, even if the wage premium does not fully reflect the productivity differential, it is nonetheless a premium and not a discount: what we are talking about now is not whether FDI enriches or impoverishes workers, but rather by how much these workers are enriched!) If this were to be the case, that the wage premium did not reflect the differential, it would fly in the face of economic reasoning. This reasoning holds that a firm's profits are maximized only when it pays a wage equal to the value of the marginal product of the worker. The reason is that, in general, as more and more workers are hired, the marginal product of an additional worker falls (at least beyond a certain level of total employment). Hence a firm could increase its profits by hiring additional workers until the point is reached where the marginal product has fallen to the level of the wage.[23] Thus, if it is true that the marginal product of a typical

---

22. If this were so economic theory suggests that, under normal circumstances, output would be expanded until marginal product of labor equaled the wage paid. However, there are a number of circumstances that might plausibly apply to foreign-controlled operations in developing countries wherein this would not happen, e.g., for a variety of reasons, there might be discontinuities in the marginal product and/or marginal revenue schedules of the operation. Also, in nations where regulations make it difficult to lay off workers, firms might not hire workers during periods of economic expansion if they expect future downturns to occur; the costs associated with layoffs (or with retaining excess labor) during downturns might exceed the expected value of the additional workers.

23. This is because if the value of the marginal product of an additional worker is greater than the wage paid to that worker, the value of the additional output of that worker exceeds the cost of the worker (virtually by definition) and hence contributes to additional profit. Also, the very fact that a wage premium exists might indicate that firms do not expand their

worker employed by a multinational firm in a developing country is higher than the wage paid that worker, it is hard to conceive why the firm would not react by hiring more workers and expanding output until the marginal product of the firm equaled that wage. This would contribute to still greater demand for workers, placing additional upward pressure on wages. It is only when the point where the value of the marginal product, i.e., the marginal productivity, of a worker equals the wage that the firm's profits are maximized. As a practical matter, the exact maximum might not be realized, but the firm surely will try to get as close to this point as it is able.

To repeat, however, the matter of whether wage premiums accurately reflect marginal productivity differences remains unresolved in the empirical literature, and the case made above is therefore strictly conjectural.[24] Evidence that the wage differential is less than the productivity differential is the fact that, on average, US-based multinationals in the manufacturing sector pay workers in the poorest countries less than one-tenth what they pay workers in the United States (table 4.1). If the technology that these firms transfer to these countries were identical to what they use in the United States, it would be somewhat unlikely that the marginal product of their workers in the host country is only one-tenth that in the United States. But there is reason to think that the technology transferred is not the same. The operations established in these labor-abundant countries are likely to be predominantly labor intensive and may not embody the most advanced technologies. In that case the 10-fold differential is not implausible. Moreover, and most important, a 10-fold differential in marginal product does not necessarily mean a 10-fold difference in average product, and it is marginal product, not average product, that determines wages (see appendix A).

Why would the ratio of marginal to average product be different in two otherwise similar operations of a firm, one of which is located in a developed country where prevailing wages are high, and the other in a developing country where prevailing wages are low? The answer is simple: in

workforces to the point where marginal product equals wages. This will be true if two conditions hold. The first is that the wage premium does not reflect greater skills of workers employed by foreign-controlled enterprises relative to workers employed by domestically controlled enterprises (on this, we have already noted that such a skill difference, however, does seem to exist). The second is that the wage differential does otherwise reflect some element of labor scarcity in the former enterprises. The latter might occur if the workers were unionized, if the enterprises functioned as closed shops (where nonunion workers are not allowed), and if the unions limited membership. This type of restriction does seem to occur. For example, Romer (1994) finds that larger numbers of workers are employed in export processing zones in developing countries than are employed in similar facilities outside these zones, and that union activity is limited in the zones. This would suggest that unions do create some restrictions on the number of workers hired.

24. This omission in the empirical studies occurs in large part because the marginal product of a worker is very difficult to measure (and is not equal to average product, as shown below).

the former, where labor is expensive, it is also conserved, for example by using machinery (a form of capital) to do things that could in principle be done manually. But in the developing country it might be economical to do these same tasks manually. Is this harmful to workers' interests in the developing country? Clearly not, because more jobs are created than if the task were done by machinery. But the effect is to widen the wedge between marginal and average product. Employing workers rather than using machines to perform such tasks lowers the average product of a worker, though only slightly. But the marginal product falls substantially: in fact, no additional output is created, but cost savings in the form of reduced requirements for machinery, power, and so forth are realized. If the difference between the reduction in cost and the wages paid to the worker is slight, marginal product will be low.[25]

Given this result, we can return to the issue of whether the wages paid by multinational firms in developing countries are less than what they might be if those countries were more unionized. First, it must be conceded that in some countries, such as Mexico, workers in some industries where FDI plays a significant role are in fact represented by unions, and their wages do seem to be higher than those paid in nonunionized sectors.[26] Indeed, their high wages might account for some significant portion of the wage premium paid by foreign-controlled firms in Mexico. But in the end, whether there is or is not scope for unions to extract higher wages rests in large measure on the issue already touched upon, namely, whether or not workers are currently underpaid relative to the marginal product that they generate. If they are underpaid in this sense, then there is significant scope for union action to raise wages. If they are not, then this scope is much more constrained.

Unfortunately, the bottom line is that we simply do not know from direct empirical evidence whether workers are in this sense underpaid. Some critics of globalization (e.g., Greider 1997) have rather boldly, and on the face of almost no evidence, asserted that they are. These authors talk about multinational operations that are as productive as those in developed countries but that employ workers at third world wages. But what these critics miss is that if a multinational firm actually did this, it would not be maximizing profits! It could produce more output simply by continuing to hire more workers until the marginal productivity of a worker fell to the level of the wage paid that worker. By doing so, the firm increases its profits without increasing its investment in the operation. Surely these critics do not mean to imply this—indeed, they typically criticize multinational firms for being greedy and putting profit above all

---

25. Furthermore, less-skilled workers are likely to be employed in this type of task, and it is precisely these workers who, as shown above, are the most likely to be left behind by globalization.

26. Moran (2000).

other considerations. But, if these firms do attempt to maximize profit, they will not pay workers "third world wages" while hiring just enough of them so that the marginal productivity of the worker is equal to that of a counterpart in a high wage country.

Thus, in short, whether or not workers employed by multinational firms in developing countries are underpaid relative to the marginal product they generate is a matter on which the empirical evidence is admittedly scant. But the empirical evidence that does exist is more consistent with these workers being paid their marginal product than with their being paid significantly less. More important, it simply does not make economic sense that workers are not paid their marginal product. If this were so, firms would be forgoing opportunities to reduce costs or increase output by employing still more workers in these operations. Rather than that multinationals are failing to pay workers the value of their marginal product, it is much more likely that these firms take advantage of lower wages in developing countries to employ workers to perform manual tasks that might be done using machinery in a developed country. And if this is so, workers in the developing country unequivocally benefit, because additional employment opportunities are created. Moreover, at least some of these benefits might be available to less skilled workers who otherwise might not be employed at all.

Globalization and the Sweatshop Issue

For some labor activists, the main grievance against direct investment in developing countries is not that direct investors pay their workers substandard wages, however defined.[27] Rather, the complaint is that workers in these countries are forced to work under what amount to sweatshop conditions.[28]

"Sweatshop conditions" are by their nature rather difficult to define. But like pornography, you know them when you see them. Typically, a sweatshop is a manufacturing operation where some combination of the following circumstances prevails: workers put in long hours, the facility is crowded, working conditions are unsafe or unsanitary, lighting and/or ventilation is poor, or treatment of workers is harsh.

---

27. A lengthy study by the US Department of Labor (Bureau of International Labor Standards 2000) addresses whether or not wages meet workers' needs in the apparel and footwear industries of 35 countries that are the largest exporters of apparel and footwear to the United States. The study's executive summary reports that "For the countries considered, there appears to be little conclusive evidence on the extent to which wages and nonwage benefits in the footwear and apparel (sic) meet workers' basic needs."

28. "Forced to work" here is meant in the sense that better opportunities for these workers do not exist. As odious as sweatshops are, they do not employ slave labor.

It would be hiding one's head in the sand to assert that sweatshops do not exist, or that, if they exist, they are in no way associated with international trade or investment. Indeed, this author has visited facilities in a number of developing countries that meet the "you know it when you see it" test. Nor is it any defense that sweatshop facilities are not limited to developing countries—that they can be found even in New York, San Francisco, and the suburbs north of Paris. But no one would dispute (even if the fact is not well documented) that sweatshops are more commonly found in developing than in more developed countries.

All the sweatshop facilities that I have visited were producers of apparel destined for export. Even in this industry and in these countries, however, my experiences have been mixed. For example, although conditions in some apparel facilities I have seen were little short of appalling, other facilities were clean and well lit, and the workers were treated well by any reasonable standard.

Importantly, none of the sweatshops I visited were actually owned or run by multinational enterprises, nor, indeed, are the operations often cited by activists (e.g., suppliers to Nike or The Gap). Rather, they are owned and managed by local entrepreneurs in the economies in which they operate. Many do, however, produce apparel products under contract for international companies. In some cases, these companies are brand-name retailers of apparel, but in most cases they are Hong Kong-based wholesale distributors who supply product to mass marketers in the United States, Europe, and Asia. Thus, activists might claim—with reason—that although the facilities are not actually part of any multinational firm, they are under the de facto control of such firms. In some cases the subcontractors for international retailers are themselves foreign owned. For example, Korean investors own apparel and footwear plants in Guatemala and Southeast Asia.

My visits taught me some of the complexities of the sweatshop issue. For instance, it is easy, from the vantage point of a country like the United States, to argue that no factories in any location or under any circumstance should be allowed to employ children. In Bangladesh, however, I visited one apparel factory where children (in this case, girls in their early teens) were employed. This factory was owned by a local entrepreneur but served as a subcontractor to an international apparel maker. On the face of it, such employment might seem shameless. But this particular facility was clean and well lit, wages were more than adequate by local standards, and most important, the young women were required as a condition of employment to spend several hours a day in a company-run school where they were taught to read and write.[29] This was in a country where, at the time, the illiteracy rate among women bordered on 90 percent, and one

---

29. The factory owner, who sought to project an image of a hard-headed businessperson and not that of an altruist, indicated that he provided schooling for these employees because the operation was beginning to use computer-driven process controls, whose implementation required that the production workers be literate.

could not help but notice that hordes of children lived on the streets of the capital and earned their keep by begging. Also, in much of rural Bangladesh, where most of the population lives, extreme poverty is endemic. Rural women typically are married and bearing children by the time they reach the age of the workers in the apparel factory. Thus, compared with most of their compatriots, these young women were well off.

However, it must be stressed that, in other facilities I visited, conditions were very much worse. Others have observed and reported even worse practices than any I saw, and some of these are discussed below. But the only general statement that one can make regarding the conditions I witnessed was that they varied greatly from plant to plant, from deplorable to commendable. In some, by any definition, sweatshop conditions did prevail.[30] But in others it was hard to find significant fault with working conditions.

The question then becomes, How prevalent are sweatshops in developing countries, and to what extent are they associated with direct investment or export activities? Some antiglobalist authors have claimed that essentially all foreign-owned facilities in developing countries are sweatshops.[31] But this is simply not true. I am not aware of any effort that has been made to collect comprehensive data on the incidence of sweatshops, but most of the anecdotes (including my own) seem to involve the footwear, apparel, toy-making, and sporting goods industries, with most of the problems apparently in the first two.[32] These industries are not dominant ones in the global economy. Products originating in these four industries combined accounted for less than 10 percent of world exports of merchandise in 1997, and for well under 7 percent of the stock of US direct investment abroad in 1998.[33] If indeed sweatshop conditions are con-

---

30. However, the worst working conditions I observed were to be found in locally owned plants that did not serve the international market. Rosen (1999) finds similarly that working conditions in foreign-controlled, export-oriented plants in China are typically better than in plants controlled by state-owned enterprises with a domestic market focus. This would seem to belie the claims made by some antiglobalists that it is international trade and investment that create the sweatshop conditions and that the answer is local control of economic activity. See Goldsmith (1996).

31. That sweatshops are the rule is essentially the claim of Wallach and Sforza (1999), for example.

32. Perhaps for this reason the US Department of Labor, in its efforts to determine if export sectors in developing nations employ child labor (Bureau of International Labor Standards 2000), has concentrated on the apparel and footwear sectors.

33. World Trade Organization (1998, table iv.1), Bureau of Economic Analysis (1998). Unfortunately, footwear products are not broken out separately in the WTO statistics, and thus the assumption is made that these are equal in value to clothing exports. If this is so, then textile products account for 2.9 percent of world merchandise exports, and clothing and footwear 3.3 percent each. In the BEA data, the footwear, textile, and apparel industries are not shown separately but are included in "other manufacturing." The total stock of "other manufacturing" represents about 6.6 percent of the total stock of US direct investment abroad.

centrated in these industries, they do not represent the greater part of globalized economic activity.[34] And as already noted, not all facilities even in these industries are sweatshops.

Also, even if these industries are ones where sweatshops tend to be prevalent, it does not follow that the answer is to shut down international trade and investment in these industries and for all countries to make these products locally, as some antiglobalist authors suggest.[35] In fact, in a number of once-poor economies, the establishment of export-oriented apparel and footwear operations has been the first step on a long journey to prosperity. Hong Kong, Korea, Singapore, and Taiwan all began their successful marches out of poverty and into the ranks of the middle- and high-income economies in just this way.[36] And the evidence is robust that developing countries that foster export-oriented activity do much better at alleviating poverty than do those that maintain inward-looking regimes (see, e.g., Krueger 1998 and Dollar 1992).

None of this, of course, excuses the worst sweatshops, wherever they are found. Indeed, one of the benefits of modern technology is that buildings virtually anywhere in the world can now be lighted properly, ventilated adequately, and equipped with sanitary restrooms at reasonable cost. There is simply no longer any excuse for subjecting workers to such degrading working conditions. A few years ago the chief executive of Nike offered to send basketball star Michael Jordan to inspect Nike's overseas suppliers for bad working conditions. Labor and human rights activists countered, possibly accurately, that all such overseas facilities could be upgraded to remove the objectionable conditions for a fraction of what Nike was paying Jordan at that time to endorse its basketball shoes.

What are the offensive practices that occur in sweatshops? Some that have been reported are the following.[37]

Inadequate Wages and Unfair Wage Practices

As already noted, there is not much evidence one way or the other on whether sweatshops in developing countries pay wages sufficient to meet the basic needs of their workers. However, the anecdotal evidence sug-

---

34. However, just as it is clear that not all textile, apparel, or footwear factories in developing countries are sweatshops, neither is it clear that sweatshops do not exist outside of these industries. On this matter, as noted, little systematic evidence exists.

35. See, for example, Morris (1996) for an exposition of this view.

36. Will other countries follow in their footsteps, such that apparel and footwear exports will lead a significant number of countries that are today among the world's poorest out of poverty? For some differing views, see Varley (1998, chapter 3).

37. All of these are taken from Varley (1998); for each practice listed, there is at least anecdotal evidence to suggest that it has actually taken place. However, as noted earlier, one problem is that there are no data to indicate exactly how prevalent such practices are.

gests that wages are often so low that they cover only the barest minimum of living standards. In addition, there is evidence that some employers delay paying their workers what is owed them (sometimes, it would seem, for months). Overtime pay is often nonexistent, and many such operations pay on a piece-rate basis, where the basic unit of pay is very low. Some of the worst cases that have been uncovered (e.g., the stitching of soccer balls by young children in Pakistan) involve work done at home on a piece-rate basis.

Excessive Overtime

Complaints are commonly heard from around the world that, during busy times, workers are required to work overtime, often with no overtime bonus and in excess of statutory maximums, and that during such times workers are sometimes forbidden from taking breaks, even to use the toilet. Some of the relevant industries in which sweatshops are common (especially apparel) are highly seasonal, so that suppliers are often forced to meet short production deadlines. Even so, situations that require workers to be on the job for periods of time that are excessive to the point of being inhumane seem commonplace.

Abusive Treatment of Workers

Abusive treatment can take several forms, one of which is that workers are sometimes required to work under conditions where they are exposed to undue risks of injury or disease. Cases have also been reported where workers are punished abusively—that is, subjected to the risk of bodily harm—for violation of work rules. Also, given that many factory workers in developing countries are young and female, cases of sexual harassment by male supervisors are often reported. In extreme (but apparently not uncommon) cases, such workers can be required to grant sexual favors to supervisors virtually as a condition of employment.

Bonded Labor

Under bonded labor schemes, a worker pledges his or her labor for a specified time in return for a loan. In some countries, parents pledge the labor of their children in this way. The worker thus in bondage is virtually a slave. Numerous variants have been reported. For example, in some reported cases, workers pay a deposit for the "right" to work in a distant operation, are transported there, and receive back the deposit only if they stay a minimum specified time. During this time they are little more than slaves.

Child Labor

Child labor is one issue on which reasonably accurate data do exist, and they are not comforting. According to the International Labour Organisation, 250 million children worldwide under the age of 14 are working, although more than half of these work only part-time. As my experience in Bangladesh showed, not all these children are employed in sweatshop conditions, but it is a safe bet that a large percentage are. In some cultures child labor is socially acceptable and indeed part of the culture. And in many countries children may have few alternatives to starting work at an early age. Indeed, the children who work might be considered more fortunate than their contemporaries on the streets.

However, in today's world, in every culture no matter what its norms and traditions, a child needs education if he or she is to grow into an adult with a promising future. How can a child who is working full-time hope to receive an education? As my visit to Bangladesh also shows, a lucky few may receive education from their employers, but such cases are likely to be rare.

In many countries this problem is compounded by inadequate educational infrastructure: there are simply not enough public schools to educate all the country's children. And in most of these countries the vast majority of parents cannot afford to send their children to private schools. In these countries there is no real alternative for many children except to work. This situation simply cries out for the provision of a better educational infrastructure. If there is a case to be made for increasing the flow of concessional aid to the world's poorer countries, that case surely is strongest for aid to build and staff public schools.

What Is the Solution to the Sweatshop Problem?

At the end of the day, there simply is no excuse on humanitarian grounds for sweatshop conditions to prevail anywhere. If at least some apparel factories in Bangladesh can provide for their workers a living wage, humane working hours, and a clean, safe, and harassment-free working environment, and still earn a profit for their owners, surely the same can be accomplished in virtually any industry and in any country.

But what is the best way to achieve this? Unions and human rights activists in the United States advocate imposing sanctions on imports from countries where sweatshops exist, to induce those countries to improve working conditions. Would sanctions work? This is not an easy question to answer. But clearly it makes no sense to impose sanctions on a whole country for labor standards violations by a relative few employers. That would be to punish the innocent along with the guilty, for again, not even all apparel, toy, or footwear factories are sweatshops. It would not serve a useful purpose to subject the employers and employees of the good facilities to possible shutdown and loss of employment in an attempt to root out the bad facilities. This would only deprive workers of the chance to earn a living, and in some cases even deprive them of the chance to become literate.

A fairer (and effective) approach would be to sanction only the products of those specific facilities that do not implement good labor practices. Indeed, in the United States itself, labor unions target for punitive action only those employers, not whole sectors or regions, against which workers have legitimate grievances. Admittedly, selective imposition of sanctions would not be easy. In Dacca, Bangladesh, at the time of this author's visit, there were upward of 800 firms producing garments for export. To distinguish the bad from the good among these firms, it would be necessary to devote sufficient resources to enable impartial inspectors to visit each of these firms for purposes of certification.

Difficult though this would be, it would not be impossible. Indeed, one means of doing it is already being implemented, through associations under which firms agree to adhere to voluntary codes of labor standards. One of the more ambitious of these is the Fair Labor Association, under which firms agree to rather stringent, but self-enforced, standards of monitoring. This group has been organized by the Apparel Industry Partnership, a private industry group, with the backing of the US Department of Labor.[38] A large number of US universities have joined this association to ensure that clothing bearing their logos is not made in operations in which workers are mistreated.

Skeptics might question whether such voluntary associations that follow codes of conduct, or even associations that require that members implement monitoring procedures, will be effective at curtailing the more egregious labor practices. Their effectiveness could be enhanced if such associations were open to inspection by outside agents. For example, inspection teams from recognized human rights advocacy groups could be allowed to spot-check factories supplying firms that are members of the association.

Some role for the multilateral organizations might not be out of the question here. For example, the WTO could allow its members, if they choose, to apply tariffs on products imported by firms that elect not to join an effective monitoring association. Alternatively, sanctions might be allowed on products that the International Labour Organisation (ILO) determined had to have been made in operations that do not meet ILO basic labor standards. This latter would necessitate the creation of a corps of inspectors within the ILO whose mission it would be to visit plants around

---

38. The charter of the Fair Labor Association is available on the Internet at http://www.dol.gov/dol/esa/public/nosweat/partnership/aip.htm.

the world to determine if core standards were violated.[39] Such a corps would not necessarily have to be large to be effective. Its existence might create a large incentive for firms to comply with ILO standards.

US Direct Investment Abroad and Employment in the United States

Let us now turn to the effects of direct investment abroad on workers in the home country, again focusing on the United States. To stylize somewhat, labor leaders critical of FDI maintain that multinational firms typically shut down factories and other operations in their home countries and replace their production with new factories in countries where wages are lower. Alternatively, they use the threat of relocation to bargain for lower wages in the home country. Thus, these critics maintain, the effect of outward direct investment on the home country is either that jobs are lost (unemployment rises) or that wages are reduced below levels that would otherwise prevail.[40]

As this section will show, the first allegation simply does not stand up to careful examination of the relevant evidence. There is, in fact, little or no evidence to link outward US direct investment to rising overall unemployment. To the contrary, in those industries where FDI is prevalent, the evidence is actually consistent with the notion that FDI leads to job creation, not net job loss. At least this is so in those countries where this issue has been studied in some depth, notably the United States, France, and Japan.

The second allegation, however, is not so easily dismissed. We finish this section by addressing this issue.

But, to begin, a simple fact is worth noting: most US direct investment abroad does not occur in low-wage areas. Table 4.3 shows that the vast bulk—almost 80 percent—of the stock of US direct investment abroad at the end of 1997 was located in other high-income countries such as those of Western Europe, Canada, Australia, New Zealand, and Japan. Nearly all the rest—18 percent of the total—is in the world's middle-income countries. Only about 1.5 percent of the stock of US outward direct in-

---

39. Other antisweatshop initiatives and proposals are evaluated in Varley (1998), which surveys the whole issue of sweatshops much more comprehensively than is possible here.

40. In this view, it is not only the threat of plant relocation and the consequent bargaining down of wages that reduces wages. If plants in some sectors are shut down as the result of FDI, but workers from these plants are reemployed in other sectors, there could be a reduction in average wages (but no net loss of jobs) if wages in the sectors to which the workers relocate are lower than those in the sectors from which they came. Kletzer (1997) shows that this can indeed happen when workers are displaced by imports in durable goods sectors, and at least some of this displacement might be caused by plant relocations.

Table 4.3 US direct investment position abroad by host-country income, 1997

Income group	Billions of dollars	Percent of total
High-income countries	679.7	79.5
Middle-income countries	162.2	19.0
Low-income countries	13.2	1.5
All countries	855.2	100.0

Source: Calculated by author from Bureau of Economic Analysis (1998).

vestment is located in low-income countries.[41] (Table 4.4 indicates which countries are classified as high income, middle income, and low income.) To the extent that US FDI goes to other high-income, high-wage countries, the threat of firms relocating abroad to obtain cheaper labor would appear to be a hollow one.

Skeptics might counter that the stock of FDI largely reflects overseas investments made decades ago—what if the more recent acceleration of globalization has led to a rising trend in current FDI *flows* to poor countries, which the stock measure obscures? But this is not the case: the official statistics do not reveal any marked shift in recent flows of direct investment toward these countries. Figure 4.1 breaks down dollar flows of outward US direct investment since 1983 by the income category of the host. Figure 4.2 does the same in terms of percentages of annual totals. As figure 4.2 shows, the percentage of these flows going to high-income countries did drop somewhat during the late 1980s but was quite stable during the 1990s. Moreover, the corresponding rise in the 1980s was registered not by the low-income countries but rather by the middle-income countries. The share of US outward direct investment received by this group of countries in fact rose sharply between 1988 and 1990 but has remained quite stable since then. There has been no trend toward a greater share of these flows going to low-income countries.

Figures 4.1 and 4.2 are based on country income classifications published by the World Bank as of 1995. During the past 10 years, however, certain countries have changed their income category. In most cases this happened as countries "graduated" from the middle- to the high-income category. Thus, a number of countries that had been classified as middle-income in 1985 were reclassified as high-income countries by 1995. This could bias upward the observed share of FDI in high-income countries in the later years. Figures 4.3 and 4.4 therefore use the 1985 income classifications for the entire period. (In addition, appendix A lists which countries fell into which categories for both 1985 and 1995.)

As one would expect, this reduces somewhat the percentage of FDI flows going to the high-income countries, because some countries are

---

41. A small amount of this investment ($4.4 billion, or about 0.6 percent of the total) is classified as "international," that is, not allocated to any specific country. In table 4.3 and figures 4.1 through 4.8, this investment is omitted.

Table 4.4 Countries in the sample by income category in 1985 and 1995

High-income countries		Middle-income countries		Low-income countries	
1985	1995	1985	1995	1985	1995
Australia	Australia	UK islands	UK islands	China	China
Austria	Austria	Argentina	Argentina		Honduras
Bahamas	Bahamas	Barbados	Barbados	India	India
Belgium	Belgium	Brazil	Brazil		Nigeria
Bermuda	Bermuda	Chile	Chile		
Canada	Canada	Colombia	Colombia		
Denmark	Denmark	Costa Rica	Costa Rica		
Finland	Finland	Dominican Rep.	Dominican Rep.		
France	France	Ecuador	Ecuador		
Germany	Germany	Egypt	Egypt		
	Hong Kong	Greece	Greece		
Ireland	Ireland	Guatemala	Guatemala		
	Israel	*Honduras*			
Italy	Italy	*Hong Kong*			
Japan	Japan	Indonesia	Indonesia		
	South Korea	*Israel*			
Luxembourg	Luxembourg	Jamaica	Jamaica		
Netherlands	Netherlands	*South Korea*			
Neth. Antilles	Neth. Antilles	Malaysia	Malaysia		
New Zealand	New Zealand	Mexico	Mexico		
Norway	Norway	*Nigeria*			
Saudi Arabia		Panama	Panama		
	Portugal	Peru	Peru		
	Singapore	The Philippines	The Philippines		
Spain	Spain	*Portugal*			
Sweden	Sweden		Saudi Arabia		
Switzerland	Switzerland	South Africa	South Africa		
	Taiwan	*Singapore*			
UAE	UAE	*Taiwan*			
United Kingdom	United Kingdom	Thailand	Thailand		
		Trinidad & Tobago	Trinidad & Tobago		
		Turkey	Turkey		
		Venezuela	Venezuela		

Note: Countries that switched groups between 1985 and 1995 are in italics.

Source: World Bank, *World Development Report*, various issues.

classified in the middle-income category throughout the period that were in the high-income category in figures 4.1 and 4.2. But the basic message is the same. In particular, even with the reclassification, the share of US direct investment flows to high-income countries fell during the 1980s but has been quite stable during the 1990s. The middle-income countries received a growing share of these flows from roughly 1988 through 1991, but that share stabilized thereafter. And even with the reclassification,

**Figure 4.1   Outflows of US foreign direct investment by
host-country income** (1995 income categories)

billions of dollars

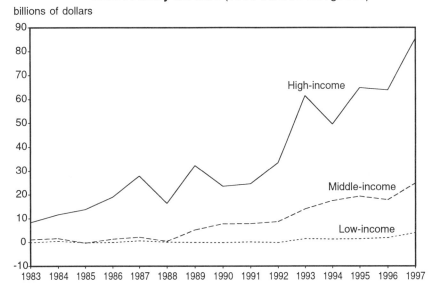

Source: Bureau of Economic Analysis (1998).

**Figure 4.2   Shares of US foreign direct investment outflows by
host-country income** (1995 income categories)

percentages

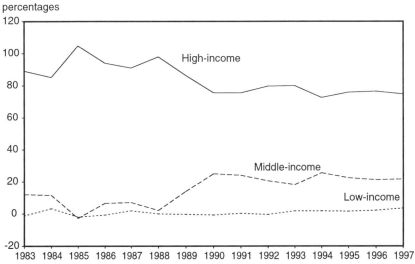

Source: Bureau of Economic Analysis (1998).

Figure 4.3   Outflows of US foreign direct investment by host-country income (1985 income categories)

billions of dollars

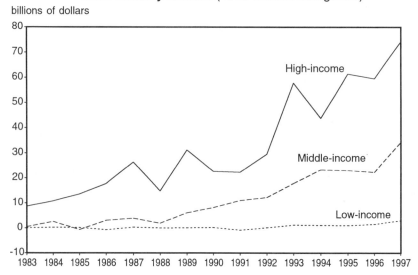

Source: Bureau of Economic Analysis (1998).

Figure 4.4   Shares of US foreign direct investment by host-country income (1985 income categories)

percentages

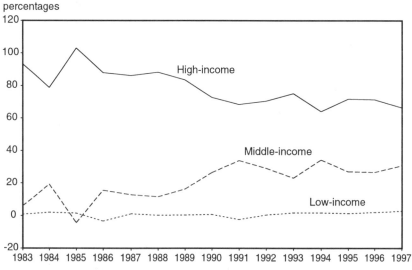

Source: Bureau of Economic Analysis (1998).

Figure 4.5   Outflows of US equity capital by host-country income
(1995 income categories)

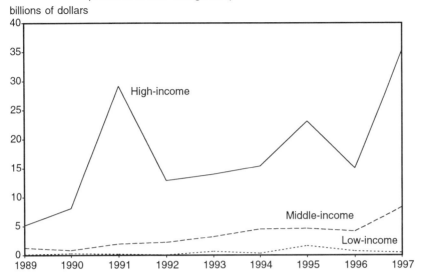

billions of dollars

Source: Bureau of Economic Analysis (1998).

there is no suggestion of a growing share of US direct investment flows into low-income countries in recent years.

The direct investment flows depicted in all four of these figures are total flows, which consist of three components: equity flows, retained earnings, and intracompany loans. It might be argued that the second and third of these components are at least in part determined by a country's historic stock of direct investment, and that this might also bias the picture of where new US direct investment is flowing. Hence, figures 4.5 through 4.8 show only equity flows by country income category. These flows represent, to the best the aggregated figures are capable of showing, new direct investment abroad by US firms.[42] (Figures are shown only after 1989 because the 1980s saw significant divestment of equity abroad by US firms and this distorts the numbers. In fact, in 1985, 1986, and 1988, this divestment exceeded equity outflows.)

Again, the bottom line is that the vast majority of US equity flows have gone to other high-income countries. From 1991 to 1994 there was some slight trend toward an increased share going to both middle- and low-income countries. Even so, the share of the high-income countries in these equity flows has remained close to 80 percent, more than went to these

---

42. The correspondence is not exact. The figures include new equity to existing affiliates as well as equity flows to finance the establishment or acquisition of new affiliates. However, in most years the former is a small fraction of the latter, because the greater part of internal financing of existing affiliates comes from retained earnings rather than new equity.

Figure 4.6   Shares of US equity capital outflows by host-country income (1995 income categories)

percentages

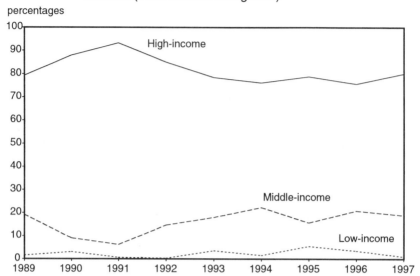

Source: Bureau of Economic Analysis (1998).

Figure 4.7   Outflows of US equity capital by host-country income (1985 income categories)

billions of dollars

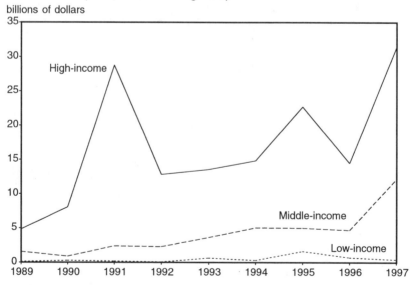

Source: Bureau of Economic Analysis (1998).

Figure 4.8 Shares of US equity capital outflows by host-country income (1985 income categories)

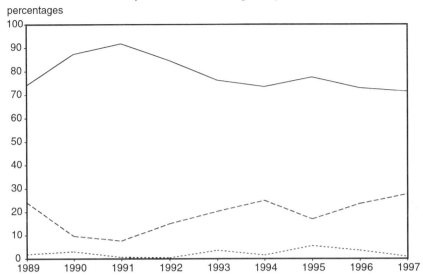

percentages

Source: Bureau of Economic Analysis (1998).

countries in the early 1980s.[43] Also, this share seems to have stabilized since 1994, although it is too soon to say for sure.

It is clear, then, that US direct investment abroad does not flow to any significant degree to countries where the average income is very low. Indeed, US direct investment abroad is not to any great extent a story about closure of plants in the United States in order to ship the activities of these plants to low-wage countries. Bolstering this observation is the following. It was once conjectured that US direct investment abroad should occur largely in labor-intensive activities. The reasoning was that the United States, with its capital-intensive, high-wage economy, would have comparative advantage in the production of capital-intensive goods, that is, goods whose efficient production requires the use of a large amount (or, more correctly, a large value) of capital goods per worker. Labor-intensive goods—those requiring relatively less capital per worker—would be more efficiently produced elsewhere. US firms making these goods would find it worthwhile to move offshore, to countries where the costs of labor are relatively lower[44] than in the United States, whereas firms producing capital-intensive goods would remain at home, where the cost of capital is relatively lower than overseas.

---

43. In 1983, for example, only 60 percent of US equity outflows went to other high-income countries (using the classification based on 1995 income levels), and in 1984 this figure was 69 percent.

44. The adverb "relatively" is necessary here because, strictly speaking, the requirement is that the cost of labor *relative to capital* be lower in the offshore location.

Table 4.5 Net fixed assets of foreign manufacturing affiliates of US multinational corporations and of US manufacturing firms, by host-country income, 1996

	Thousands of dollars per employee
All foreign manufacturing affiliates	51.06
High-income countries	62.20
Middle-income countries	26.64
Low-income countries	18.95
US manufacturing firms	81.71

Source: Bureau of Economic Analysis (1996, table III.B.7; 1998).

Of course, the data presented in table 4.3 and figures 4.1 through 4.8 do not support this conjecture. US direct investment abroad flows mostly to other rich countries, where the relative costs of capital and labor are roughly the same as in the United States (and where, in some cases, wages are actually higher than in the United States). Indeed, as is shown in appendix B, there is a strong correlation between per capita income of a country and US direct investment in that country. What this shows, above all else, is that US direct investment is attracted to countries with affluent markets, not ones with low wages.

Table 4.5 shows much the same result from a different perspective. In this table, the fixed assets per employee—a crude measure of the capital intensity of operations—of overseas affiliates of US firms in the manufacturing sector are compared with the fixed assets per employee of manufacturing operations in the United States. As can be seen, net fixed assets per employee are indeed lower in the overseas affiliates of US firms than in the domestic manufacturing sector. Some of this difference, especially with respect to affiliates in high-income countries, is due to "selection bias": US direct investment abroad in the manufacturing sector is distributed differently among sectors overseas and domestically.[45] Even so, it is clear that fixed capital per worker is significantly lower in affiliates of US firms located in middle- to low-income countries than in domestic US operations, and that this difference is not likely to be accounted by selection bias. This indeed does suggest that operations transferred to these areas tend to be, on balance, more labor intensive than those retained at home.

Given all of this—that US direct investment abroad does not to any great extent flow to low-wage countries but, when it does, it seems to entail relatively labor-intensive operations—what are the effects of US direct investment abroad on overall US employment? The answer is, precisely none. It is in fact fundamentally wrong to impute any overall effect of di-

45. Alas, publicly available data are not sufficiently detailed by industry to allow one to calculate how much of the difference results from selection bias.

rect investment on the total number of jobs in the US economy, because the level of employment, in the long run at least, is driven by the supply of labor and not the demand for labor. If the supply of labor, at prevailing wages, does exceed demand (i.e., if there is net unemployment), the Federal Reserve Board can boost demand by increasing the money supply. What constrains its ability to do so is, of course, the Fed's obligation also to control inflation. It is generally accepted by economists that there exists a nonaccelerating-inflation rate of unemployment (NAIRU) below which additional monetary stimulus cannot be applied without sending prices upward. It is the NAIRU, rather than US direct investment abroad or any other factor, that constrains job creation in the United States. Remarkably, however, even this constraint does not appear to be a binding one today. Unemployment in the United States in mid-2000, as this book went to press, is remarkably low, well below the level that as little as five or six years ago would have been considered the lower bound of the NAIRU.

More telling for this discussion is the fact that, between 1992 and 1999—years during which the stock of US outward FDI grew rapidly—US unemployment fell significantly, from 7.4 percent of the domestic workforce in 1992 to 4.7 percent at year-end 1997 (table 4.6).[46] Since then, unemployment has continued to decline. Thus, recent evidence would suggest, if anything, an inverse relationship between outward direct investment and overall domestic unemployment.[47] However, consistent with theory, it is safer to postulate that there is no such relationship at all.

Advocates for the labor unions might concede that US direct investment abroad has no effect on overall US employment—the total number of workers employed—but assert that such investment does affect the quality of those jobs. In other words, it is alleged that US investment abroad reallocates employment opportunities away from high-paying to low-paying ones through effects on the sectoral composition of employment. In fact, as will be shown shortly, the evidence supports rather the opposite conclusion, that US outward direct investment actually stimulates the creation of high-paying jobs at the cost of suppressing lower-paying ones. This comes about as a consequence of the effects of this investment on US trade.

---

46. Adam Posen (forthcoming) conjectures that in fact the increased globalization of the US economy has had a salutary effect on the NAIRU, actually reducing the minimum level of unemployment that is consistent with noninflationary economic growth.

47. In particular, this analysis is not meant to suggest that outward direct investment actually creates jobs, on net, in the United States. The point is, rather, that outward FDI has no effect on domestic employment once certain adjustments are made (these adjustments, again, include both job creation and job destruction). The recent experience suggesting an inverse relationship between outward FDI and unemployment might, however, suggest that labor scarcity in the United States has induced firms to locate certain activities abroad. If this is so, then the direction of causality would be the opposite of that argued by many critics (and indeed even some proponents) of FDI.

Table 4.6 US FDI and US unemployment (percent)

	1990	1991	1992	1993	1994	1995	1996	1997
FDI growth[a]	12.8	8.7	7.3	12.4	8.6	14.1	11.2	10.7
US unemployment[b]	6.3	7.3	7.4	6.5	5.5	5.6	5.4	4.7

a. Figure is an annual growth rate of US FDI abroad measured at historical cost bases.
b. Unemployment is the end-of-year figure.

Sources: US Department of Commerce, http://www.doc.gov, and the US Department of Labor, http://www.dol.gov.

Brief reflection should suffice to show that, if US direct investment abroad has any effect on the composition of US employment, that effect must come largely through trade.[48] If this investment were, for example, to stimulate US exports, the effect would be to create jobs in the industries where these exports originate. In that case, US direct investment abroad and US exports would be, in a sense, complementary. If, by contrast, direct investment abroad were to supplant US exports, jobs would be destroyed in these industries. In that case, US direct investment abroad and US exports would be substitutes. Likewise, if direct investment were to stimulate imports, it would destroy jobs in those industries that compete with these imports. Finally, if direct investment were to supplant imports (a very unlikely possibility), it would create jobs in the import-competing industries.[49]

All these statements have little bearing on whether outward direct investment increases or decreases the total number of jobs in the United States. Rather, they bear upon the sectoral distribution of jobs created or lost, without considering whether there are offsetting effects in other sectors. It could be, for example, that direct investment has the effect of creating jobs in the export sector but that other, offsetting effects cause jobs to be lost in other sectors. In the parlance of economics, what we are considering here are the "partial equilibrium" effects of outward direct investment.

As for the effect of direct investment on exports, in principle it could go either way: it is theoretically possible that direct investment creates exports, but it is also theoretically possible that it displaces exports. Suppose, for example, that a US firm currently produces widgets in the

48. Another possibility is that, all else equal, US direct investment abroad represents an outflow of saving that, if not offset by increased saving elsewhere, could result in higher real interest rates and hence lower desired levels of investment in the domestic economy. Over time this could suppress the capital-labor ratio and depress real wages. This effect, however, is likely to be very small; in 1996, US equity capital outflows represented less than 2 percent of gross domestic saving. Also, this flow of US direct investment abroad *has* been largely offset, by foreign FDI *into* the United States during the past 15 years or so. Thus, the net effect on US saving of all direct investment, outward and inward, has been practically nil.

49. These statements all assume that there is no effect on the level or composition of US aggregate demand.

United States and exports them to France. If this firm were to find that it could produce those widgets more cheaply in France and therefore decided to open a plant there, the result would be to substitute production in France for these US exports. And all else remaining equal, US jobs would indeed be destroyed in the widget industry.

Of course, all else might not be equal. The reason the firm wishes to produce in the foreign location might be to meet new local competition. Without the local plant, it might lose some or all of its local market share. In this case, the jobs destroyed in the US widget industry would have been destroyed anyway, whether or not the firm built the plant in France. Indeed, if the plant enables some exports to continue that otherwise would have been lost, it is difficult to claim that the plant caused any US job loss—it might be more plausible to argue that the plant has saved US jobs.

Furthermore, to build the plant in France and to produce widgets there, this company might find it necessary to buy the necessary capital goods in the United States. Once the plant is built, the firm might also find it economical to ship certain necessary inputs from the United States to the French plant rather than obtain them locally. The exports of these items— the capital goods needed to build the plant, and the intermediate goods necessary to produce widgets there—would be complementary with the direct investment abroad.

Which of these effects would dominate: the substitution of widget exports by production abroad, or the generation of complementary exports? It is hard to know. A first calculation might suggest that the value of the widgets displaced must be greater than the value of the intermediate goods. After all, the latter are inputs to the former, and if the end product is to be sold at a profit, the value of all inputs must be less than the value of the output. Thus, if the volume of goods sold in the overseas market were to remain unchanged from what it was before the direct investment was made, the substitution effects must dominate the complementary effects. However, because the direct investment reduces the total cost of delivery of the goods to the foreign market—after all, this presumably is why the investment was made in the first place—the firm might well be able to increase the volume of goods sold in this market. And if that increase in volume is sufficiently great, the resulting total value of US exports could be greater than before the direct investment was made. In that case the complementary effects of the direct investment would dominate the substitution effects.

The direct investment might stimulate US exports in other ways. For example, distribution and after-market service facilities might be created as a result. These might in turn enable the firm to sell other products in the French market that it could not have sold there before, including products shipped from the United States. On the other hand, some of the output of the overseas facility might be shipped back to the United States,

Table 4.7 Trade in goods among foreign affiliates, their US parents, and unaffiliated firms by host-country income, 1995 (billions of dollars)

Host-country income category	With US parents	With unaffiliated firms	Total
All countries			
Exports	145.5	24.5	170.0
Imports	123.9	19.4	143.3
Balance	21.6	5.1	26.7
High-income countries			
Exports	129.0	20.8	149.9
Imports	94.0	15.1	109.1
Balance	35.0	5.7	40.7
Middle-income countries			
Exports	28.9	5.4	34.3
Imports	31.5	1.9	33.4
Balance	-2.6	3.5	0.8
Low-income countries			
Exports	1.6	0.2	1.8
Imports	1.8	0.4	2.2
Balance	-0.2	-0.2	-0.4

Source: Bureau of Economic Analysis (1998, table 19.2).

displacing domestic output. In this case, the direct investment would complement both increased US imports and increased US exports.

Which effect will dominate—the substitution of US exports and/or creation of US imports, or the creation of complementary exports—cannot be determined on theoretical grounds. Rather, it must be determined empirically. Let us therefore turn to the facts.

The first question to ask is whether or not US parent firms actually trade with their overseas affiliates. The facts on this score indicate that such trade is substantial. Table 4.7 shows US exports and imports of goods to and from majority-owned affiliates of US firms overseas in 1995; once again, the figures are disaggregated by income category of the host countries. These data show that US exports to overseas affiliates of US firms were almost $170 billion in that year, or about 29.5 percent of all US goods exports. That same year US imports of goods from these affiliates were $143 billion, or about 19.1 percent of all US goods imports. Thus, in the aggregate, the United States ran a surplus in goods trade with the overseas affiliates of US firms (that is, exports exceeded imports) totaling $27 billion in 1995. By contrast, the United States ran an overall trade deficit in goods of $174 billion in that year. The surplus with overseas affiliates was registered entirely in the high-income countries. The United States did run a small trade deficit with affiliates of US firms in the middle- and low-income countries. This deficit, however, at $1.52 billion, was well below 1 percent of the total US trade deficit in goods.

Furthermore, Bergsten, Horst, and Moran (1978) found that US industries that were highly unionized but whose firms invested abroad tended to export a higher percentage of their US output than did industries that were highly unionized but whose firms stayed at home. This result still seems to hold today (Moran 2000).

These facts and figures are of some considerable interest. Critics of FDI, however, would argue that the main issue is not the level of the current trade balance created by intrafirm trade, but rather the counterfactual, that is, the value of US exports that have been lost because of overseas production. As is always the case with counterfactuals, hard data to prove or disprove this claim are lacking. In other words, we cannot say for sure whether or not the direct investment that created these overseas affiliates has, on a net basis, substituted for US exports or complemented them.

More sophisticated analysis can, however, yield a plausible answer, and such an analysis is presented in appendix B. Table 4.8 presents some summary results from this analysis. The calculated regression coefficients in the table can be interpreted as follows: if the coefficient is positive in sign, there is a complementary relationship between US direct investment abroad and US exports (or US direct investment abroad and US imports), whereas if the sign of the coefficient is negative, there is a substitutive relationship. The figure in parentheses below each coefficient indicates the statistical significance of the coefficient.[50] If this number is greater than 2.0, the coefficient is usually deemed significant. Coefficients are shown for all countries, and for countries by level of income.

What this analysis shows is that US direct investment abroad and US exports are net complements. This is true whether the direct investment is located in high-income countries or low- and middle-income countries. Indeed, the magnitudes of the regression coefficients are similar, which suggests (along with the supporting t-statistics) that the relationships between US exports and US direct investment abroad are not greatly different for any income group. Put simply, US direct investment abroad seems not to displace US exports but rather to create them. (The coefficients indicate that of two effects that happen simultaneously—in this case the displacement of some exports and the creation of others—the latter dominates the former.)[51]

---

50. In this instance, the issue is whether the sign on the coefficient can be trusted. A t-statistic greater than 2.0 indicates that the sign is correct as indicated to a degree of confidence of 95 percent or greater.

51. Other analyses have produced results consistent with these. See Chedor (2000) for France; Graham (1999b), Urata (1995), and Buiges and Jacquemin (1994) for Japan; Pearce (1990) for 458 large multinational firms; Blomström, Lipsey, and Kulchycky (1988) for Sweden; and Lipsey and Weiss (1984 and 1981) for the United States, using different data and methodology than reported here.

Table 4.8 Coefficients indicating relationship between US exports or imports of manufactured goods and US direct investment abroad

| | All countries | | Income category of host country | | | | | |
| | | | Low | | Medium | | High | |
	Coefficient	t-value	Coefficient	t-value	Coefficient	t-value	Coefficient	t-value
US direct investment abroad and US exports	4 .67	2.04	1.30	1.92	1.59	3.34	1.59	18.91
US direct investment abroad and US imports	− 2.97	1.18	0.79	1.91	0.33	1.03	− 0.39	− 4.51

Note: See appendix B for detailed explanation.

Source: Author's calculation.

The analysis also suggests that US direct investment abroad is a net substitute to US imports from both low- and high-income countries. In other words, an increase in direct investment in these countries seems to generate a modest decrease in imports from these countries. This result, however, does not make much sense from an economic perspective; there is no plausible reason why this should happen. The result is thus probably best interpreted as a spurious correlation. In fact, if this result is interpreted to mean that there is no relationship between US outward investment and US imports of manufactured goods, this interpretation is likely wrong. Rather, the result is better interpreted as indicating that the imports from developing countries can be well-explained by factors other than FDI. But, even so, it is clear that US firms have indeed established operations in some developing countries such as Mexico as a means to outsource production of labor-intensive products, including both intermediate and final goods. Some imports from these countries thus are directly linked to direct investment.

These results are consistent with the proposition advanced earlier, that US outward FDI simultaneously creates and destroys jobs in the US domestic economy. The good news in this regard is that the jobs thus created are concentrated in export-generating activities, where a wage premium prevails. But the bad news is that those jobs that are destroyed are concentrated in import-competing activities. The net effect might be to increase the demand for high-skilled workers, the kind that typically are in demand in export-generating activities, but to reduce the demand for lower-skilled workers whose services are demanded in import-competing activities. These workers might not readily find reemployment in other activities.[52]

These results, along with the raw figures on intrafirm trade, bear on one of the more sensitive issues raised by the US labor movement, that of outsourcing of input components by US firms. The story as told by some US unions is that outsourcing creates a net job loss within the US economy. But the results presented here are more consistent with a story of worldwide integration of operations by multinational firms, where specific plants specialize in the production of certain goods (including components) and ship these to other locations so as to reduce total costs of the final products. The point behind this story is that outsourcing is reciprocal from the point of view of the United States: on intrafirm account, at least, US multinationals export as much if not more intermediate and final product than they import.

---

52. On the basis of careful empirical work, Slaughter (1995) finds little evidence that outsourcing by US multinational corporations has directly contributed to wage divergence within the US economy. The main source of this divergence seems rather to be technological advance. Leamer (1997) notes, however, that this advance itself might be in part a by-product of increased global competition.

This analysis provides no reason to believe that outward FDI either creates or destroys domestic jobs on a net basis.[53] On the other hand, there seems little question that FDI can contribute to a redistribution of jobs among activities. But generally, this redistribution is from lower-paying to higher-paying jobs. That, of course, is good news for US workers as a group.

However, there is also little question that this process has a downside: it adds to the difficulties faced by less skilled workers, whose lot in the US economy is, by virtue of a number of trends, not a very happy one. In particular, it is demonstrable that the earnings of less-skilled workers in the United States have fallen relative to those of more-skilled workers. But how much of this is due to outsourcing? This issue, as it turns out, is not easy to answer and, indeed, it has led to something of an intellectual food-fight among economists, including some of the most prominent.[54]

At the heart of the controversy is the fact that there are plausible reasons why increased trade could reduce the relative wages of unskilled workers, even if there were no changes in occurring in the domestic economy. But there are equally plausible reasons why changes in the domestic economy could have much the same effect even if there were no changes occurring in patterns of US trade. Furthermore, it is clear that there have been significant changes both in the domestic US economy and in the patterns of US trade that potentially could affect relative wages. And it is difficult to sort out, on the basis of actual data, which of these sets of reasons is dominant.

The change in the domestic economy that is most likely to be a cause of growing wage inequality is technological change. At issue is whether this change is "factor biased" or "factor neutral." Factor-biased change, as it occurs, changes the relative demand for differing factors of production, holding constant the relative prices of these factors. For example, if, as is generally supposed, technical changes in today's US economy have the effect of increasing demand for workers with university-level education relative to demand for workers with high school or less education, given today's relative wages the result will be that, in order for labor markets to clear, the relative wage of well-educated workers must rise. But factor-neutral change has no such effect. Unfortunately, there is no direct way to measure whether technical change is factor biased or factor neutral, although for the United States the case can be made that certain facts strongly suggest that recent changes have been factor biased. These facts are that (i) the supply of well-educated workers relative to the supply of

53. See also Brainard and Riker (1996). FDI by at least some other countries also seems to have little effect on employment in the home country: see Blomström, Fors, and Lipsey (1997) for results for Swedish FDI.

54. For the most recent outbreak of this food fight, see Leamer (2000), Krugman (2000), Deardorff (2000), and Panagariya (2000).

less-educated workers has sharply risen over the past thirty years or so; and (ii) the wages of the former relative to the latter have also risen. These facts would indeed virtually nail shut the case that technical change has been factor biased were it not for the fact that imports of manufactured goods into the United States from developing nations have risen as well.[55]

But imports can figure. To see why, let us assume (wrongly, of course, but in order to conduct a "thought experiment") that there has been no technological change in the US economy nor any other domestic changes that might affect relative wages but that there has suddenly opened a new source of imports from outside the United States of manufactured goods that require intensive inputs of less-educated (hence, presumably, less-skilled) labor, and that these imports are priced below those that prevail in the United States at the time of this opening. Although why this opening has occurred is not really relevant to the thought experiment, we could assume that this has been the result of outsourcing of this good by a US-based multinational firm. Price of this good, relative to other goods, would fall. It is easily analytically shown that, under plausible assumptions, this implies a drop in the relative price of the factor used intensively in the good, in this case unskilled labor, in the United States.[56] This is because these imports, in effect, increase the supply of unskilled workers available to make goods that are purchased in the United States.

To summarize at the risk of some oversimplification, factor-biased technological change in the United States would increase the demand for well-educated workers, whereas new sources of imports of low-priced, non-skill-intensive goods effectively would increase the supply of less-educated workers. The effects of both are to reduce the relative wages of the latter.

But which is correct? Most economists would agree that both factor-biased technological change and changes in trade have had an effect on relative wages, and that the remaining issue is to measure the relative impact of each. But the food fight alluded to above is still on—economists cannot fully agree on how to do this measurement. One approach that has been widely taken is to calculate what is the net factor content of US trade (how much net skilled and unskilled labor is embodied in the total of US exports and imports), to add this net factor content to domestic supplies of the same factors, and then to estimate what would be the factor prices implied by autarkic production of the same bundle of goods and services consumed by the US economy given this augmented supply of factors. The difference between the estimated relative factor prices and those actually observed are then adduced to be caused by trade. Any residual

---

55. See Lawrence and Slaughter (1993).

56. See, e.g., Krugman (2000). This is an example of the well-known "Stolper-Samuelson" effect. For the original, see Stolper and Samuelson (1941).

change is adduced to be due to changes in the domestic economy, e.g., technological change.[57]

Is this a valid technique? The answer is, it might be but no one is really sure. Economists have developed models that, if correct, would suggest that this technique is indeed valid, but these models do embody certain restrictive assumptions that might not hold in the real world.[58] Alas, whether these assumptions are really necessary (as opposed to sufficient) for the model to correctly depict reality is still not wholly resolved.

Using a souped-up version of such an approach, Feenstra and Hanson (1999) look at this issue of factor-biased technical change, outsourcing, and wage inequality. Their techniques in fact enable them to consider the former, to the extent that it has been associated with growing expenditures in the United States on computers. They conclude that factor bias created by computers has had about double the impact on wage inequality as has outsourcing, a conclusion shared by others.[59] This conclusion—that the major impact on growing wage inequality over the past thirty or so years has come from technical change rather than trade (including, of course, trade created by FDI)—is accepted by a majority of economists but rejected by a minority. And the food fight is not over.[60] The consensus thus is that the main difficulty less-skilled US workers face is that technological advance in the US economy is reducing the demand for low-skilled workers while increasing the demand for more highly skilled workers, and this places downward pressure on the wages of the less skilled. The logical remedy to this problem would be, if possible, to upgrade the skills of the less-skilled workers, but for a variety of reasons (the age of many of these workers, their innate aptitudes, lack of funding for training programs), this is not easily done. Thus what to do about the problems faced by this category of workers is a vexing issue. Defenders of direct investment must recognize that this downside does exist and that remedies must be found.

---

57. Thus, for example, suppose that for a nation, between the years t and t', relative wages of skilled workers rose by 50 percent. Using the factor content approach as described, economists calculate that, in year t', at autarky, relative wages of skilled workers would be only 10 percent higher than with trade as actually took place in that year. It is adduced that trade (note: not necessarily changes in trade that took place between t and t') has caused a 10 percent relative wage differential. The residual observed change (40 percent differential) must be caused by other things, e.g., changes in factor demand occasioned by technical change. As is apparent (and for reasons that are not so apparent but are covered in the references), this calculation is not airtight, hence the food fight. The issue comes down to, is this not-airtight calculation allowing large drafts to occur, or is it tight enough to give a useful approximation?

58. Deardorff (2000) details these.

59. For example, Autor, Katz, and Krueger (1997) find that the computer revolution alone explains from 30 to 50 percent of the increase in wage inequality in the United States since the early 1980s.

60. See also Cline (1997) for an extended discussion of these issues.

As noted in the introduction to this chapter, even if US direct investment abroad does create jobs in the higher-paying export sectors, the possibility remains that the threat by firms to relocate operations abroad alters the bargaining position of firms relative to labor, to the latter's disadvantage. Thus, even though jobs are created in the export sector, and these jobs are relatively high paying ones, it is still possible that the wages received by workers are less than they would have been if globalization had not eroded the bargaining position of workers in general. We address this issue next.

Does Globalization Reduce Workers' Bargaining Power?

The quick answer to this question is probably yes. But this quick answer must be carefully nuanced. The extent to which a firm can use the threat of relocation as a bargaining ploy depends to some degree on the structure of the market in which the firm operates.[61]

To see why this is so, let us begin by noting that multinational firms tend to be more prevalent in certain industries than in others, and that these industries are most often ones characterized as oligopolistic.[62] An oligopolistic industry (or, more precisely, an oligopolistic market) is one in which the number of sellers is small, but greater than one (that is, the market is not a monopoly). In such a market, firms typically make major decisions, especially investment decisions, based in part on their expectations of what their rivals will do in response to these decisions.

The behavior of firms in oligopolistic markets can vary widely. At one extreme, such a market can be characterized by highly rivalistic behavior of sellers, where firms constantly try to outdo each other in bids to achieve higher market share or some other gain in performance. Such a market might have a high degree of price competition and rapid rates of innovation in product and process technologies. But at the other extreme, firms in an oligopoly might collectively behave almost like a monopolist (in which case they may be termed a cartel). Prices in such a market will tend to be high and relatively inflexible, and rates of introduction of new technology will be quite low.

The extent to which any oligopolistic market tends toward either of these extremes depends in large measure upon whether the market is contestable. A contestable market is one in which new firms can be expected to enter if the incumbent firms raise prices in an attempt to earn monop-

---

61. On this same issue, see Rodrik (1997). The conclusions reached here, however, are somewhat different from Rodrik's.

62. This was noted by Hymer (1976). Caves (1995) surveys the evidence.

oly rents, that is, higher-than-normal profits.[63] The degree of contestability of any market depends on a number of factors. An important one is whether or not there are government-imposed barriers to entry, including regulatory barriers. Another is the magnitude of the costs that must be expended up front in order to gain entry. (These costs may in turn depend upon whether there are governmentally imposed barriers.)

The main issue here is the effect of an oligopolistic market structure on wages. No general answer is possible. There is no general reason to expect that firms operating in such a market will pay lower wages than those operating in a more competitive market. Even if the market in which a firm sells its product is oligopolistic, the market in which it buys labor may be competitive, and the firm must hence pay labor its marginal product in order to attract workers (see appendix A).

However, the opposite might be true: firms selling in the oligopolistic market might pay higher than prevailing wages. Suppose, for example, that a market is oligopolistic because it is not highly contestable. There might be large upfront costs associated with entry that serve as a bound on the number of firms that can participate in the market. Under such circumstances, incumbent firms might be expected to earn rents. But suppose further that these firms are unionized, and that the unions restrict membership, so that firms also face barriers to new hires. Under these circumstances, the workers might well be able to appropriate a portion of the rents for themselves, and their wages thus would be higher than normal. As long as the return to the firms' shareholders on their investment in the firm remains satisfactory,[64] the firm might have little reason to resist this capture of part of its rents.

This brings us to the main issue: Can globalization reduce these workers' wages by altering their bargaining positions relative to the firms that employ them? As indicated earlier, the answer is probably yes. A firm that has the option of relocating its operations offshore can use that threat to bargain wages down to competitive levels, if these wages include an element of oligopoly rent.

As argued earlier, however, such a threat, to be effective, must be credible. And a minimum condition for credibility is that the expected cost savings from relocation must exceed the costs of relocating. Further, if the firm's market position is such that its oligopoly rents are secure, it has little incentive to relocate even if the potential cost savings would seem to warrant such a move—it does not have to lower its costs to remain prof-

---

63. On this, see Graham and Lawrence (1996).

64. If capital markets are efficient then, indeed, the return to new shareholders should be a market-determined "normal" return even if the firm does earn rents. This is because any expected rent accruing to shareholders will result in the share prices of the firm's stock being bid up until the returns on these shares (adjusted for risk) are equal to those on other firms' shares.

itable. Thus, as long as an oligopolistic firm is confident about retaining its market position, it might be willing to allow its workers to appropriate some portion of its rents, even if it could regain these rents by threatening to move offshore.

Globalization itself, however, can threaten a firm's rents.[65] For globalization is a two-way street. The same phenomenon that allows a particular firm's operations to be transferred more easily to other locations also implies lower barriers in that firm's own market to entry by firms headquartered elsewhere. If the incumbent firm's home market was heretofore an oligopoly, the newly created competition can act to bid away its rents. Indeed, if the new entrant does not pay its workers wages that embody some share of a rent, its labor costs will be lower, and it might therefore be able to supply the market at lower cost than the incumbent firm. This in turn could force the incumbent firm to try to reduce its own costs, and this might include playing the card of threatening to relocate if its workers do not accept lower wages. The net result could very well be reductions in wages in certain sectors.[66]

Is this an argument against globalization? The answer depends largely on one's point of view. From the point of view of a worker employed by a firm that was earning oligopoly rents, it certainly is: the loss of these rents implies a loss of future income, for which no amount of benefit from globalization may be able to compensate. In the United States in the second half of this century, workers in two major industries, steel and automobiles, almost surely have been compensated at rates that embodied an oligopoly rent. In 1950, in the steel industry, production workers were paid wages that averaged 124 percent of the average wage of production workers in the manufacturing sector as a whole. That figure rose to 157 percent by 1980. In the automobile industry, the comparable figures were 126 percent and 143 percent. One of these industries, automobiles, has been characterized by considerable amounts of outward US direct investment, but the other, steel, has not.[67]

Thus US direct investment abroad did not cause wage erosion in autos relative to steel. Hourly compensation of unionized workers in both industries thus did grow, in fact, to exceed by far average compensation in

---

65. This is in fact the main them of Whitman (1999). Whitman, a former General Motors executive, notes that a globalized economy carries more risk for established firms, and that one major consequence is reduced commitment of such a firm to its workers.

66. How great are these wage reductions? This is impossible to estimate because of the problem of establishing the counterfactual, a matter touched upon below.

67. See Vernon (1971) on the reasons behind this outcome. Outward direct investment by US automobile firms has a long history that predates unionization of this sector in the United States. US automotive FDI began in the 1920s. By the 1950s and 1960s, the two largest domestic manufacturers, General Motors and Ford, were also among the largest manufacturers in Europe. Both firms began extending their operations into developing countries during the 1970s. The early FDI activities of Ford are chronicled by Wilkins and Hill (1964).

the US manufacturing sector.[68] But since both industries became increasingly contestable over the past twenty years or so, some of the rents have disappeared. Domestic firms in these industries have thus been increasingly unable to compensate their workers at levels well above those that prevail in the rest of the manufacturing sector. Thus, by February 2000, the average wage in the US steel industry had fallen to 135 percent of the US manufacturing average, and the figure in the automobile industry was 134 percent. Further, the greater contestability of both industries has doubtless been due in large measure to globalization, as measured by the share of the relevant US markets captured first by imports and later, during the 1980s, by the product of local subsidiaries of foreign-controlled firms.

Workers might not be the only losers from the loss of rents. Communities in which the workers reside stand to lose tax revenue as these workers' incomes fall. Local merchants might suffer from workers' reduced spending, as they adjust to take into account their lower disposable income.

But there are also winners from the increased contestability of markets. The oligopolistic firms acquire their rents by raising prices and reducing output. As the markets served by these firms become more competitive, prices will fall and output will increase, benefiting consumers. Furthermore, as already noted, oligopolistic firms operating in noncontestable markets often tend to be slow to introduce new product and process technologies. Increasing competition in their markets can serve to increase the rate at which new technology is developed and deployed, to the further benefit of consumers. In fact, in many cases, improvements in the rate at which new technology is created and utilized can increase the productivity of workers and thus restore at least some of the real wages that were lost with the firm's rents. In the case of the steel industry, for example, labor productivity has increased sharply during the past twenty years. Would this have occurred without the increased competition brought on first by imports and later by the entry of mini-mills and the takeover of laggard domestic firms by foreign rivals? It is hard to know for sure, but it is quite plausible that it would not have happened.

As noted previously, significant outward direct investment from the United States has occurred in the automobile industry but not in the steel industry. For both industries, however, the case can be made that globalization has had a depressive effect on domestic wages, in the sense that differentials between wages in these industries and other US manufacturing industries have eroded over the past twenty years, and that globalization has had something to do with this. In both industries, in fact, domestic oligopolies were eroded, first, by significant import penetration into the US market and, later, by significant *inward* direct investment into the United States.

---

68. Both industries, however, were unionized only during the late 1920s and early 1930s. Significant wage premiums over the average US manufacturing sector wage in both these industries were recorded in 1932, the earliest year for which data are available.

But was the erosion of the wage differential greater in automobiles than in steel, given that outward investment occurred in the former but not in the latter?[69] The answer seems to be no. Although such erosion has occurred in both industries, it has, if anything, affected steelworkers more than auto workers. From 1980 to 2000, the wage premium in the steel industry fell from 57 percent to 35 percent, a fall of 14 percent of the total wage. In automobiles, this fall was only about 6 percent. Thus, in the end, whether or not outward US direct investment has resulted in lower US domestic wages than would otherwise have prevailed in the automobile industry remains controversial. The even greater fall in the wage premium of steelworkers suggests that greater competition accounts for this erosion (in both industries) and that the erosion has little to do with outward investment by the US automobile producers.

To sum up, the issue is whether outward direct investment by US firms serves to diminish the bargaining position of the US workers who work for these firms and, hence, to reduce their compensation. In cases where firms have historically been able to garner economic rents, and workers have been able to appropriate some of these rents, this line of argumentation is not implausible. But the experience of the US steel industry shows that direct investment is certainly not the whole story behind this erosion. There the erosion of wage premiums created by the capture of rents has been among the most pronounced of any industry, even though US steel firms have neither engaged nor threatened to engage in any significant direct investment abroad.

Summary and Conclusion

Much of the opposition to the MAI, in the United States especially, has come from the organized labor movement. This opposition reflects a long-held position of organized labor that FDI, or at least US direct investment abroad, hurts both the interests of US workers and the interests of workers that are employed by US firms overseas.

To hear some US labor activists speak, one would think that US investment abroad flows mostly to low-wage countries, that the overseas affiliates of US firms pay less than prevailing wages in those countries, and that large numbers of jobs in the United States are eliminated as a result of this investment. The facts, however, argue strongly against the first two of these claims. With respect to the third, although the empirical evidence does not yield completely unambiguous results, the case is stronger that US direct investment overseas in net creates jobs in the United States than that it destroys US jobs. The analysis in this chapter in fact shows strong

---

69. And noting that, as far as can be determined, US steel firms have never even threatened to relocate their activities abroad if US steelworkers would not accept lower wages.

evidence that outward US direct investment creates jobs in higher-paying sectors, and somewhat weaker but still credible evidence that it reduces jobs in lower-paying sectors.

Another position often taken by organized labor, that outward investment and associated outsourcing weaken the bargaining position of unions relative to the management of multinational firms, is more plausible than the argument that outsourcing actually reduces domestic jobs. This weakening might in fact be symptomatic of a number of social ills created (or at least fostered) by the increased competition brought about by globalization.

Whatever the merits of its case, the labor movement does seem to have succeeded in capturing much of current US policy with respect to international trade and investment issues. This is especially true with respect to US policy on whether or not there should be multilateral rules on investment. This is a subject to which we return in chapter 7.

5

Globalization, Foreign Direct Investment, and the Environment

Many of those who demonstrated against the Multilateral Agreement on Investment outside the OECD's Paris headquarters in the fall of 1998 were members of, or sympathetic to the causes of, environmentally oriented NGOs. Environmental activists were present in still greater numbers one year later outside the World Trade Organization's ministerial meeting in Seattle. The reason for their presence was a passionate belief, held by many (but not all) environmentalists, that expanded international trade and investment will lead to further degradation of the natural environment. And of those environmentalists who are not categorically opposed to growing international trade and investment, many nonetheless believe that the current multilateral rules governing global commerce act against, or at least are highly insensitive to, environmental interests.

A substantial majority of the environmental community also believe that new rules on investment such as those that the MAI would have embodied would act to increase environmental degradation. As discussed in some detail in chapter 2, some specific provisions of the MAI, notably those on definition of investment, expropriation, and dispute resolution that might have been applied to regulatory takings, especially upset the environmental community.

However, the even larger presence of environmental protesters in Seattle, almost a year after the demise of the MAI, illustrates that the concerns of this community with multilateral trade and investment rules go well beyond the specific issue of regulatory takings. One reason the WTO has become the target of environmental activism is that some recent WTO panel rulings (and some earlier rulings by dispute panels convened under its predecessor, the General Agreement on Tariffs and Trade) were perceived by the environmental community as threatening to the environment.[1] Most of the recent decisions have involved cases brought against the United States. One of these was a 1996 WTO panel ruling on US Environmental Protection Agency rules pertaining to imported gasoline. In this case, a WTO panel found that certain provisions of the US Clean Air Act pertaining to reformulation of gasoline to produce less pollutants were applied on a basis that discriminated against imported gasoline, and hence contrary to GATT Article III, part 4. This article states that "national treatment" be applied to imports, i.e., that imports be granted treatment under domestic law and policy that is "no less favourable than that accorded to like products of national origin. . . ." The panel ruled that the discriminatory treatment was not justified under a defense argued by the United States based on GATT Article XX, part g, which states that a WTO member can apply measures "relating to conservation of exhaustible natural resources. . ." providing that these measures do not "constitute a means of arbitrary or unjustifiable discrimination between countries where the same conditions prevail, or a disguised restriction on international trade. . . ." The finding was largely upheld by the WTO Appellate Body.[2] It is noteworthy that the panel and the Appellate Body did find that the United States could impose measures to ensure that gasoline was reformulated to reduce emissions and, in particular, that clean air is an "exhaustible resource" in the meaning of GATT Article XX(g). What the panel found at fault was that imported gasoline was held to somewhat different and, in its view, discriminatory standards.

This case, as do other cases with environmental overtones that have come before the WTO, raises issues that can be difficult to balance. Environmentalists have maintained that the somewhat different standards were in fact required to ensure that the imported gasoline was as clean as the domestic product. Trade experts might counter that the United States could have met its WTO obligations by imposing restrictions on domestic gasoline as strict as those imposed on imported gasoline and that to have

---

1. Wallach and Sforza (1999) offer a full litany of WTO and GATT panel decisions that have gone against environmentalist concerns. Their list also indicates why environmentalists disapprove of each of these decisions. However, the reader is warned that Wallach and Sforza treat these cases as might a lawyer presenting evidence in a trial. That is, they present those facts that support the point they want to make, but omit other important facts that do not. (The next footnote provides an example.) Fortunately, all the facts and considerations that bore on these decisions are public information. The full texts of the WTO panel and appellate body reports pertaining to the turtles case and the gasoline case mentioned below, as well as other cases, are published on the WTO web site, at http://www.wto.org/wto/dispute/distab.htm.

2. The combined texts of the panel report and the Appellate Body report on this case are available on-line from WTO at http://www.wto.org.

done so would "have raised the bar" with respect to environmental standards, not lowered it.

Another such case was a 1998 WTO ruling on US efforts to ban imports of shrimp from countries that do not require shrimp fishermen to use turtle excluder devices, or TEDs. In this case, which has become a cause célèbre among environmentalists, a WTO panel again found that the US ban was in violation of WTO obligations. The main reason for the WTO decision was that the US import bans did not distinguish between shrimp caught by shrimpers who used TEDs and those who did not. Rather, the bans applied to all shrimp imports from countries whose governments did not require use of the devices. Complainant countries were able to show that at least some shrimp subject to sanctions were in fact caught by shrimpers who used TEDs. This fact figured importantly in the decision of the WTO Appellate Body to uphold the panel findings against the United States. The Appellate Body did indicate that, were the US law administered so as to distinguish between shrimp actually caught using TEDs and shrimp not thus caught, it would be WTO-consistent.

This finding so outraged environmentalists that, in Seattle, the sea turtle became an icon of the activists assembled there.[3] Indeed, the decision in the turtles case, which seemed to reinforce some of the concerns arising from the earlier GATT decision on tuna imports (see chapter 2), led many environmentalists to conclude that WTO panels would routinely place the interests of international commerce over environmental protection. This doubtless contributed to the intensity of the protest both in Paris in 1998 and in Seattle in 1999.

However, the issues raised by the environmental community go beyond specific WTO panel decisions as well as beyond the specifics of the MAI.[4] This chapter therefore tries to examine some of the larger issues

---

3. It also stands as an example of the point made in the previous footnote, namely, that Wallach and Sforza (1999) omit material facts in their treatment of WTO cases. Nowhere do they mention that the main reason the appellate body (rightly or wrongly) ruled as it did was that the US law, as implemented, failed to distinguish between shrimp caught using acceptable and unacceptable means.

4. In what follows, the author has tried to extract from a number of sources the precise nature of the environmental activists' concern over globalization. This is surprisingly difficult, because most of the activist literature is specifically focused on the WTO and the perceived anti-environmental bias of recent cases; almost nowhere is laid out an integrated view of why activists believe that increased international trade and investment inevitably impact negatively on the environment. Thus, for example, absent entirely from Wallach and Sforza (1999) is any discussion of whether increased international trade is, in and of itself, inimical to the goal of environmental preservation. A major exception is a collection of essays edited by Mander and Goldsmith (1996). Several of these are cited in the discussion below. Even so, the reader is cautioned that this discussion represents this author's possibly flawed interpretation of a number of strands of thought found in these works. See also Charnovitz (1994) for a review of the activist literature. For a contrasting view, that liberalized trade and investment are *not* important causal factors of environmental degradation, see OECD (1998, chapter 6).

raised by environmentalists with respect to globalization in general and FDI in particular. It begins by acknowledging that expanded international trade and investment, to the extent that these are associated with greater economic growth, are almost sure to lead to some degree of environmental deterioration in much of the developing world and perhaps in the developed world as well. Such deterioration is particularly predictable during the early phases of rapid development when incomes are rising sharply, as has been happening in a number of large developing countries such as China and, very recently, India.

The good news is that, in the long run, growth in these countries' incomes will almost surely enable measures to be taken to alleviate this environmental distress. The reasons for this are developed later in this chapter. But even so, in much of the world these measures remain in the somewhat uncertain future. An important issue then becomes how to manage the trade-off between the benefits of globalization, which has great potential to raise incomes in regions of the world that remain desperately poor, and the benefits of measures to protect the environment, where these conflict with globalization. Can measures be employed that will both enable real income growth in poor areas of the world and adequately safeguard the environment? Does globalization hinder or advance the rate at which such measures are likely to be implemented? And do multilateral rules (including possible future rules on investment) act, or have the potential to act, to increase the environmental degradation brought about by globalization?

The Environmental Impact of Globalization and Growth

What are the most basic issues that globalization raises for environmentalists? Starkly stated, the principal one comes down to the following: that the economic growth that globalization brings, combined with the consumerism that this growth fosters, puts ever increasing stress on the limited resources of the earth.[5] For example, one major concern is that an expanding world economy results in the destruction of wildlife habitat. Habitat is certainly being lost from human encroachment of numerous wetlands and tropical rainforests all over the globe, in developing countries and elsewhere. And those habitats that are not actually destroyed may be altered by the encroachment of human beings in ways that threaten their flora and fauna. This can happen even if there is no physical encroachment at all. For example, humans do not actually inhabit the world's oceans, but large areas of the ocean are being polluted by the disposal of effluents in their waters.

---

5. See the chapters by Korten, Daly (1996a), and Goodland in Mander and Goldsmith (1996).

The main reason for habitat encroachment is that the share of the global biomass appropriated for human activity has expanded considerably over the course of the last two centuries, that is, since the beginning of the industrial age.[6] According to some environmentalists, further growth in this share would be unsustainable.[7]

However, with respect to both habitat encroachment and human appropriation of the world's biomass, the effects of economic growth are not unequivocally bad. In fact, rising incomes often give countries the wherewithal to preserve more habitat than they could otherwise. For example, it is mostly the relatively rich countries of the world that have been able to designate large tracts of land as national parks or wilderness areas, where development is limited or forbidden so as to preserve natural habitat. By contrast, in the world's poorest countries, habitat is often destroyed as impoverished farmers cut down forests in order to raise crops on land that is, at best, marginal for agriculture. Even where such homesteading is prohibited, natural habitat can be put under stress or destroyed as people who cannot afford other fuels are forced to cut down trees for firewood. Alleviation of poverty in these countries could go a long way toward preserving their wilderness areas and saving their tropical rainforests from destruction.[8]

Perhaps the greatest contribution that income growth makes to preserving habitat is that it seems to put a brake on population growth. In the thirty years from 1970 to 2000, the world's population has grown from about 3.7 billion persons to almost 6 billion.[9] But in most of the world's richest countries, population growth has stabilized, and in some (e.g., Japan) the population is forecast to decline. (The United States is an exception, but mainly because of continued immigration.) Population growth has been greatest, by contrast, in the world's poorest countries. This growth is doubtless due in large measure to poverty itself (e.g., people living in rural poverty seek to produce numerous offspring simply in order to increase the numbers of workers on the land).

Thus, many environmentalists acknowledge and accept that the elimination of poverty is wholly compatible with the preservation of wildlife habitats. Indeed, there is a demonstrable positive relationship between a

---

6. Vitousek et al. (1986). See also French (2000).

7. Daly (1996a).

8. A closely related issue is overpopulation, which in many areas of the world is a major source of environmental stress. A negative relationship can be demonstrated between income per capita and the rate of population growth. Thus, alleviation of poverty should also reduce environmental stress where overpopulation is a major cause of that stress. See WTO (1999). Charnovitz (2000) provides a critical review.

9. Brown, Gardner, and Halweil (1998) discuss population growth and the environmental stress it causes.

country's income level and its environmental performance.[10] But environmentalists also point out that increasing affluence can place mounting stress on habitat, even if rich countries do designate some lands as wildlife preserves and national parks. The filling of coastal wetlands to create new space for urban and suburban expansion is one example.

A second major consequence of economic growth that environmentalists find troubling is the production of ever increasing amounts of waste products from human activity, including toxic wastes, that must be disposed of.

Waste products in turn cause deterioration of air and water quality. To environmentalists, both air and water are scarce resources and ones that the market system undervalues. Many economists would agree. To be sure, rich societies are often able to develop means to dispose of at least some of these wastes without environmental harm, a point to which we return shortly. But some environmentalists maintain that, even so, the production of wastes is growing so rapidly that the planet will soon reach a point where it can no longer absorb additional wastes without suffering irreparable harm. Thus, boiled down to its essence, a basic issue raised by environmentalists is that *both* mass affluence and mass poverty can produce considerable effluence and much destruction of habitat that cannot be sustained without grave consequences.

It is all but self-evident that the emission of a number of types of wastes by affluent societies can lead to significant environmental degradation unless adequate measures are taken to dispose of those wastes. Anyone who has been to Los Angeles on a smoggy day can attest to the fact that such degradation occurs even in the richest of the world's economies. Likewise, it is all but self-evident that the clear-cutting of trees in wilderness areas to meet the burgeoning demand of affluent populations for wood products has the same effect on wildlife habitat as the cutting of the same trees by poor people seeking firewood. If growing numbers of poor people are a threat to environmental preservation, so are growing numbers of rich people.

However, much of the degradation resulting from unchecked emissions can be reduced or even reversed by the application of advanced waste disposal technologies and techniques. Both the development and the deployment of these technologies and techniques are driven at least in part by higher income and wealth. This is simply because an affluent society can better afford to undertake the necessary investments than a poor society can. Further, affluent societies might, for reasons discussed later in this chapter, place a higher relative value on clean air and water than do poorer societies with unmet basic needs, and their greater purchasing power increases the effective demand for environmental improvement. Thus,

---

10. Dasgupta, Mody, Roy, and Wheeler (1995); see also Lucas, Wheeler, and Hettige (1992).

whereas affluence at least creates a necessary condition for reversal of environmental degradation, albeit not a significant one, poverty does not.

One consequence is that, alas, significant environmental degradation is occurring in some poorer countries today that could easily be reversed or at least alleviated by the application of known technologies. The problem is that these countries cannot afford to make the investments necessary to put these technologies in place. The opportunity costs of using these countries' scarce resources for this purpose are very high, given their other priorities.

These considerations give rise to the possibility that the relationship between a country's income per capita and the pollution it generates follows what economists call a Kuznets curve.[11] The Nobel prize-winning economist Simon Kuznets theorized that the relationship between a country's average income per capita and the inequality with which income is distributed in the country would follow an inverted U-curve. Inequality would rise with income at low levels of income, but as income continued to rise, inequality would reverse direction and begin to fall. Analogously, an environmental Kuznets curve (figure 5.1) would predict certain forms of environmental degradation to rise with income per capita in the poorest countries as they industrialize and begin to move up the income scale. Beyond a certain level of income per capita, however, as the effective demand for environmental quality in these countries grows, this upwardly sloping curve would turn and begin to decline. This decline would occur in some cases because of the development and adoption of technologies that curtail or abate discharge of the effluent. But also, in some cases, rising incomes would enable a shift away from products and services that cause environmental harm and toward others that can satisfy the same need but with less environmental damage.[12]

However, environmental economists point out that although certain types of environmental degradation do seem to follow a Kuznets curve, others apparently do not.[13] One of these is the emission of carbon dioxide and other so-called greenhouse gases believed to cause global warming. Also, in some cases at least, the observation of a Kuznets curve in one country may result simply from the transfer of certain of its polluting activities to other countries. For example, heavily polluting paper mills might be shut down in the United States, but the paper they formerly produced might instead be imported from newly built but equally polluting

---

11. OECD (1998). See also Selden and Song (1994) and Carson et al. (1997).

12. In 19th-century and early 20th-century London, for example, the use of untreated coal for home heating and industry produced "black fogs," which caused widespread respiratory problems. With the switchover to the use of cleaner-burning fuels for home heating, however, black fogs are now a thing of the past. This switchover would probably not have been possible had it not been for rising incomes in the United Kingdom.

13. Grossman and Krueger (1993).

Figure 5.1 Income and pollution

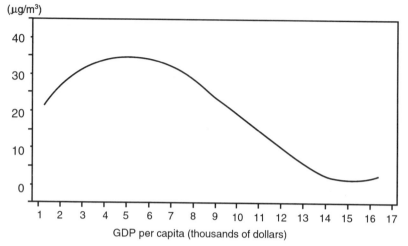

Additional units of sulfur dioxide
(μg/m³)

GDP per capita (thousands of dollars)

Concentrations of sulfur dioxide rise with income at low levels of per capita GDP, fall with income at middle levels of GDP, and eventually level off in the most advanced economies. The estimated turning point comes at a per capita income level of about $5,000 (1988 dollars).

Note: μg/m³ = micrograms per square meter of air.

Source: Grossman and Krueger (1993), MIT Press. Reproduced with permission from the authors and publisher.

paper mills abroad. Arguably, such a transfer might actually be desirable if it improves air quality in a congested region that suffers from especially polluted air, even if it causes some deterioration of air quality in another, less populated region where air pollution is low and the additional emissions can be easily absorbed. Some environmental activists, however, view emissions in any location, populated or not, already polluted or not, as equally bad.

New technology can of course cause environmental damage as well as undo it. For example, agricultural chemicals, including man-made fertilizers, have done such harm. These chemicals have been in widespread use for only about fifty years and have greatly enhanced agricultural productivity, alleviating hunger in many parts of the world where it was once commonplace. But they have also created environmental problems that were largely unknown before their introduction. One major problem is increased contamination of inland and coastal waters by agricultural runoff, as the use of chemicals encourages the expansion of agriculture. Another is that the use of pesticides has fostered the evolution of pesticide-resistant insects, not to mention a range of human health problems where regulation of these toxic substances has been lax. Unfortunately, the United States and other advanced countries where certain pesticides are now banned nonetheless continue to allow export of these same chemicals to other countries where their use is unregulated.[14]

Many environmentalists, while conceding the theoretical existence of Kuznets curves for some types of environmental degradation and the clear environmental benefits of eliminating poverty, argue that in fact the net effect of higher levels of affluence worldwide has been ever increasing environmental harm.[15] The reasons given are twofold. First, despite the introduction of emissions-reducing technologies, economic growth has caused pollution to rise and spread faster than these technologies can contain it. Second, as we have seen, technological advance also creates new types of environmental problems that did not previously exist.

Are these environmental pessimists correct? Some authors have argued, with evidence to back their case, that the converse is true: that prosperity and technology will increasingly lead to a cleaner, not a dirtier, environment.[16] In this view there is, as it were, an aggregate Kuznets curve that governs the sum total of environmental degradation. Most of the evidence supporting this argument comes from the United States. Goklany (1999), for example, shows that the United States has witnessed an overall decline in the emission of five major air pollutants: particulates, sulfur dioxide, volatile organic compounds (and the ozone that these create when airborne), carbon monoxide, and nitrous oxide.[17] These declines can largely be attributed to the introduction of new technologies to control pollution, or to the substitution of cleaner fuels such as oil or gas for dirtier ones such as coal. Somewhat controversially, Goklany argues that these substitutions and introductions of technology have occurred largely

---

14. French (2000, chapter 5). But is the answer to this problem for countries to ban the export of pesticides if their use is banned at home? Or should there be a worldwide ban on their use? There is no easy answer. Defenders of open trade might argue that, as a means of regulating these substances, use of the multilateral trade rules is a poor substitute for sound domestic environmental policy. Without effective domestic bans on the use of pesticides, an export ban would likely only result in local production being substituted for imports of the pesticide. But environmentalists might counter that, even if the first-best solution, a ban on usage in all countries, cannot be achieved, a trade ban would be better than no action at all. In other words, a trade ban would be an acceptable second-best solution.

15. See Daly (1996a) and Goodland (1996) for arguments that economic growth places stresses on the planet that will ultimately prove unsustainable.

16. One problem that bedevils this debate is that data on, for example, the atmospheric concentration of many classes of pollutants do not go back very far. Systematic collection of data began only during the 1970s. And since then, changes in the way air quality is measured and monitored have resulted in some time series being inconsistent, so that what was being measured in 1979 might not be exactly the same as what is being measured today. This makes it hard to establish empirically whether Kuznets curves actually exist.

17. These downward trends would appear to exist even after accounting for discrepancies in the data, as described in the previous note.

in response to local initiatives rather than federally mandated pollution abatement programs.

But Goklany also notes that the data for airborne lead contamination do not indicate a downward time trend as clearly as for the five pollutants listed above.[18] Thus, the empirical studies he cites offer both good news and bad news (but mostly good) with respect to the long-term trend of environmental degradation in the United States. Furthermore, environmentalists argue, even if there has been a net improvement in air and water quality nationally, the same is not true for all regions. In the Los Angeles Basin, for example, where automotive emissions are the main cause of air pollution, increased use of pollution abatement technology has failed to hold the line against an overall deterioration of air quality. The main reason is that a reduction in emissions per vehicle has been more than offset by an increase in the use of vehicles. The deterioration would have been far worse, of course, had the technologies not been employed. And it is possible that further advances in clean car technology ultimately will enable the deterioration of air quality in places such as Los Angeles to be reversed. But, or so argue environmentalists, this has not happened yet.

A definitive answer to the question of whether growth in developed countries will lead to net environmental degradation or net environmental improvement may depend in large part on scientific evidence not yet at our disposal. For example, it may depend on the determination of whether global warming from increased carbon dioxide emissions will create irreversible net damage to the planet.

How do globalization in general, and FDI in particular, fit into this picture? The basic link is that globalization and FDI are drivers of economic growth.[19] Thus, if growth is responsible for increasing environmental

---

18. Goklany's finding however does not seem consistent with information presented in the Economic Report of the President 1999 (Executive Office of the President of the United States 1999, 197), indicating that lead emission has fallen faster than all other automotive emissions, due to the phasing out of the use of leaded gasoline. The apparent inconsistency might be resolved if (1) there is a significant time lag between reduction of lead emission and its disappearance from the air, such that Goklany's data do not reflect recent reduction of emission or (2) there is some significant source of airborne lead contamination other than automotive emission that Goklany's data pick up. It is not clear which, if either, of these explanations is correct.

19. As reported in chapter 4, Borzenstein et al. (1998) find that FDI does contribute to increased growth in countries that exceed a certain human capital threshold. Substantial evidence also links a greater volume of international trade with positive income growth (see, e.g., Frankel and Romer 1998). But whether or not open trade *policy* is associated positively with income growth is another matter. A number of recent empirical studies tend to confirm this relationship (e.g., Dollar 1992, Ben-David 1993, Sachs and Warner 1995, Edwards 1998). However, a recent study by Rodriguez and Rodrik (1999) suggests that this apparent positive relationship may be spurious, because factors other than trade policy might so dominate the trade policy variable that no significant relationship between this variable and income growth can be ascertained. But even the evidence in Rodriguez and Rodrik (1999) does not

degradation, then trade and FDI must be counted among the underlying causes of that degradation.

Further, even for those types of degradation that are subject to Kuznets curves, if trade and FDI do significantly contribute to growth in the world's poor countries, the *initial* effect is almost sure to be greater, not lesser, environmental degradation. Many of these countries are still on the uphill side of the curve and may take years or decades to reach the income threshold beyond which higher income leads to reduced degradation. Likewise, only with time will income levels reach the thresholds where rising incomes lead to stabilization of population growth.

On the other hand, for some types of environmental degradation subject to Kuznets curves, FDI may in some cases actually reduce the income level at which the turning point occurs. This would happen to the extent that multinational firms transfer their latest, best, and cleanest technologies to their operations in developing countries.[20]

Environmentalists might nonetheless argue that, even if some such technology transfer is achieved, it will be insufficient to prevent net environmental degradation in the affected areas. The degradation of air and water quality along the US-Mexican border, where many US firms have located *maquiladora* operations just inside Mexico, is often cited as an example. One reason is that environmental regulation in some countries is lax or even nonexistent. Indeed, environmentalists argue that some countries go so far as to offer lax environmental regulation as an incentive to attract foreign investors. This, it is argued, is leading countries into a "race to the bottom" in terms of environmental regulation, as countries eager to attract or retain investment lower their environmental standards in response to other countries doing so.[21] The worst fear is that such a "race to the bottom" would undo much existing environmental regulation even in high-income countries as well as create a major disincentive for countries, especially poorer ones, to pass and enforce new regulation.

However, although the specter of a "race to the bottom" runs deep in the environmental activists' opposition to globalization, there is very little evidence that any such race is under way. Chapter 4 showed that the vast majority of FDI worldwide flows into developed countries, which

---

point to a negative relationship; rather, their results suggest simply that no relationship exists. This last point notwithstanding, it is clear that many countries have experienced faster growth following implementation of policy packages that contain trade and investment liberalization (Krueger 1998). What is at issue is whether, at the margin, the trade liberalization portion of these packages significantly affects the outcome.

20. Dua and Esty (1997).

21. If this is true, one solution would be for countries to negotiate international rules to forbid the use of lax environmental regulation as an incentive. Ironically, although the issue was unsettled at the time the MAI negotiations came to a halt, there was a serious proposal to include in the MAI certain provisions that would do just that. This matter is discussed further below.

have on the books (and actively enforce) laws and regulations to protect the environment. No one has uncovered evidence that these nations have lowered their standards to attract this investment.[22] It is in general the world's poorest countries that have the weakest environmental regulation, but a very small fraction of recent FDI goes to these countries. This suggests in fact that there is not a strong incentive for multinational firms to locate activities in countries with lax environmental standards. And if no such incentive exists, it is difficult to imagine why countries that do currently apply high standards would seek to lower them to attract investment.

Why do lax environmental standards seem to be so ineffective as investment incentives? Almost surely, the main reason is that, in most instances, there is very little cost saving to be achieved by relocating an activity from a country where environmental standards are high to one where they are low.[23] Many of today's product and process technologies have been developed or refined to meet environmental standards in the developed countries; their environmentally friendly features are thus embodied in the current technology and cannot be stripped away.

The technology of a modern automobile, and especially its engine, serves as an example. Large, multinational automaking firms typically produce their product in many countries and, indeed, the automobile industry is one of the most "global" of all industries. Also, worldwide, automobiles have been one of the major sources of air contamination. In response to societal pressure to reduce automotive emissions, since the 1970s the basic design of automobile engines has been extensively modified to reduce the volume of pollutants in the exhaust. In most engines this reduction is achieved mostly by means of a catalytic converter. Of course, a catalytic converter can be uncoupled from the engine, but the engine runs well only when the converter is in place. Moreover, state-of-the-art engines are designed to run on unleaded fuel, both because catalytic converters require unleaded fuel and because regulatory mandates exist in developed countries to reduce lead emissions. Indeed, it would be difficult to run most modern automobile engines so as to produce the same levels of pollution as the typical engine of the 1960s—and it would actually be costly to modify them to pollute. Cars using these engines will produce much less pollution than cars of older design, and this is true irrespective of whether local air quality standards are lax.[24]

In fact, automotive manufacturers seek air quality standards (and, importantly, standards for formulation of automotive fuel) that are consis-

---

22. See Eskeland and Harrison (1997) for an effort to try to find such evidence; they find little.

23. See Lucas et al. (1992) and Oman (2000).

24. At least this is true if the car is run on gasoline formulated for the engine. One problem in some developing countries is that such gasoline is not available, and locally available gasoline causes even modern engines to produce a dirty exhaust.

tent across nations. And the standards that are sought by multinational firms are at the high end. Thus, for example, automotive manufacturers joined environmentalists in seeking a ban on the use of MMT in gasoline in Canada on grounds that MMT might interfere with emissions control devices (see chapter 2). In Indonesia, gasoline still contains lead, which raises costs of imported cars because they must be modified to use leaded gasoline. Representatives of several firms interviewed by this author indicated that their interests would be served by Indonesia raising air quality standards and requiring use of unleaded gasoline. Indonesia has been reluctant to do so, apparently, because higher air quality standards would put domestically owned manufacturers of vehicles at a disadvantage relative to importers or local subsidiaries of multinational firms.[25]

Much the same can be said about many process technologies often thought of as "dirty." For example, state-of-the-art petrochemical processing equipment inherently does not emit nearly as large a volume of organic pollutants as does equipment of older design. There is no cost saving to be had by placing the new equipment in locations with lax pollution standards.[26] Nor is it often cost-effective to transfer an older, more-polluting facility to a country with lax standards; rather, it is usually more economic to build a modern facility. In some process industries, as for multinational car companies, costs are actually raised by lack of clean air standards, e.g., if process equipment must be modified to accept locally produced "dirty" feedstock.

Also, it can actually raise a firm's indirect as well as direct costs to relocate highly polluting activities to areas where environmental standards are lax. For example, because such pollution worsens health and living conditions in the surrounding area, the pollution can add to the cost of production by reducing worker productivity. Even if some firms might be tempted to relocate polluting activities to countries that have low pollution standards today, they face the risk that standards in those countries might later be raised, after they have made the investment. They would then have to retrofit their polluting operations to meet the new standards, which might be more costly than if they had built clean facilities to begin with, and they might even be held liable for health hazards created by these activities or for past environmental damages.[27]

---

25. This could change soon. A "national car project" that was promoted under ex-President Suharto has been scuttled, and the Indonesian government is under pressure from domestic NGOs (and some of its own ministries) to take measures to improve the quality of air, which is rapidly deteriorating in some parts of the nation, especially the capital city of Jakarta.

26. See Oman (2000). Some environmental activists (e.g., French 2000) nonetheless worry that if a multinational firm does locate a plant in a country with lax standards, the firm will find ways to take advantage of these low standards once there. Examples in the text, however, suggest that the opposite can be true, i.e., that these firms can have reason to push for higher standards.

27. These arguments are further developed in Schmidheiny (1992).

To be sure, while the remarks of the past several paragraphs apply to many activities, they do not apply to all. In some activities and industries there are indeed cost savings to be gained from operating in a country with lax environmental standards. One such sector is mining. Most mining operations do create serious environmental problems, and fixing them can be quite costly. Mines must often be located in ecologically fragile areas such as mountainous regions, where measures to prevent environmental damage are extremely costly. Environmentalists are quick (and correct) to point out that, in many such cases, the outcome has been environmental damage of almost immeasurable magnitude. An example of a particularly dirty large-scale mining operation in the Indonesian province of Papua (formerly Irian Jaya) was reported in the normally probusiness *Wall Street Journal*.[28] The environmental damage caused by this mine figures in the fact that Papua has become one of several provinces in Indonesia seeking autonomy or independence from the Indonesian state.

But perhaps the extreme case is logging. Here the potential for environmental damage is so great that, in some cases, the only acceptable solution may be to ban the practice altogether. The cutting of forests, especially old-growth forests, reduces biodiversity, leads to soil erosion and flooding, and, by destroying a major absorber of carbon dioxide (trees), contributes to global climate change. Commercial logging, however, is not the largest contributor to loss of the world's forests; the cutting of trees to create new agricultural land and to provide firewood, activities largely associated with population growth in the poorest countries, are more important factors (French 2000). But commercial logging is nonetheless an important factor, and the industry has expanded significantly worldwide during the past thirty or so years.

Even so, the importance of these industries for economic globalization must be put in perspective. Mining and logging operations account for only a minuscule share of international trade and investment. Mining, for example, accounts for less than 1.4 percent of the total stock of US direct investment abroad, and logging for less than 0.2 percent. Abuses in these sectors (and, indeed, abuses wherever they occur) that have adverse impact on the environment should be curtailed. But, as with abusive labor practices (see chapter 4) that affect only a small fraction of globalized economic activity, these should not become reasons to "throw the baby out with the bathwater." It would not make sense to forgo the benefits of globalization in order to curtail the abuses, given that the magnitude of the former are very much larger than of the latter, and that the latter can, at any rate, be curtailed without loss of the former.

Moreover, it is not clear that globalization is the primary culprit in the loss of forestland worldwide, or even for that portion of the problem cre-

---

28. Peter Waldman, "Hand in Glove: How Suharto's Circle and a Mining Firm Did So Well Together," *The Wall Street Journal*, 29 September 1998, A1.

ated by commercial logging. Here French (2000), speaking for the environmentalist cause, seems to commit a logical error. She notes that world trade in forest products has grown much faster over the last twenty years than world production of such products, which is true. But she then implies that expanded world trade therefore is responsible for a growing part of the problem of lost forests. This conclusion does not necessarily follow; indeed, growing world trade in these products might have reduced rather than increased the loss of forestland. This is because trade can create efficiencies that would likely not otherwise exist.

For example, suppose that in country A there are substantial supplies of hardwood, and in country B substantial supplies of softwood, but that each country lacks the other type of wood. Without trade, country A might choose to make from hardwood certain products that are more efficiently made from softwood, so that more trees are consumed than would be the case if softwood were available. Likewise, country B might overconsume hardwood because it is forced to use it for products better made from softwood. If instead country A were to export some of its hardwood to, and import softwood from, country B, these inefficiencies would be eliminated, and trees would be saved. If complementarities of this type are widespread, increased trade in forest products likely would result in less, rather than more, cutting of trees to make wood products than would have been the case in the absence of trade.[29]

Although globalization of activities such as mining and logging does clearly have an environmental impact, other activities that figure prominently in globalization have little or none at all. Many service operations, for example, create few if any environmental problems, and indeed services now account for about 60 percent of US outward FDI flows. Thus, although environmentalists are correct to worry about the problems created by international trade and investment in mining and logging operations, they should also recognize that most of the problems they cause are peculiar to those activities. Again, it does not seem appropriate to lump these problem sectors together with other sectors that do not create environmental problems.

There also are some cases where environmental regulation might have the effect, intended or unintended, of sheltering domestic activities from international competition, even where such competition would have desirable environmental consequences. For example, in the Ethyl Corporation's dispute against the government of Canada (see chapter 2), one reason for Canada's imposition of regulation may have been to protect Canadian ethanol producers against competition from Ethyl's additive

---

29. In any case, trade of softwood for hardwood between these countries would create gains for consumers even if it resulted in no net reduction in cutting of trees. Also, the opening of trade would likely not produce any increase in logging. Thus the net effect of trade would be that the same numbers of trees are cut but that better use is made of them.

MMT. The ethanol producers claimed that their product was less environmentally harmful than MMT, but this is not wholly clear. The two substances both have adverse, albeit quite different, specific impacts on air quality. The question of which is the less desirable is open to debate, because the answer depends upon which impacts are judged to be the more harmful. What is clear in the MMT case in Canada is that ethanol producers' claim that their product was an environmentally friendly alternative to MMT should have been treated more skeptically than it was by environmental advocates (Soloway 1999). How widespread such regulatory sheltering might be is not known, but a number of cases can be identified.[30]

Despite these arguments, for some environmental extremists the ultimate answer to all these issues is simply to stop globalization in its tracks.[31] After all, if globalization creates environmental problems in the first place, putting an end to globalization must surely be the answer. And if international trade and FDI are the major drivers of globalization, the curtailment of international trade and investment would be to the benefit of the environment.[32] The obvious problem, however, is that this alternative would almost surely leave most of the world's poor people—that is, most of the world's people—mired in poverty.

Unfortunately, although this dilemma, like the problem of environmental degradation itself, is all but self-evident, many environmental activists have yet to show a willingness to confront or even acknowledge it. Instead, many environmental activists line up behind the proposition

---

30. See Rugman and Soloway (1998).

31. This seems to be, implicitly at least, the solution favored by many, if not most, of the contributors to Mander and Goldsmith (1996).

32. Whatever the views of the Mander and Goldsmith (1996) contributors on economic growth generally, they are explicitly in favor of curtailing international trade and investment. See in particular the chapters by Morris (1996), Daly (1996b), Norberg-Hodge (1996), and Hines and Lang (1996). Some of these authors attack trade and international investment precisely because of the greater efficiency in production to which they lead. This is a curious position for self-professed conservationists to take, for greater efficiency, in the end, means nothing more nor less than the elimination of waste in the use of inputs. To the extent environmental degradation is caused by the overuse of inputs (including natural resources) and the greater volume of waste products generated by this overuse, environmentalists should applaud, indeed demand, greater efficiency. Unfortunately, none of the Mander and Goldsmith authors ever clearly explain why they perceive a conflict between greater efficiency and environmental preservation. On the other hand, at least one of them (Morris) seems to recognize the logical inconsistency, because he seeks to resolve it by claiming that international economic activity does *not* in fact enhance efficiency. But if so, why do profit-seeking companies engage in this activity? Alas, no answer is given. In fact, the propositions that greater efficiency is one outcome of expanded trade, and that this creates potential complementarities between trade and environmental policies, have long been accepted by economists working both on the environmental (e.g., Repetto et al. 1993) and on the trade side of the street (e.g., Anderson and Blackhurst 1992).

that, if only globalization could be done away with, the world could somehow eliminate both third world poverty and environmental degradation. After all, if globalization benefits only that portion of the world's population that is already rich, and works to further impoverish, if not enslave, the rest, then abolishing globalization would cause economic harm only to those wealthy few. And who but they could object?

But as chapter 4 argued, the proposition that globalization benefits only the rich is simply wrong on the facts. Rather, the hard evidence suggests that workers in developing countries who are employed by local affiliates of multinational firms tend to be paid more than other workers in the same countries. Thus, to reverse the trend toward globalization would condemn much of the world's poor to continuing poverty.

Indeed, for many of the world's poor, globalization represents the best way, if not the only way, out of their poverty. The alternative advanced by antiglobal activists, stripped to its essence, amounts to a move to autarky. Indeed, Hines and Lang (1996) openly call for a "new protectionism." But the world has seen any number of "new protectionisms" in the past, all of which have been tried and failed. In some countries, "new protectionism" has taken the form of import substitution policies (see chapter 4), which failed dismally as a means of alleviating poverty.[33] And for decades the most autarkic, inward-looking countries in the world were the Soviet Union, its Eastern European allies, and China under Mao. In all these countries, autarkic policies not only failed to eliminate poverty but proved disastrous for the environment as well. The experience of China, in particular, showed that, from an environmental perspective, small is not necessarily beautiful. During China's "Great Leap Forward" of the 1950s and 1960s, for example, that country learned that letting tens of thousands of small blast furnaces bloom in an equal number of villages produced a lot of toxic fumes but not a lot of usable steel.

Thus, the antiglobalist position that globalization causes both global environmental degradation and worldwide impoverishment is contradicted by the facts, and the antiglobalist solution—autarky—is both simplistic and counterproductive. If they want to both eradicate poverty and protect the environment, antiglobal advocates must present an effective alternative to globalization as a means to achieve the former. Absent such an alternative, they must acknowledge that there is an unavoidable trade-off between globalization and growth in developing countries, on one hand, and some measure of environmental degradation on the other. Many environmentalists do accept that this trade-off exists and must be addressed. But unfortunately, many others maintain, despite all the evidence, the chimerical view that somehow autarky can both lead the world to prosperity and save the earth.

---

33. This is a point stressed in WTO (1999) and Organization for Economic Cooperation and Development (1998). See also Burtless et al. (1998).

The questions that remain even after one has accepted this trade-off are many, and difficult in their own right. Can, for example, globalization be made more environmentally friendly without destroying the benefits that it brings, especially to the world's poorer countries?[34] Could the multilateral rules governing international trade and investment be revamped in a way that achieves greater global environmental protection without stifling the income growth that developing countries so desperately need? Can FDI be made part of the solution to the problem of environmental degradation? In the next section we start with the last of these questions and work our way backward.

Foreign Investment: Can It Be Made Part of the Solution to the Environmental Problem?

It would be useless to pretend that FDI has never been part of the problem. In many instances the operations of multinational firms have indeed been guilty of serious environmental damage. The worst of these, as already noted, have tended to be found in activities related to natural resource extraction, such as copper mining, smelting, and logging. But at least some foreign manufacturing operations are represented in the hall of environmental shame as well. In some such cases, lax management has led to local environmental and human disaster. For example, at Bhopal, India, in 1986, a facility controlled by the US firm Union Carbide accidentally released methyl cyanate gas into the air, killing as many as 6,000 people. Arguably, this accident would not have happened had the plant been held to the same standards of industrial safety as the US facilities of the same firm.[35] Fortunately, such disasters are rare. But surely significant environmental damage in the aggregate results from the day-to-day activities of many foreign-owned facilities, for instance through lax control of routine waste disposal. Examples include mining operations that dump unprocessed tailings into wilderness (or even agricultural) areas, and smelters that emit untreated waste gas. Often these problems could be rectified using technologies and managerial practices already in use in other countries or other industries.

The reader should note that these statements do not contradict earlier ones that lax environmental regulation in developing nations is not leading to large-scale relocation of production facilities in these nations by firms wishing to take advantage of lax regulation. The earlier statement still holds. Nonetheless, it can be true that those facilities that are located

---

34. Encouragingly, alone among the Mander and Goldsmith contributors, Daly (1996a) at least considers this alternative, but in the end concludes that the answer is no.

35. Khor (1996).

in countries with lax standards do not embody those levels of emissions control that might be sought by domestic residents in these countries. This can be true because of some combination of the following. Governments might not be representative, so that domestic preferences of ordinary citizens are not embodied in law and policy. Plants might be old, such that they do not embody current process technologies, which as noted earlier tend to be cleaner than older-vintage technologies. In some cases, old-vintage plants might indeed have been transferred to these countries under misguided policies of protection for the establishment of local industry. Such programs have enabled multinational firms to hold domestic monopoly positions in local markets for certain products. With no need to be internationally competitive, such plants often have embodied old technologies that in some cases are quite dirty. These policies are not generally in favor in current times and, indeed, economic reform in many developing nations has entailed getting rid of these policies, in part because they failed to bring significant development to these nations. However, the legacy of such policies does persist.

Why do developing countries often have more lax environmental standards than more advanced countries? Economists often answer this question by arguing that the populations of poorer countries prefer a different point on the trade-off between additional income and a cleaner local environment than do those of richer countries. Given its many unmet needs, a dollar (or rupee or peso) of additional income is worth more to a poor society than the amount of environmental improvement that it would achieve by forgoing that income. The conclusion is that poor countries tend to be willing to accept dirtier types of activity than rich countries are, if these activities generate additional income. But although this trade-off doubtless does exist, at least to some extent and in certain situations (this is discussed further later in this section), appeal to it to justify dirtier-than-necessary operations being located in developing countries is fallacious. Even if the residents of a developing country are willing to accept dirtier activities than the residents of a developed country would tolerate, they might still want these activities to be as clean as possible. This might be true even if there is some price to pay in terms of income forgone. Why, then, would plants built and operated by foreign investors (or, indeed, by any investor) fail to adopt what local residents regard as the optimal level of control of emissions?

There is no contradiction between the point made here—that firms may have incentives to put fewer resources into pollution abatement technologies than is socially optimal—and the earlier assertion that firms may have little incentive to locate economic activity where environmental standards are lax. The main reason why the latter is true is that much modern process technology embodies pollution abatement technology, which itself has been developed in response to demand for a cleaner environment. In such cases, transfer of this technology in response to lax environmental standards simply does not make economic sense. The present argument deals with why, once an operation is in place in a particular location, the optimal level of pollution abatement might not be implemented.

One reason can be market failure. The market in which the firm purchases its inputs may fail in the sense that the firm does not bear the full costs, including the environmental cost, of its activity. That cost is instead shifted to those in surrounding areas who suffer from the resulting environmental degradation. This cost not borne by the firm is termed an "external cost" or an "externality."

For example, suppose that a firm generates waste gas that is emitted into the air, and that these emissions create health problems for those who must breathe the contaminated air. These health problems in turn create real costs for the local community, both in the form of additional health care expenses and in the form of lost output from workers who become ill from the polluted air. (The increased risk of a Bhopal-like disaster might be another uncompensated cost.) If the firm does not have to pay these costs (that is, if the costs are not "internalized"), it is likely to underemploy pollution abatement techniques and technologies that would serve to curtail these costs. In this context, "underemploy" means that the community affected by the pollution would choose to have the firm use these techniques and technologies even if it had to pay some price to enable the firm to do so. The costs to the local community might not be direct. For example, the community might be willing to accept some reduction of employment opportunities, and hence some reduction of wages, in exchange for increased deployment of pollution control. This might not necessarily reduce the community's overall economic welfare; for example, if public health were to improve as the result of less pollution, there would be offsetting gains from lower costs of health care.

If one could accurately measure both the full costs of pollution (including the external costs) and the costs of cleaning it up, one could, in principle, arrive at a level of pollution that is optimal. ("Optimal" here means that this level attains the country's preferred trade-off between more income and more environmental preservation; figure 5.2). As suggested earlier, this level might vary from country to country, such that higher levels are tolerated in poor nations. But, although the optimum for a low-income society might allow for more pollution than that for a high-income society, even in the former case the result is not likely to be a total absence of pollution abatement. Likewise, even in the high-income society, the optimum likely will not be to remove all pollution. In both cases, in fact, the optimum occurs where the marginal cost of further pollution abatement equals the marginal social gain from this abatement. The marginal social gain is then exactly equal to the net reduction in total costs to society of the pollution that is removed.

Some environmentalists will argue that the only good level of pollution is no pollution. But this is again to deny the existence of a trade-off be-

Figure 5.2 The optimum level of pollution control

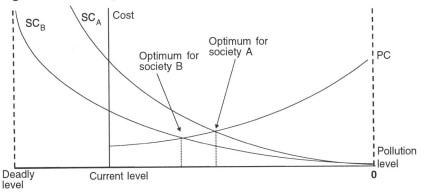

Curved SC$_A$ represents the total social costs, including external costs, of pollution for society A, and curve SC$_B$ that the society B. The curves are convex with respect to the origin because these costs increase at an increasing rate as pollution itself rises. The two curves differ in steepness because of differing preferences in the two societies—society B places a lower value on health per capita than society A—but the costs for both societies approach infinity as pollution becomes so high as to be deadly to human life. Curve PC represents the total cost of bringing pollution down to the indicated level. It, too, is convex because, in general, the cost of abating still more of the pollution rises as the remaining pollution falls to low levels. But it is less convex than the SC curves because the cost of abatement is always finite. At no point are abatement costs zero, because some costs (e.g., the cost of developing cleanup technologies) are large and fixed. The intersection of a society's SC curve with the PC curve represents the optimal level of pollution, which will always be greater than zero, and the optimum level of pollution control. The cost of additional abatement (to the right of the intersection) would exceed the cost imposed by the pollution that would be removed. This suggests that the optimum amount of abatement is lower (and the amount of pollution tolerated higher) for society B than for society A.

tween economic benefits and environmental benefits. But, even acknowledging that a tradeoff does exist, many environmentalists argue that it is not actually achieved and that activities are dirtier than society would choose.

In theory, an optimal level of pollution abatement can be achieved in either of two ways. First, the community could charge the polluting firm for all the external costs that its pollution creates. This would give the company an incentive to install appropriate pollution abatement devices. If the cost of doing so is less than the cost of continuing to pollute, the company will install the equipment. If not, the community will be compensated for the costs it is forced to bear. This approach is sometimes termed the "polluter pays" approach.

Suppose that a spectrum of abatement technologies were available, so that the firm could choose (on a rising scale of cost) anything from zero abatement to full abatement. Suppose also that the "pollution tax" is gradated such that the additional tax assessed per unit of additional pollution is exactly equal to the marginal cost of that pollution to the community, taking into account the total level of pollution. Then the company would choose a level of abatement that was optimal, in the sense that the marginal cost of abatement exactly equaled the marginal savings to the community from eliminating the additional pollution. As a practical matter, however, pollution abatement technologies do not generally come so finely tuned, nor is it generally possible to establish a schedule of pollution taxes that exactly reflects the cost to the community of additional pollution.

But should the polluter be charged the marginal external cost associated with its pollution or some other measure of the cost (e.g., the average cost)? This matters because the external costs of the pollution created by any one firm are a function of the total amount of pollution generated by all firms. For example, if levels of pollution are already high, the marginal cost to society of an additional unit of pollution may be higher than it would be in an area where total pollution is currently low. This issue is discussed further below.

The alternative would be for the community to offer to pay the polluter a sum equal to the total external costs that would be eliminated by deploying the abatement technology, provided the firm actually deploys the technology. Again, if the sum offered exceeds the cost of deployment, the firm will choose to deploy the technology. But if it does not, it will not deploy the technology (and will refuse the payment).

It should be clear that the environmental result is the same under either alternative: each achieves the point on the community's income-environment trade-off that it seeks. This result, in fact, is an illustration of a well-known economic theorem called Coase's theorem, named after another Nobel prize-winning economist, Ronald Coase. (This theorem was introduced in Coase 1961.) According to this theorem, an optimal level of pollution abatement can be achieved whether the polluter or the affected community pays the costs of abatement, provided the sum paid (or received) by the firm is exactly equal to the external cost created by the pollution. What is different about the two alternatives is, of course, who pays.

A large literature has grown up, based on Coase's theorem, on how to achieve this optimum balance between clean air (for example) and the cost of cleaning up activities that cause air pollution, where the costs of pollution are external to the activities that create it. It should be obvious from this description, however, that many practical obstacles exist to the application of Coase's theorem, not the least of which is that it is difficult at best to determine the true external costs of pollution.

One approach is for the public authorities to forbid all of a given type of pollution beyond the amount that achieves the optimum balance, and then issue quantitative licenses that in total would allow just that amount of pollution. If this optimum cannot be determined, maximum allowances could be set at or below some level determined by experts on health and environment to be acceptable; with luck, that level would be close to the theoretical optimum. In practice, different licenses would have to be created for different types of pollution. A business that produced more than one category of pollutant would have to hold licenses for each category. Firms would then be allowed to bid for the licenses; in effect, they would be auctioned to users.

Alternatively, the licenses could simply be issued on a first-come, first-served basis until they were depleted. Thereafter, firms wishing to enter the market (or to retain their existing operations, if licenses have been depleted before all incumbent firms have obtained them) would have to bid to buy licenses already held by other firms. This would set up the dynamic described below. Licenses could also be assigned to certain final-use products, such as automobiles. The idea is essentially the same. Cars that produce emissions would have to be licensed to do so, and the cost of the license would be passed on to the owner in the form of higher prices. Clean cars then would cost less than dirty ones, giving the consumer an incentive to buy the former.

The bidding (either in an initial auction or in a secondary market) would establish a price that a firm would have to pay to emit a certain amount of effluent. Those firms that could clean up their unlicensed emissions at a cost below the price of an additional license would do so. But those for which the cleanup cost exceeds the price of a license would be forced to pay the price of an additional license.

This scheme, in fact, automatically takes care of the issue of who exactly is the marginal polluter. All firms must bid for the licenses, and hence the price of a license is driven up to the level that the marginal polluter would just be willing to pay to acquire a license. If the total amount of pollution created by license holders were less than the total allowable amount, the price of a license would be low (or zero). This reflects the fact that, at overall low levels of pollution, the external costs associated with a marginal amount of pollution are also low. But when total pollution began to approach allowable levels, the price would rise to the point where highly polluting firms could not afford to buy licenses. They would be forced either to clean their operations or to shut them down.

But what about a firm that was a new entrant to a market? To enter, this firm would have to buy unused licenses from other firms; indeed, the ability to trade licenses is at the heart of this scheme, and the reason these licenses are commonly called "tradable pollution rights." Trading of pollution rights is a concept that some environmentalists find offensive, but in fact such trading would create incentives for especially dirty operations to shut down and for their licenses to be acquired by less polluting activities. If the price of a license were to rise, so that the cost of a license exceeded the value of staying in business, the owner would be better off selling the license. Having done so, the owner would then have no choice but to either shut down the business or install pollution abatement equipment so that the business no longer pollutes (and hence no longer requires a license). A third alternative might be to relocate the business to an area where licenses were cheaper, but the lower price would signal that, in this area, the pollution does less damage.

One attractive feature of this system is that, as the price of a license rises, it becomes increasingly possible for a business to finance the installation of pollution abatement equipment through the sale of at least some of its tradable pollution rights.

Also, the dirtier an operation, the higher would be the total price of the licenses required for that operation to stay in business. Likewise, were the price of a license to rise, the total value to an owner of a business from selling its licenses would be higher for a dirty business than for a clean one. This is simply because the relatively dirty business must hold more licenses to emit pollutants than the relatively clean one as a condition of being in business. If, say, the former business has license to emit fifteen million units of a pollutant per day and the latter has license to emit two million units per day, and if then the price of a license to emit one million units per day rises by $100,000, then the value of closing the operation and selling the license rises by $1.5 million dollars for the dirty business but only $200,000 for the clean business. The incentive for the dirty operation to shut down is therefore higher than for the clean business to do so.

Such a scheme also creates an incentive for firms to deploy clean technologies when establishing a new facility, because the less pollution the new facility creates, the fewer licenses it must purchase. In the limiting case, of course, a facility that does not pollute at all requires no license.

Any scheme of tradable pollution rights of course requires adequate monitoring, to ensure that firms actually comply (i.e., that they do not emit more pollutants than they have licenses for). Firms found polluting without a license should be subject to fines, set to approximate the full cost of the additional externality. This would give a firm in violation a strong incentive to correct the violation. Fines collected from violators could be used to offset the cost of monitoring.

Can such schemes work in practice? The most extensive experiment to date to implement such a scheme has been a scheme allowing emitters of sulfur dioxide to trade pollution rights enacted as part of the Acid Rain Program of the US Clean Air Act of 1990. Sulfur dioxide emission resulting from the burning of coal to generate electrical power is believed to be the main agent responsible for "acid rain" that has adversely affected forestland throughout the world. In North America the areas worst affected by acid rain have been in the eastern parts of the United States and Canada, and large coal-fired power plants in the US middle west are believed largely responsible. Thus, the Acid Rain Program has implemented a cap on sulfur dioxide emission and a program of allowed trading in emissions rights that operates along the lines of the tradable pollution rights scheme just outlined. The Acid Rain Program was much criticized by some environmentalists both on ethical grounds (the program created pollution entitlements and linked these to a right to trade, which were seen by some environmentalists as effectively creating rewards for polluters) and practical grounds (environmentalists worried that the program would not prove effective to reduce emissions, or that it would create so-called "hot spots," i.e., zones where emissions actually increased).

However, after five years of operation, the Acid Rain Program appears to be a major success. There is no evidence that "hot spots" have been created (Swift 2000) and, furthermore, there has been achieved a 25 percent reduction in acid deposition in the heavily affected eastern states. Also, the price of emission allowances has averaged in the range of $150 per unit of emission, far below initial estimates of $250 per unit and up, indicating that emissions abatement has been achieved at lower costs than originally expected (US Environmental Protection Agency 1999). A comprehensive evaluation of the Acid Rain Program and the role of tradable pollution rights is contained in Ellerman et al. (2000).

An even bigger experiment in tradable pollution rights is envisaged in the 1997 Kyoto Protocol to control emissions of greenhouse gases. In this scheme, pollution rights would be traded among countries, not among firms. As of this writing, the Kyoto Protocol has been ratified by only a handful of countries, and the scheme has not yet been implemented. Also, a number of problems have emerged, the principal one being how to determine the initial allotments of rights. These allotments are meant to result in a net worldwide reduction of carbon dioxide emissions by 8 percent from the baseline year. One problem is that the baseline year (established not at Kyoto but rather at the 1992 Rio Earth Summit) is 1990, and since that time, the economic collapse in the former Soviet bloc has caused greenhouse gas emissions in certain former Soviet countries to drop, giving them a windfall in terms of allotments in excess of current emission. Similarly, the European Union has experienced a net reduction of emissions since 1990, in part because of the absorption of the former East Germany and the replacement of highly inefficient thermal power generating facilities there with more efficient ones.

The second and bigger problem is that, under the protocol, developing countries would be given very low initial allotments, or at least so if initial allotments were to be based on historical emissions. As a result, these countries might have to buy a large number of emissions rights in order to sustain high growth rates. They would also be competing in the market for emissions rights with rich countries such as the United States, which has so far not been able (or, perhaps more accurately stated, has not been willing) to reduce its carbon dioxide emissions. Indeed, US emissions have grown significantly since 1990. Developing countries see the initial allotments as imposing an unfair restraint on their development, and the sense of unfairness is heightened by the fact that these countries have not been a principal cause of the problem—in 1990, developing countries collectively accounted for only a small fraction of total greenhouse gas emissions.

Despite these problems, there is in principle no reason why the Kyoto Protocol should not work. The main obstacle is, at root, political in nature. For example, will the United States be willing to impose some sort of discipline on itself to reduce its emissions, so as to free up some allotments for developing countries?

Can tradable pollution rights schemes be implemented at the national level in developing countries? Given many of the obstacles to effective environmental regulation in these countries, such schemes might work relatively better there than any other form of regulation. For example, in many developing countries, strong environmental regulations do exist but corruption is widespread so that officials can be easily bribed to overlook violations. Arguably, a licensing scheme would make it somewhat harder for a corrupt official to look the other way. This would be especially so if effluents were to be monitored by international agencies. If these agencies were to find unacceptably high levels of pollution, but that licenses traded at low prices, this would indicate that something was amiss. It would then be hard for local officials simply to ignore the situation.

Whatever the merits of tradable rights schemes as a means of controlling pollution, the main point is that externalities do exist and do bear upon foreign direct investors as well as upon local entrepreneurs. In other words, foreign direct investors do face incentives not to abate pollution, even where it is economically feasible to do so, if they do not internalize the costs associated with the pollution. This, of course, applies to all classes of investors and not just foreign investors.

However, it is worth asking whether foreign direct investors face incentives not to abate pollution that are stronger or weaker than those faced by domestic investors. For reasons already touched upon, foreign direct investors might very well face weaker incentives. As discussed in chapter 4, one of the competitive advantages that foreign direct investors typically have over domestic rivals is better technology. "Better technology" here does not necessarily mean better pollution abatement technology, although this might often be the case. Rather, often the foreign investor's production or process technology is better in the sense that it is more efficient. And a more efficient technology, virtually by definition, is one that uses less input per unit of output. As we have seen, greater efficiency itself generally implies a favorable environmental outcome.

China, for example, sorely needs to curtail its emissions of sulfur dioxide. The major source of this sulfur dioxide in China, as well as in the US, is waste gas from electrical power generation. The problem is most intense in older-generation, coal-fired facilities. Since the early 1990s, China has invested heavily in new generating facilities, most of which do embody modern technology. However, given the growth of demand for electrical power in China during that decade, the new facilities have largely augmented capacity rather than replaced old capacity. These facilities are, for the most part, technologically antiquated and hence less efficient than they could be.

Replacement of current facilities with more modern ones—an endeavor in which China is seeking foreign investor participation—could therefore result in as much as a 50 percent reduction in emissions of sulfur dioxide. At the same time, reductions could also be achieved in the emission of carbon dioxide, associated with global warming. All this could be achieved with no decrease in the amount of electricity supplied.

Further reductions in sulfur dioxide, but not carbon dioxide, could be achieved through deployment of such devices as flue gas scrubbers.[36] But significant reductions can be achieved even without any such deployment, simply through increased efficiency of the primary production technology. And, again, foreign firms often possess the most efficient technology.

There is a second reason multinational firms might have some advantages over domestic rivals in the deployment of pollution abatement technologies. This is that multinational firms operating in developing countries can transfer their own experience from their home operations to their own affiliates at lower cost than could be achieved were the same transfer attempted in a manner external to the firm. Thus, a multinational firm often can transfer pollution abatement technology at lower cost than can a nonmultinational rival. Or, put slightly differently, even if substantially the same technology is available to both the multinational and the domestically owned firm, the former might be able to deploy it more economically than the latter if the former has experience in its home country with the use of the technology.

This ability to transfer a technology within a firm at lower cost than could be achieved via an external transfer, termed by economists an economy of internalization, is not trivial. Indeed, it has long been postulated that economies of internalization are absolutely vital to explain the very existence of multinational firms.[37] One of the reasons China, in the example above, is seeking foreign participation in efforts to modernize and clean up its electrical power generation sector is to take advantage of such economies.

Environmentalists thus have recognized that multinational firms can have advantages over domestic rivals in the ability to deploy pollution abatement techniques effectively (e.g., Dua and Esty 1997). Specialists in economic development have recognized it as well (see UNCTAD 1994). Indeed, for the developing countries of the Asia-Pacific area, Esty and

---

36. The 50 percent reduction would require, however, that steam created by the plant also be used for space heating. See Zhang et al. (2000) and references therein.

37. The classic work on this subject is Buckley and Casson (1976), who borrow extensively from Coase (1937).

Gentry (1997) conclude that only foreign direct investment can meet the need for environmental infrastructure.

Indeed, one quandary for developing nations is that possession of superior environmentally friendly technologies by multinational firms can give these firms advantages over domestically owned firms over and above those advantages that multinationals already possess. Further, implementation of domestic environmental regulation accentuates this advantage of multinationals.

One response by developing nations has been to renew calls for technology transfer on terms favorable to developing nations, e.g., that multinational firms be required to license their environmental technologies at rates favorable to local rivals. However, multinationals are likely to resist such a requirement for obvious reasons; after all, the firms might argue, why should they give away an asset that was costly to develop in order to benefit a potential rival firm? This resistance will be magnified by the fact that, as already developed, the environmentally friendly component of new process and product technologies is often deeply embedded in those technologies such that it cannot be separated. It would thus often be difficult or impossible for a multinational firm to license to a local rival in a developing country just its emission abatement technology without licensing (or at least revealing) other technology as well. Thus, developing-nation policymakers might be faced with a politically difficult choice: either to implement measures to improve environmental quality, knowing that these will impart additional advantages to foreign-owned versus domestically owned firms, or to promote domestic firms at the expense of environmental quality.

With respect to this issue, it can be argued that the best choice of governments is to take the steps necessary to achieve the level of environmental quality demanded by its citizens and not to be upset by the possibility that these will impart advantages to foreign-owned firms. After all, the objective of the government should be to enhance the welfare of its people, and if this implies foreign ownership of economic activity (and all of the benefits this brings), so be it. However, it is clear that governments face intense political pressures not to enact measures that favor foreign-owned enterprises over domestically owned ones.

Toward Global Rules That Are Environmentally Friendly

Environmental activists sought to block the MAI because they felt that, if implemented, the agreement would have diminished, rather than enhanced, the ability of societies to regulate against activities that damage the environment. Later, having succeeded in halting the MAI negotiations, activists vowed to defeat any new rules on investment that might be negotiated in the WTO.

However, careful reflection should persuade almost anyone that blocking the negotiation of new investment rules might not move the world at all toward solving the problems of environmental degradation. To begin with, no comprehensive, binding multilateral rules governing investment are currently in place, yet direct investment is burgeoning (see chapter 1).[38] Thus, even if it could be proved that this investment is a major cause of environmental degradation (or of world poverty), clearly it is not multilateral investment rules that are creating the problem. Furthermore, and ironically, had the MAI negotiations continued, negotiators from at least some countries, including most importantly the United States, were willing to introduce new measures into the draft agreement to create environmental safeguards (see chapter 2). Thus, by helping to defeat the MAI, the environmental movement might have shot itself in the foot. They halted an exercise that had become an anathema to the movement, but in doing so they blocked what might have become the first multilateral commercial agreement to incorporate a strong environmental safeguard, and one that might have been subject to dispute resolution procedures to enforce that safeguard. To be sure, no one knows quite what sort of safeguard might have been created had the MAI negotiations been carried to completion. But, arguably, any safeguard that might have resulted almost surely would have been better, from the environmentalists' point of view, than nothing at all. Also, by opposing the agreement, the environmental community gave up a chance to play an advisory role in creating these safeguards.

In fact, to the extent that globalization of economic activity through direct investment does create environmental problems, an effective solution requires that multilateral rules be enacted that work to safeguard environmental interests at the local level. Indeed, many environmentalists accept this argument.[39] After all, even if environmental problems were to derive from multinational companies evading environmental regulation by locating activities from jurisdictions where regulation is strong to ones where regulation is weak, the only real answer would be to beef up regulation in the weak jurisdictions. In this light, defeat of the MAI does not prevent multinational firms from transferring dirty operations from strong to weak jurisdictions, if that is what these firms are actually inclined to do (we of course have argued that this is in fact a serious problem only in a limited number of sectors). Passage of an environmentally friendly MAI, on the other hand, could have worked to improve regulation where it is lax.

---

38. The rules on investment within the WTO, in the agreement on trade-related investment measures and the General Agreement on Trade in Services, cover only narrow aspects of investment and, for the most part, have not yet even come into force.

39. See French (2000, chapter 9) and von Moltke (2000).

If global rules pertaining to investment should contain environmental safeguards, what form should these safeguards take? Here negotiators must think both globally and locally. Safeguards are needed both to protect the "global commons," that is, to protect against pollutants such as greenhouse gases that have global consequences, and to protect the local environments of cities, countries, and regions. (Some environmental ills, of course, such as deforestation of the Amazon basin, have both global and local repercussions.) The most effective approach to the former would be to implement tradable pollution rights on a global scale, as is being attempted under the Kyoto Protocol for greenhouse gas emissions. This is one multilateral endeavor that many environmentalists support.

As noted earlier, tradable pollution rights can also be implemented on a national or a local scale, and in most cases they would be the most desirable way to achieve local environmental protection. Rights would be issued by national authorities, which would also enforce compliance, to ensure that firms not holding such rights do not generate emissions.

However, even at the local level there could be a role for multilateral institutions. For example, a global agency such as the Global Environmental Organization (GEO) advocated by Esty (1994) could play several important roles. It could provide technical assistance, including helping national authorities to set maximum pollution levels against which to issue licenses. It could also help national authorities monitor compliance.

Such a role for an international agency, however, has little to do per se with multilateral trade or investment rules. Such rules could nonetheless serve to ensure that any system of tradable rights is indeed a global system. A WTO investment agreement could oblige countries to require that firms obtain and hold such rights as a condition of doing business in the country. National governments could be given considerable leeway with respect to how much pollution to allow, but they would have to have in place a licensing system to ensure that limits on pollution are met. This does not mean that governments could set limits unreasonably high. The GEO could be authorized (perhaps through a process of negotiation among countries) to set standards for maximum allowable levels of pollution. Governments would then be free to set higher standards than those recommended by the GEO, including higher standards for some regions than others. But they would not be free to set lower standards.

Furthermore, alleged violation of such an obligation might then be subject to dispute settlement procedures. In this matter, however, WTO remedies would not suffice. Rather, a modified version of remedial procedures envisaged under the MAI for violation of an investment obligation would be preferable. Specifically, the government of a country found in violation of its environmental obligations might be given a certain amount of time to correct the violation. But if it failed to do so, it would not be subject to trade sanctions, the remedy of last resort under the WTO. Rather, the government of the country would be subject to fines, assessed to approximate the social costs of the pollution resulting from the violation. Such a fine might induce the government to impose fines against those firms whose activities were causing the problem in the first place. And as noted above, this is exactly how government enforcement agencies should treat individual violators of pollution standards.

Would global implementation of tradable pollution rights satisfy the concerns of the global environmental activist community? Many activists would not be mollified, largely because they are ideologically opposed to the whole idea of such rights. These activists advocate instead an autarkic, "small is beautiful" approach. (See, e.g., the essays in part IV of Mander and Goldsmith 1996.) Such a "solution," as already argued, might actually do little to preserve the environment. In any case, it simply would not be acceptable to the majority of the world's population, especially that portion of the population that now lives in poverty. Thus, to advocate a return to rustic living is, for all practical purposes, to advocate something that will not happen. It would serve the activist community far better to open their minds to approaches that properly account and compensate for the social costs of environmental degradation, to give business firms incentives to pursue clean options in pursuing their legitimate activities. And until a better plan is advanced, a system of tradable pollution rights is the only game in town.

Conclusion

The reader will surely have detected that this author is, at root, sympathetic to many of the concerns raised by environmental activists, but not to the solutions that some of them propose. For example, one might note that the population of China is currently about 1.2 billion, and that more than 70 percent of these people live in rural areas. In Korea in the early 1960s, about the same percentage of the population lived in rural areas; today, after less than forty years of rapid economic growth in that country, that share has dropped below 10 percent. If income growth in China results in the same shift from rural to urban areas there over the next forty years, it will mean almost three-quarters of a billion people moving into Chinese cities—even with zero population growth. This would create the equivalent of over 60 new urban complexes, each roughly the same size as Los Angeles or Seoul. If these new complexes were to create the same amount of urban air pollution as do Seoul or Los Angeles today, the environmental damage would be monumental. Environmentalists are right to wonder if the planet, let alone the eastern portion of the Eurasian landmass, could sustain this amount of air contamination and remain fit for human (or animal) habitation.

However, it is equally true that such massive urbanization will have effects that will at least partially offset the rising effluence that results from the increased affluence. Relative energy prices will rise around the world, inducing energy conservation. (Indeed, even Americans might get over the delusion that every household needs at least one large sports utility vehicle that gets only 10 miles to the gallon.) The demand, indeed the necessity, for cars that are clean as well as energy conserving will increase. The resources devoted to developing environmentally friendly technologies will also increase. At the same time, greater affluence will lead to greater demand for wilderness and habitat preservation, even in countries where this is today a low priority.

The problems nonetheless are very real, and environmental activists are right to worry that, even allowing for the positive changes brought about by rising affluence, the coming decades could still see significant net environmental deterioration worldwide. Certainly some major problems with global ramifications exist for which no effective solution is in place. Greenhouse gas emissions, leading possibly to global warming, are one example, given that no one is confident that the Kyoto goals will be met.

However, activists should also realize that the answer offered by certain members of their community—a worldwide return to simple, organic, rural lifestyles—simply is not an answer at all. The nearly three-quarters of China's population that live in rural areas already have this lifestyle, and it is one that most of them are eager, if not desperate, to escape. Globalization of the world's economy provides for these people the beginning of a way out of a life of poverty and deprivation.

Furthermore, to place globalization at the forefront of the causes of the problem, as some environmentalists do, is itself erroneous. Some aspects of globalization might indeed have the effect of worsening environmental problems, or of retarding the implementation of effective solutions. Fixing these problems is a worthy priority. However, much of globalization is far removed from environmental concerns. In India, for example, globalization has enabled the spectacular rise of a local software sector. Some of this activity in India is driven by multinational firms, but even the part that is homegrown depends on a growing global market for software. In either case, it would be difficult indeed to link this activity directly to any form of environmental degradation—programming computers generates little if any pollution. Here the only significant link to environmental problems is through the rising incomes that this industry is generating. And as this chapter has argued, rising incomes are more part of the solution to environmental worries than they are part of the problem.

Furthermore, as emphasized in chapter 2, the environmental activist community missed its best opportunity to date to fix one of their concerns in a multilateral context. This opportunity was the MAI. The negotiating countries, at the time the negotiations were terminated, were quite open to changing the text in response to environmental concerns. But rather than push for continuation of the negotiations to accomplish these changes, most activists joined in the fray to kill the whole exercise, and then turned to planning for the demonstrations in Seattle. It might have been briefly satisfying to the demonstrators in Paris to know that they had played some role in bringing the MAI negotiations to a halt, and later in delaying the WTO ministerial meeting in Seattle for a day or two. But, in the end, no changes in the multilateral rules that might have worked to meet the goals of these activists were accomplished. This, in the end, may prove to be the real shame of the failure of the MAI.

6

The MAI and the Developing Countries

In this chapter and chapter 7 we return to some of the specific issues raised by the MAI, issues that remain relevant even in the wake of the negotiations' failure. This chapter examines certain of these issues from the perspective of developing countries. This discussion does not center on whether or not globalization itself or foreign direct investment is in the interests of these countries. Chapters 4 and 5 have already dealt with such issues as how FDI affects growth, wages, and environmental conditions in the developing world. Rather, this chapter focuses on whether new multilateral rules on direct investment are something that developing countries might support and, if so, in what form.

Chapter 1 noted a main reason that the MAI was negotiated at the Organization for Economic Cooperation and Development rather than at the World Trade Organization. It was that the industrialized countries feared that, had the latter venue been chosen, a blocking coalition of developing countries would have prevented a high-standards agreement from being implemented. The expected leaders of such a coalition were India, Egypt, and the ASEAN nations led by Malaysia. By no means all developing countries would have joined this coalition; a number of important countries might actually have sought implementation of an effective agreement in the WTO. Indeed, while the MAI negotiations were being pursued, some developing countries, mostly in Latin America, indicated an interest in participating in the finished agreement. However, the pro-MAI developing countries were a minority, and enough countries would have joined, or would have at least been sympathetic to, the blocking coalition to have prevented a WTO negotiation from reaching consensus on an effective agreement. Or at least that was the view of officials of most of the OECD countries in 1995 when the talks were launched.

This chapter examines the major potential differences between the developing and the developed countries over what might be contained in a multilateral investment agreement. Such an examination is greatly complicated by the fact that, since no negotiations involving developing countries took place, it is difficult even to guess what would have been the developing countries' position on specific provisions. In any case, the developing countries do not hold uniform views on what an investment agreement should contain, or even agree that such an agreement is desirable.

Therefore, this chapter instead takes a normative approach, attempting to identify what the position of most developing countries on these issues "should" be. Needless to say, the result will be largely judgmental and will not necessarily reflect the actual position of any developing-country government, much less any consensus view among such governments. It will, however, be based in large part on interviews with officials of a number of developing countries, most of whom spoke on condition that they not be cited. (At these conferences, officials often speak in a "personal capacity," meaning that they do not necessarily reflect official views.) In addition, the author has attended a number of conferences at which officials from developing countries have spoken on this issue, again, in most instances, on condition of anonymity.[1] Finally, this section draws on the official statements of a number of developing countries on the issue of trade and investment. These were submitted to the WTO as background documents before the 1999 WTO ministerial meeting in Seattle.[2] But in the end, the views expressed here are judgment calls with respect to what should be, rather than what is.

What is perhaps surprising is that, when the issues are examined normatively, most of the features of an agreement on investment that would be "friendly" to developing countries do not diverge markedly from the actual provisions of the April 1998 MAI text. The positions of developing and developed countries on investment rules would seem to be much closer than were, say, the initial negotiating positions of the United States and most developing countries over the substance of the Uruguay Round Agreement on Trade-Related Aspects of Intellectual Property Rights. That

---

1. These include conferences sponsored by the Overseas Development Council (in Washington, 7 October 1997), the Asia Pacific Economic Cooperation forum (Hong Kong, 28-30 October 1997), the United Nations Conference on Trade and Development (Glion, Switzerland, 8-9 June 1998; Geneva, Switzerland, 21-22 September 1998; Kingston, Jamaica, 28-29 September 1998; and Caracas, Venezuela, 6-7 December 1999), and the Inter-American Development Bank (Barbados, 25-26 October 1999). The author has particularly benefited from exchanges with A. V. Ganesan, former Commerce Secretary of India, at several of these conferences.

2. National statements are available at http://www.wto.org/seattle/english/state_e/state_e.htm

agreement was one, of course, on which consensus among developing and developed countries was eventually achieved. Agreement on an MAI would therefore, at first blush, seem easier. This is not to say that there are no significant differences between developing and developed countries on investment issues, but rather that these do not seem so intractable that the only imaginable outcome is a complete impasse. Although some of these differences have the potential to create major stumbling blocks, they do not appear to be wholly irreconcilable.

The Changing Position of Developing Countries on Foreign Direct Investment

That the potential seems to exist to reach an agreement on investment between developing and developed countries reflects, in large part, a considerable evolution in attitudes toward direct investment in developing countries during the past twenty years or so. As noted in previous chapters, during the early 1980s there was considerable negative sentiment within these countries toward multinational firms, and official policies tended to reflect this sentiment. To a very large extent, this sentiment has been replaced by an appreciation that multinational firms can bring to developing countries a large bundle of benefits.

The emerging view among experts in many developing countries that FDI can play a powerful and significant role in development is underscored in the 1999 issue of *World Investment Report,* an annual publication of the United Nations Conference on Trade and Development (UNCTAD). That organization has itself been a focal point for criticism of multinational firms by developing countries in the past. The 1999 report contains an extensive discussion of FDI and development, written by a team of experts under the direction of Sanjaya Lall of Oxford University, an often-cited expert on multinationals and development. That discussion stresses the role of FDI and multinationals in increasing the financial resources available to developing countries, to enhance their technological capabilities, boost their export competitiveness, and generate employment. The discussion is not wholly about benefits; some of the disadvantages of FDI are also discussed. But overall the emphasis is on the positive aspects.

Such a positive view would not have been common among experts on developing countries 25 or even 15 years ago. Lall himself, although not known as a critic of multinational corporations (MNCs), had argued in the 1970s, on the basis of empirical studies of various authors, that developing-country subsidiaries of multinational firms tended to increase those countries' current account deficits substantially.[3] Until well into the

---

3. See, e.g., Lall (1973, 1980) and Lall and Streeten (1977). For a much more extreme view of the negative role of MNCs in developing nations, see Hymer and Rowthorne (1970).

1980s, developing-country experts often tended to view multinational firms as exploiters, transferring wealth from developing to developed countries while creating little of value in return.[4] Furthermore, these firms were typically perceived as vehicles that their home-country governments used to project their own power. ("Neoimperialism" was a recurring term in the 1970s discourse about multinational firms and their roles in developing countries.)

This perception was in large measure a legacy of quite a long history of FDI and multinational operations in the raw materials-producing sectors of what we now call the developing countries. Earlier in the 20th century, large raw materials-based multinational firms were often successful in striking deals in resource-rich developing countries on terms that greatly favored the firms. Not uncommonly, these deals were backed by what amounted to gunboat diplomacy on the part of the firms' home-country governments.[5] Before World War II, of course, much of what is today the developing world was under the colonial domination of the industrial powers. But even in those developing countries that were independent, it was not uncommon in the early 1900s for powerful industrial countries to regularly intervene in these countries' affairs. Some went so far as to topple governments to ensure that the commercial interests of the home country were safeguarded.

Most of the colonies of the industrial powers acquired their independence in the years following World War II. This period also saw the end of the most overt forms of gunboat diplomacy, although some such incidents continued, and some aspects of the earlier era survived well into the postwar period. During the height of the Cold War, for example, efforts by the US government to protect the interests of US investors in some developing countries became closely intertwined with efforts to prevent governments from coming into power in those countries that might be sympathetic to the Soviet Union. In particular, because leaders in developing countries who sought to renegotiate raw materials contracts were often leftist in political orientation, the US government tended to view them with suspicion, as potential Soviet sympathizers. Although history is likely to judge the efforts of the United States to promote US foreign policy interests as legitimate overall, in the process it became associated with efforts to resist renegotiation of what often were truly lopsided raw materials contracts. At times, the element of gunboat diplomacy in such efforts was all but unmistakable, at least in the eyes of the intelligentsia of the developing countries. Did the United States, for example, back the violent overthrow of democratically elected governments in Guatemala in 1954,

---

4. Stewart (1981) provided a thoughtful and sympathetic examination of the developing world's case against multinational firms as it was articulated during the 1970s, and of the changes in the international economic order that spokespersons for the developing world sought in this regard.

5. For example, see Moran (1976) on US direct investment in the copper industry of Chile.

and Chile in 1973, primarily because these governments represented real security threats, or because they had expropriated or threatened to expropriate local subsidiaries of US-based firms?[6] It is doubtful that historians will ever reach a unanimous verdict on this issue.[7]

The perception that FDI was bad for development also extended to certain manufacturing operations that multinationals established in some developing countries. Often these operations produced for local consumption goods that proved to be higher in cost (and/or lower in quality) than substitute goods that might have been imported. As noted in the previous chapter, these operations were in most cases the result of ill-advised import substitution policies, under which host-country governments sought to establish a local manufacturing industry almost irrespective of economic considerations. Such policies were largely homegrown in the developing countries, not imposed from without, and were eagerly pursued by governments seeking to reduce ties between their domestic economies and the world economy. To lure this investment, developing-country governments often used a number of incentives, including high levels of protection against imports and, all too often, the granting of local monopolies to multinational firms. Not surprisingly, the outcomes of such policies were for the most part unsatisfactory (we take a closer look at this issue later in this chapter). Nonetheless, it was typically the multinational investors rather than the misconceived local policies that were blamed for the poor performance, at least until governments in many developing countries much later began to reexamine their own policies and to implement reforms.

One irony is that, by the early 1970s, when antimultinational fervor in many developing nations reached its peak, the basis for this fervor was already being severely eroded. In the raw materials sectors, the Cold War notwithstanding, old deals were being renegotiated and new ones agreed on terms much more favorable to host countries. The reasons for this were many, but economic factors played a major role. For example, many natural resource industries saw considerable new entry by firms that had not participated in international markets during the years immediately following World War II. Consequently, as time passed, developing countries could increasingly pick and choose their business partners from a grow-

---

6. Interestingly, when the rightist government of Augusto Pinochet replaced the leftist government of Salvador Allende in Chile in 1973, there was no effort to undo the Allende government's expropriation of properties of two large American copper firms. Nor did the Nixon administration in Washington issue any strong demand that this be done.

7. Even those authors who were favorably inclined toward multinationals tended to be critical of the political power that these firms exerted at that time. See, for example, Vernon (1971). Also, one of the most stridently anti-multinational-firm works in the literature on these issues (Barnett and Mueller 1974) came not from a developing country but from the United States. A counter to this book is Bergsten, Horst, and Moran (1978).

ing list of suitors. This effectively broke the quasi-monopoly power in these sectors once held by certain large firms or oligopolies.

Also, host-country governments began to realize that certain other economic realities played, over time, to local advantage even in the absence of new entry. Prime among these was the fact that development of natural resources typically requires that an investor sink considerable money into start-up costs. Investors accept these costs in the expectation that future returns will amortize them. It follows that, once this cost is sunk, but before the revenues begin to flow, the investor cannot easily walk away from the undertaking without suffering considerable losses. One implication is that, during the early stages of negotiation of a raw materials deal, before the sunk cost is incurred, the negotiating advantage tends to lie with the investor, which can always walk away from the deal if the terms are not to its liking. Also, because the start-up costs are so large, the host country might have few if any alternative means of moving the project forward. However, once the deal is consummated and the costs have been sunk, bargaining power shifts to the host country. At this stage, the investor is largely locked in and cannot afford to walk away from the venture. This is especially true if the deal as struck provides some form of economic rent to the investor (that is, returns in excess of those needed to induce the investor to make the investment in the first place). In that case the investor can typically be induced to accept new terms more favorable to local interests than negotiated originally.[8] The ultimate weapon that the government holds in this regard is the threat to nationalize the undertaking.

Importantly, however, once both investors and governments fully grasp the implications of the "obsolescing bargain" generated by a large sunk investment, both have an incentive to strike a deal from the outset on terms that both can live with in the long run. On one hand, the investor recognizes that if the initial terms are too much in its favor, they can be undone once the investment is in place. On the other hand, governments quickly learn that playing the nationalization card to force renegotiation of a contract on terms unfavorable to the investor has long-term costs for the country. Most important, it can lead to the country's being effectively blacklisted by other investors. Raw materials deals between international investors and developing countries thus represent one of a number of types of negotiating situations where experience and learning tend to drive the negotiating parties toward an optimal outcome.[9]

Learning on the part of host-country governments also played a role in improving the performance of FDI in developing countries. For example, by the mid- to late 1970s, the governments of many developing countries had become much more sophisticated at evaluating investments in local production of manufactured goods. Officials of developing-country gov-

---

8. This dynamic was described by Vernon (1971), who termed it the "obsolescing bargain."

9. See Axelrod (1984) for a treatment of learning and its effects on outcomes of negotiations.

ernments worldwide have, for example, learned to apply the techniques of cost-benefit analysis to this task, in part as a result of advice from experts from multilateral institutions such as the Investment Advisory Service of the United Nations and the Foreign Investment Advisory Service of the World Bank. These agencies have instructed many developing-country officials in techniques of effective analysis and negotiation of investment projects. And indeed, these officials themselves in many nations have, over the years, become better trained in economics. By the 1980s, younger officials in many countries were already highly technically qualified before assuming their posts, many having obtained their doctorates in economics from top universities in the United States and elsewhere. Their counterparts of previous generations often lacked college degrees, let alone a graduate-level education (or at least this was true in some countries; in others, e.g., India, there is a long tradition of officials having university degrees).

Outcomes of negotiations with multilaterals might conceivably have been even more favorable had developing countries simply gotten out of the business of screening or otherwise restricting FDI altogether. They might indeed have been better off ending all preferences to local affiliates of multinational firms, such as protection of local markets. However, few developing-country governments have been bold enough to adopt such a laissez-faire approach. In many governments, therefore, even if intelligent intervention is in some sense a second-best policy, the adoption of effective techniques of investment analysis and negotiation has gone a long way to improve the performance of local operations of multinational firms. Some of these governments might, as a result, now be prepared to adopt less interventionist policies.

But we are getting ahead of the story. These developments notwithstanding, the late 1970s and early 1980s were a time when developing countries held much antipathy and antagonism toward multinational firms. During this period, these countries took steps to create three different codes within the United Nations that would be binding on multinational firms. The first was a code of conduct, negotiated but not adopted at the United Nations; the second was a code on restrictive business practices, negotiated at UNCTAD and adopted on a nonbinding basis in 1980; and the third was a code on transfer of technology, also negotiated at UNCTAD but never adopted. The basic assumption behind all of these codes was that multinational firms were inherently likely to behave in a manner contrary to the interests of developing countries, and that the world needed enforceable rules to temper this behavior.

The 1970s also witnessed a number of nationalizations of affiliates of these firms by developing countries, in some cases through outright expropriation, and in others as a result of negotiation between the investor and the host government. Also, many developing-country governments, recognizing that they needed foreign capital to achieve their development goals, deliberately sought to replace FDI with funds borrowed directly from international banks. One result was that FDI to developing countries largely dried up during the second half of the 1970s, a situation that would persist for about a decade and a half. And although sovereign borrowing flowed massively during the second half of the 1970s, this wave of borrowing ended in the sovereign debt crisis of the early 1980s.

This crisis served to bring home to the by now heavily indebted developing countries the problems inherent in using bank debt to finance large-scale developmental projects. All too often the proceeds of this borrowing were invested in ill-advised undertakings that yielded little or no return, leaving the country unable to service the debt.[10] The upshot of the debt crisis was that new lending was curtailed, and some lenders sought immediate repayment of the outstanding debt. Many developing countries were forced to reschedule their debt, in effect going into default. One consequence was deep recession in most of the heavily indebted countries. For some of them, especially in Latin America, the 1980s became known as the "lost decade."

These circumstances soon led political leaders of many developing countries to take another look at FDI. Many of these leaders began to recognize that direct investment has at least three advantages that sovereign borrowing does not. First, the direct investor cannot simply pull its investment out at short notice, because unlike bank debt it is bolted down in the form of factories, equipment, and other tangible goods. Second, if host-country policies are properly designed and implemented, FDI will lead to efficient economic outcomes and, importantly, a satisfactory return on the funds invested, giving investors the needed incentive to reinvest in that country. The significance of these first two features is that FDI is generally not associated with balance of payments or liquidity crises. Third, direct investment can bring with it external benefits that manifest themselves in positive spillovers, such as the transfer of technology and managerial skills. Additionally, it became increasingly widely recognized in the late 1980s and early 1990s that competition within national markets brings about its own long-run advantages, and that direct investment in most cases tends to increase competition within the markets of developing countries. This new perception was, of course, in sharp contrast to that of the 1970s, when multinationals were most often perceived as monopolistic. The overall perception thus was swinging, by the mid-1990s, from one that saw FDI as a hindrance to economic development, to one that saw it as making a very positive contribution.[11]

---

10. Cline (1995) provides a detailed analysis of the 1980s' debt crisis.

11. This perception was bolstered by empirical studies. For example, as noted in earlier chapters, Borzenstein et al. (1998) showed a strong and significant positive relationship between FDI in developing countries and economic growth, provided that the host country has a sufficient level of "human capital." The "demonstration effects" of other countries' experiences

Even so, when this investment began to surge internationally in the mid-1980s, at first it flowed largely among the OECD countries, rather than from these countries to developing countries. Only during the 1990s did this investment begin once again to flow to developing countries in significant amounts, and even then by far the greater part of this investment went to only a handful of developing countries.[12] But those countries that did receive large amounts of direct investment also reaped significant benefits, as a number of studies have confirmed.[13] By the late 1990s, in a large number of developing countries, the pendulum had swung from antipathy and antagonism toward FDI to active efforts to attract as much of it as possible.

Changing Attitudes Toward Multilateral Rule Making

Along with these changing attitudes toward FDI came changing attitudes with respect to the desirability of multinational rules on investment. In this regard, a landmark event was recorded in 1995, when one developing country, Mexico, entered into the North American Free Trade Agreement with two developed countries, Canada and the United States. In signing that accord, Mexico agreed to very strong rules pertaining to treatment of foreign investment from the other NAFTA countries. Beyond that, however, Mexico subsequently went so far as to grant to all countries that were home to investors with investments in Mexico most-favored-nation treatment with respect to their investments. In effect, Mexico thus extended its NAFTA investment obligations to all countries. (MFN treatment did not, however, extend to NAFTA chapter 11, part B, obligations, pertaining to dispute resolution; extension of these provisions to other countries would have required that these countries themselves participate more broadly in NAFTA.)

In agreeing to the NAFTA investment obligations, Mexico was arguably ahead of the times. Although official attitudes toward such obligations in

---

with FDI have also been persuasive. Here the striking case is that of China, where direct investment was effectively discouraged until the late 1980s but where, since 1990, it has been encouraged, albeit with conditions attached. Chinese economic growth was spectacular throughout the 1990s, and it is clear that FDI has been a major factor behind this growth. See Lardy (1998).

12. According to various issues of *World Investment Report*, the developing countries received an average share of 18 percent of world direct investment flows between 1985 and 1990. By 1996 this share had risen to 37 percent of a much larger total. It should be noted that these data do not contradict those presented in chapter 4. The data presented here are for developing nations' share of US outward FDI. A substantial portion of the total FDI in developing nations is from other developing nations.

13. Relevant studies are reviewed in World Bank (1997), Moran (1998), UNCTAD (1999).

developing countries were shifting, it must be remembered that, only slightly more than ten years ago, these attitudes were mostly hostile. For example, during 1986-93, developing countries participated in the negotiation of what would become the WTO Agreement on Trade-Related Investment Measures (TRIMs). This exercise showed that there already had developed a rift among developing nations over trade and investment issues. A relatively few countries, mostly Latin American ones, were quite willing to bind themselves to new obligations pertaining to investment. Nonetheless, even these countries sought that the TRIMs agenda be kept fairly narrow, e.g., that it address performance requirements but not restrictions on entry. They might, however, have been willing to accept wider coverage of the TRIMs agreement than that which was actually agreed upon, e.g., that the agreement cover additional performance requirements that were not covered in the final agreement. But they did so with notable reluctance and, indeed, under the presumption that this agreement would be minimalist in content.

By the late 1990s, however, some developing countries that had earlier opposed a wide TRIMs agenda were expressing a willingness to become signatories to the MAI. These included Latin American countries such as Argentina and Chile that had been among the most willing to accept wider TRIMs obligations than actually were agreed to. This was true even though the draft MAI would have imposed much heavier obligations with respect to investment than had ever been envisaged, let alone concluded, in the TRIMs. In addition, other developing countries, although not yet ready to sign the MAI, were at least willing to explore cautiously but seriously whether or not they might become signatories at some time in the future. These nations included Brazil, for example, and certain Asian nations.

Changing official attitudes in developing countries during the 1990s were also reflected in a greater willingness to enter into bilateral investment treaties (BITs) with the major home countries to FDI. Indeed, the 1990s witnessed the signing of hundreds of such treaties between developed and developing countries. In 1990 a total of about 400 BITs were in existence, but by 1997 this number had risen to over 1,300, with more than 160 countries participating in at least one such treaty. The vast majority of these were between developed and developing countries.

This willingness to sign BITs, however, does not imply that most developing countries now eagerly seek comprehensive multinational rules on investment. Indeed, experience in the Asia-Pacific Economic Cooperation (APEC) forum during the early 1990s was somewhat disappointing. The APEC did produce, at its 1995 ministerial meeting, a set of nonbinding investment principles, but these fell far short of unambiguous and enforceable rules. Thus, the shift in attitude among developing countries toward multinational rules is probably best characterized as a move away from outright hostility and toward cautious consideration of their merits.

Even so, this represents a dramatic change in the position of developing countries as a group. Whereas most such countries would have been inalterably opposed to such rules as recently as ten years ago, a great many are now at least prepared to examine seriously whether such rules might not be in their interests, even if they are not yet prepared to accept them unequivocally.

Developing Countries and the Provisions of the MAI

All this serves as background to a normative examination of where developing countries should stand on the obligations that the MAI would have created.[14] The goal is to determine which among the obligations laid out in the draft MAI are ones that these countries should be willing to accept as written, which are those where differences would exist but on which compromise is possible, and which are those on which agreement would be unlikely. Obligations on which agreement would likely be readily struck include the following:

- MFN treatment,
- national treatment in the postestablishment phase of investment,
- general treatment of investment (i.e., fair and equitable treatment, full and constant protection and security, and treatment as required by international law),
- obligations relating to expropriation and compensation for expropriated assets,
- obligations relating to transfers of funds by investors,
- obligations relating to privatization and monopolies,
- dispute settlement of state-to-state and perhaps investor-to-state disputes in modified form (i.e., not the form of the NAFTA), and
- obligations relating to transparency.

In each of these areas, it seems in developing countries' interest to agree to currently accepted international standards, subject to specific exceptions, as would have been agreed to under the MAI. Exceptions might include grandfather clauses to an MFN obligation, to allow continuation of special treatment accorded to investors from specified countries under existing agreements. Such an exception would be less broad than the proposed exception for regional economic integration organizations that contributed to the failure of the MAI negotiations (see chapter 3). If the US-EU differences over the Regional Economic Integration Organization (REIO) exception could

---

14. For views on these issues from the former Secretary of Commerce of India, see Ganesan (1999).

have been resolved so as to allow grandfathering of existing cases of special treatment, this likely would also have laid to rest any differences between developing and developed countries over similar exceptions.

The standards of the MAI with respect to expropriation and compensation for expropriation have become quite widely accepted among developing countries, as evidenced by the fact that these standards appear in almost all of the BITs that these countries have willingly entered into.[15] Nonetheless, developing countries might appropriately join with developed countries to add language to remove regulatory takings from the coverage of the expropriation provisions of any future multilateral agreement, for the reasons discussed in chapter 2.

Developing countries almost surely would demand, and likely could negotiate, a derogation from the free transfer of payments obligation for countries experiencing severe balance of payments problems. Such a derogation was allowed in the MAI, provided it was taken in a manner consistent with existing International Monetary Fund rules. (A similar derogation is allowed under GATT Article XVIII: B.) Developing countries also would likely demand that free transfer apply only to FDI and not necessarily to other forms of investment, but this issue could be dealt with by narrowing the definition of investment (see below).

With respect to the investor-to-state dispute settlement procedures of the MAI, the most likely source of contention between developing and developed countries is that these allow an investor to take a state to international arbitration procedures (see chapter 3) but do not allow the reverse. The reasoning for this asymmetry is that the MAI was meant to be an agreement among national governments, to which only those governments could be bound. Developing countries should accept this line of reasoning (and, indeed, many likely would do so). If they did, it would eliminate a stumbling block that would have arisen ten years ago. Then many developing countries would have insisted that a multilateral agreement also impose obligations on multinational firms, and that dispute settlement provisions enable governments to sue firms for violations of these obligations. Such an arrangement (which lay at the heart of proposed UN codes of conduct, mentioned above) would not be acceptable to the developed countries.

As discussed later in this chapter, developing-nation insistence on a binding code of conduct that would apply to multinational firms thus has the potential to become a deal breaker to any future agreement on investment. There might be, however, compromise positions that could be struck. For example, there certainly is some scope for a nonbinding code that would establish standards for conduct by multinationals in developing nations. Indeed, such a code might be welcomed by at least some multina-

---

15. For example, the US-model BIT, upon which all such treaties entered into by the US government are based, contains language almost identical to the MAI.

tional firms, as it could establish unambiguous norms against which a firm could defend its own actions. Nonetheless, such a nonbinding code would not be part of future rules that would be binding on governments.

But in exchange for accepting that only governments would be bound by the agreement, developing countries would surely seek provisions establishing narrower scope under investor-to-state dispute resolution procedures for a firm to sue a government than the MAI would have allowed. For example, developing countries might seek a provision stating that such procedures could be invoked only for violations by a government of core obligations on a postestablishment basis, and then only where other remedies in the countries themselves have been exhausted or have resulted in decisions at odds with international obligations.[16] Given recent experience with investor-to-state dispute resolution procedures under NAFTA (see chapters 2 and 3), it is quite possible that developed countries themselves would be quite ready to accept a more restricted access to these procedures for international investors than was envisaged under the MAI.

On these obligations, then, the differences between developing and developed countries are likely to be fairly minor and certainly bridgeable. Thus, we turn next to those obligations where there is greater potential for major differences to arise. We first consider those issues with some, but not strong, potential to be deal breakers. We then turn to the truly difficult issues.

One major issue is investment incentives. The case is strong that developing countries are at a disadvantage vis-à-vis the developed countries in the use of incentives to compete for FDI. Multilateral disciplines to restrain the use of incentives would therefore seem to be in the developing countries' interest.[17] This view is, of course, largely consistent with that advanced elsewhere in this volume (see chapters 3, 4, and appendix B). As noted in chapter 2, however, in the MAI negotiations the United States and certain other countries were unwilling to bind their subnational governments to any such disciplines. This position could create a major stumbling block for developing countries that would like to see such disciplines imposed.

As just suggested, however, investment incentives are not likely to be a deal-breaking issue, but for all the wrong reasons. There appears to be

---

16. In an earlier work (Graham 1996), this author proposed that investor-to-state dispute settlement procedures function along the lines just proposed. Under these proposals, international arbitration would proceed in two stages. In the first stage, the investor would have to show three things. First, it would have to show some reasonable substantive basis for lodging the complaint. Second, it would have to show that local remedies have been exhausted or are unavailable. Third, it would have to show that, where local remedies have been sought, a decision has been handed down that appears inconsistent with the country's obligations under the relevant multilateral agreement.

17. See the discussion of investment incentives in chapter 3 as well as in Moran (1998).

very little demand on the part of developing countries for restrictions on investment incentives, mainly because many developing countries currently offer such incentives (or offer subsidies that might be covered by future restrictions on incentives). This is one area where the actual position of developing countries is likely to be less of a stumbling block than would be the position that is arguably in their best interests.

Another issue that might raise problems but is unlikely to be a deal breaker is cross-border movement of personnel. Here the major problem is that certain developing countries might reasonably assert that the provisions as drafted in the MAI do not go far enough to meet their interests. India is one country that has a number of specific concerns with respect to the immigration policies of the United States and the EU countries. India would like to see far fewer restrictions on its highly trained computer software engineers, for example, with respect to temporary residence in the United States. In fact, India would advocate a provision allowing multinational firms who employ these engineers to transfer them to their home operations in the United States virtually without restriction. On this, India's government is joined by many US firms.[18]

However, other developing countries do not necessarily share India's concerns. One result is that these issues are not likely to be comprehensively addressed in the context of an investment agreement. Rather, if multilateral investment negotiations were to be initiated at the WTO, India would likely raise the issue, joined perhaps by a few other developing countries. But in the end, without a consensus among all developing countries, they would likely welcome any aspect of an investment agreement that had the effect of liberalizing to some degree the immigration policies of the developed countries. In other words, they probably would be willing to settle on an agreement that went at least as far as the MAI on these issues, without insisting on new provisions that go significantly further.

The provisions of the MAI that do have the potential to be deal breakers are those that, in some sense or another, go too far to be acceptable to most developing countries. The most important of these is preestablishment national treatment.

The reason preestablishment national treatment is a potential deal breaker is that, if the standard were implemented strictly, developing countries would be unable to pursue policies of infant-industry protection. (As explained in chapter 4, infant-industry policies are designed to protect domestic firms in the local market from competition from international firms until the domestic firms can compete successfully with their foreign counterparts.) A key issue for our normative analysis is, of course, whether or not infant-industry protection is effective in building internationally com-

---

18. Thus, for example, Microsoft Corporation's president Bill Gates has frequently testified before the US Congress in favor of reduced barriers to US residency for persons of non-US nationality with high technical qualifications.

petitive industries. On this, the evidence is mixed but, as noted earlier, mostly negative. Many efforts at infant-industry protection have fostered, as it were, infants that have never matured. In Brazil, to cite but one example, a program of protection of domestic computer manufacturers has been in place for over twenty years, accompanied by domestic content requirements placed on foreign-owned computer manufacturers operating in Brazil. The result of this policy, by most accounts, is that computers produced by domestic Brazilian firms (including foreign-owned ones) remain technologically laggard and more expensive than comparable imports.[19] In other cases, however, such as that of Korea's steel industry, infant-industry policies appear to have produced at least some firms that have become very competitive internationally.[20] Certain economists (e.g., Rodrik 1999) therefore defend infant-industry policies as viable. However, the majority of development specialists, it is safe to say now, believe that these policies have hurt development more than they have fostered it.

It should be noted that the reasoning underlying infant-industry policies often is used to justify what are ostensibly other types of policies, e.g., policies to support "strategic sectors". These latter policies are to give government support or protection to domestic firms in sectors that are considered to be in some sense "strategic". Often these sectors include telecommunications, computers, and other "high-technology" activities. Although the terminology used to justify special treatment for these sectors is often quite different from that used in the lexicon of infant-industry protection, the reasoning comes down to much the same: notably, that there is some special case for domestic ownership of these activities, but for domestically owned enterprises to thrive, they must at least temporarily be protected from competition from stronger international rivals.

But whatever the arguments for or against infant-industry protection, the governments of a large number of developing countries seek to retain the option to pursue these policies, and therefore are not currently willing to agree to rules binding them to preestablishment national treatment. Since, as we have seen, the evidence does not overwhelmingly indicate that these countries should give up such policies entirely, it is not clear that developing countries would be wrong to decline to enter into an international agreement to do so.

Even so, developing countries might wish to consider a generalization of the approach taken by the GATS on this issue. The GATS incorporates both a positive list of sectors and activities in the services sectors that are open for foreign investment, and a negative list of the applicable limitations on national treatment and market access.[21] Also, in practice, many

---

19. See Frischtak (1996)

20. See Amsden (1989).

21. The negative lists attached to the GATS commitments thus apply essentially to postestablishment national treatment. See chapter 7 for more detail.

developing countries (and, indeed, some developed ones) reserve the right to screen FDI proposals, but routinely approve them where the total amount to be invested is below a certain threshold. Thus, developing countries might be prepared to grant national treatment on a preestablishment basis for projects falling below a stated threshold but may wish to reserve the right to require approval for larger projects.

All this suggests that there is scope for a mutually acceptable compromise on the issue of preestablishment national treatment between developing and developed countries. In particular, the hybrid approach of the GATS—a positive list whereby only ventures in the listed sectors would be subject to this treatment—appears promising. It is noteworthy that the sector where such an approach has been agreed to—the services sector—is one where restrictions on entry are quite prolific (see, e.g., Sauvé and Wilkie 2000). Thus, it would seem a fairly straightforward extension to create a national treatment provision that would cut across all sectors based on this approach.

Major differences also exist between developing and developed countries on the issue of performance requirements (see chapter 3). This issue is linked to that of investment incentives, but also to that of restrictive business practices. The latter dominated discussions of investment policy between developed and developing countries during the 1970s, and the issues that were raised then have not entirely gone away. Development experts reasoned at that time that multinational firms may behave as monopolists, achieving benefits for themselves by implementing restrictive practices that are suboptimal from the host country's point of view. Among these practices are, allegedly, the withholding of technology from the host country, the suppression of exports, and the use of transfer prices to avoid taxation. These experts argued that the need for performance requirements of various types derives from the need to compensate host countries for these practices that, arguably, reduce their welfare.

The strongest argument against this position is that many of these performance requirements do not produce the desired results. Thus, in a recent study that builds on a large body of accumulated empirical research, Moran (1998) concludes that local content requirements, requirements for local equity participation, and technology transfer requirements are all typically counterproductive. Not only do they not help meet development goals, such as the development of locally owned, internationally competitive suppliers of inputs to multinational operations, and increased technology transfer into developing countries, but indeed they have the reverse effect: they retard this development and transfer. Multinational firms tend to be reluctant to transfer their best technologies to suppliers or to joint venture partners that the host government forces upon them. The crucial element of trust is often lacking in such relationships.

Moran also concludes, however, that some performance requirements, especially export performance requirements, are nonetheless effective. If multinational firms are required to achieve a certain level of exports from their operations in developing countries, the goods they produce there must be competitive on international markets. Hence these requirements create incentives for firms to use their best technologies in these operations. Of importance here is the fact that a multinational firm that faces a transparent export performance requirement at entry can choose whether or not to accept this requirement, but if it does not choose to accept the requirement, it must walk away from the venture. This can induce bargaining between the firm and the host government, which may result in the firm offering to export some categories of products, often including intermediate goods, but not others. (For example, US automakers in Mexico export certain components of cars and some classes of vehicles. But other components are imported, and some classes of vehicles are assembled for local consumption only.) If both sides bargain competently, the result can be a win-win situation. The host country receives investment in activities that enable it to realize a latent comparative advantage, and the firm gains a low-cost source of a product that it can offer on international markets. The outcome is consistent with national comparative advantage and hence tends to enhance world welfare.

Other performance requirements, by contrast, seem to be a particularly ineffective means of offsetting most restrictive business practices that are implemented to generate rents. This is particularly true in the rather common case where a performance requirement is imposed on a direct investor but to offset this the investor is granted protection from import competition or competition from other direct investors. It is difficult to imagine that a firm could successfully appropriate a rent if the host country's market is open both to imports and to additional FDI. But developing countries, in order to induce investment, have often been only too willing, in effect, to grant the local market as a monopoly to the investor. Fortunately, as noted earlier, many countries have backed away from this self-defeating practice as their governments' analytical capabilities have improved. And even markets that once were considered natural monopolies increasingly appear to be contestable, if government policy allows them to be. The bottom line is that control of abusive business practices by foreign investors in many countries and in many sectors begins with reform of domestic policy, not with the imposition of performance requirements.

Some practices, to be sure, might require regulation rather than market opening. Transfer price abuse, which in a globalized world economy is a matter of concern to developed as well as developing countries, is a clear candidate. But, as even the US government is beginning to realize, control of transfer price abuse requires an international, not a unilateral, solution (see Hufbauer and van Rooij 1992; Graham and Krugman 1995). Developing countries that are concerned about this abuse should be pressing to include taxation as part of a multilateral agenda on investment, not backing away from such an agenda.

Moran (1998, 2000) and others note that, today, certain policies and practices of developed-country governments create more formidable barriers to the achievement of their own goals than do the practices of multinational firms. These policies and practices include restrictive rules of origin and policies governing "less than fair value" (LTFV) imports, including most importantly antidumping policies. (The latter are laws by which governments impose higher than standard import duties on products that are deemed to be priced excessively low. The former are rules used to determine whether imported products should be accorded preferences under agreements such as NAFTA. Both have been used to favor domestic products over imported ones.) Government policies and practices in this area, and the creation of binding obligations relating to them, are of course the legitimate business of multilateral trade negotiations, and such negotiations could include links with multilateral investment negotiations. It follows that developing countries should be much more concerned with getting these policies and practices onto the negotiating table than with insisting that future multilateral rules on investment address firms' restrictive business practices. Indeed, Moran (1998) suggests that the "grand bargain" that developing countries should seek is to trade away *all* their performance requirements (including export performance requirements) for substantial progress toward making the trade and investment policies of the developed countries "developmentally friendly." This grand bargain would surely include disciplines on investment incentives as well as a substantial reining in of policies on LTFV imports.

Whether or not Moran's grand bargain is achievable, from a normative perspective, developing countries should not object to MAI obligations that do away with most performance requirements, for the reason noted above: they simply are not effective in achieving their objectives. Indeed, the best policy that a country can undertake to achieve these objectives is *not* to restrict entry by multinational firm B once entry has been gained by multinational firm A.

One last issue that could be a deal breaker is the definition of investment that would be covered by multilateral rules. The draft MAI's definition, as chapter 3 noted, is very broad, encompassing not only direct investment but also portfolio investment and even intangibles such as intellectual property. Developing countries are quite right to object to such a broad definition. Their governments, looking to the experience in East Asia and elsewhere during the financial crises of 1997-98, might be on quite solid ground to wish to regulate short-term capital movements but to exempt direct investors from such regulations.[22] A multilateral agreement on investment with coverage as broad as that of the draft MAI would prevent them from doing this, however.

---

22. In this they are supported by a number of prominent economists who are not generally in favor of heavy regulation (see, e.g., Krugman 1999).

But does this issue really have the potential to be a deal breaker? This author's best guess is, probably not. Given the East Asian experience of 1997-98, as well as experiences under NAFTA where investors have lodged disputes that would have been disallowed had the NAFTA investment provisions had less broad coverage, the developed countries might themselves no longer be convinced of the wisdom of a very broad definition of investment. Thus, on this issue, although the developing countries would likely be the *demandeurs* for a significantly narrower definition of investment than appeared in the MAI, the developed countries might very well offer little resistance.

Is There a Deal Breaker?

There is, finally, one issue that has real potential to be a deal breaker in any future negotiations on investment involving both developing and developed countries. That is the issue of whether multilateral rules on investment should include some binding code of conduct on multinational investors. This is something that the developed countries have long resisted. As noted earlier, an effort within UNCTAD to create such a code of conduct was undertaken in the late 1970s, but without conclusion. An effort to revive the UNCTAD exercises was attempted in the early 1990s but was quickly abandoned.

The issue remains a deal breaker for the simple reason that the developed countries, which refused to accept a binding code during the 1970s, have now been joined by quite a large number of developing countries. However, some specific remaining concerns of developing countries have merit. Chief among these is their fear that multinational investors operating in their territories might act to carry out the law or policy of a powerful home country when this law or policy is contrary to that of the host country.

This is a real issue, and indeed, the broader issue of extraterritorial application of law and policy surfaced in the MAI discussions. But as this author suggested in an earlier study (Graham 1996), a relatively simple fix can be envisioned that does not require an elaborate code of conduct that is binding on multinational enterprises. All that would need to be done is to bind the affiliates of multinational investors to obey, under normal circumstances, the laws of the host country in which they are incorporated and operate. (Exception should be made for national laws that violate international laws or conventions.) Normally, such an obligation goes without saying. The situation can arise, however, where an affiliate is required to take some action to comply with host-country law, but that action violates the law of another entity (typically the home government of its parent firm). In such an instance, the proposed provision would in effect require the affiliate to take the action required by the host country. This is an obligation that multinational firms should be willing to undertake, as it would serve to insulate them from the conflicts imposed when one country attempts to enforce its own law on an extraterritorial basis. This would be the case especially when this law conflicts with the law of some other country in whose territory the first country attempts to enforce its law.

Whatever the merits of this last argument, some developed countries are likely to reject it. The US government, for example, is inclined from time to time to enforce its own law and policy on an extraterritorial basis, and is disinclined to enter into any international obligation that might reduce its capacity to do so. And although the European Union has generally been less extraterritorial in enforcing its own law and policy than the United States has been, it has nonetheless been quite willing to reach beyond its borders in enforcing mergers policy, for example.

Is Any Negotiation on Investment Between Developing and Developed Countries Doomed to Failure?

This brings us to the final point to be made in this chapter. This is that the positions that appear to be the normatively correct ones for developing countries and developed countries, as revealed by those provisions of the MAI on which there was agreement, are not so far apart as to be unbridgeable. To be sure, for the two groups of countries to reach consensus on a multilateral investment agreement would require intense and hard negotiating. Nonetheless, the basis for good faith negotiating with some reasonable chance of success does appear to exist, whereas ten years ago any such effort would likely have led to an impasse. Thus, on this set of issues, the passage of time has changed quite a lot. Even today, a favorable outcome is not certain, but it cannot be ruled out as a nonstarter.

The bottom line seems to be that the argument used five years ago to begin MAI negotiations in the OECD rather than the WTO—that is, that developing countries would block any such effort in the WTO—no longer carries significant weight. What today most constrains the feasibility of achieving multinational investment rules within the WTO is not a blocking coalition of developing countries but rather lack of political will among the developed countries. Chapter 7 addresses this issue.

7

Where Does the Multilateral Investment Agenda Go from Here?

The failure to conclude the Multilateral Agreement on Investment within the OECD has led to consideration of whether to try again, in some other venue, to negotiate a multilateral instrument on investment. Most eyes have turned to the World Trade Organization, where there has existed a Working Group on Trade and Investment since the WTO ministerial meeting of 1996 (see chapters 1 and 2). Negotiation of such an instrument in the WTO could be part of the agenda of a larger round of multilateral trade and investment negotiations under that organization's auspices.

Indeed, it had been expected that the WTO ministerial meeting in Seattle in late 1999 might authorize such a round (see Schott 1996 on this prospective round and the possible role of investment in it). In particular, the European Union had pressed for initiation of such a round, and inclusion of investment negotiations in it, during the months leading up to that meeting. A number of other WTO members supported the European position on investment or slight variations on it. Other countries expressed views favoring this position but did not formally support it.

On the other hand, a number of countries, from Southeast Asia especially, vocally opposed the proposal. Also, perhaps deterred by labor union opposition as well as continued pressure by antiglobal activists,[1] the US government declined to endorse the European position. As late as October 1999, however, senior US trade officials indicated that the US government was not unequivocally opposed to such negotiations. Rather, the stated position was that the issue was undecided within the government.

---

1. See, for example, http://www.tradewatch.org/MAI.htm.

As events transpired, the issue of whether to launch negotiations on investment was left undecided at the Seattle meeting (as indeed were all other issues). Major disagreements as to what might be included in a new round emerged and remained unresolved. One reason was that demonstrations by activists disrupted the meeting, reducing the amount of time that ministers could spend trying to resolve their differences. The upshot was that no new round was authorized, but neither was it ruled out for the future.

Discussions between major governments have continued in the aftermath of the Seattle meeting, but as of this writing, they have failed to break the deadlock. Thus a new negotiating round remains a possibility, but only that. The European Commission continues to press for inclusion of investment negotiations but reportedly seeks a scaled-down version, which would include neither preestablishment national treatment nor investor-to-state dispute settlement procedures. This approach would increase the appeal of investment negotiations to developing countries (see chapter 6) but reduce its appeal to the business community in both the United States and Europe.

Given the state of play of efforts to launch investment negotiations, this chapter examines the pros and cons of including negotiations on investment in a new WTO round in the near future, if indeed such a round comes to pass. The chapter concludes that, in light of the deadlock that occurred in the MAI negotiations and the impasse in Seattle, it would be very difficult for negotiations in the WTO to produce a comprehensive agreement on investment that would yield tangible benefits. And in any case, given the huge flows of direct investment that have continued worldwide even as the MAI negotiations were floundering, it is reasonable to ask whether such an agreement is necessary. In light of all this, what should be done next remains an open and perplexing question.

Arguments For and Against Multilateral Investment Rules

The main substantive case for multilateral investment rules remains that presented in chapter 1. This is that such rules can help to remove, or at least reduce, the policy distortions that diminish the global value of economic activity created by international investment and, in particular, direct investment. Reduced to its essence, the case is that world GDP could be increased if these distortions were removed.

However, as chapter 1 noted, direct investment has burgeoned in recent years, even in the aftermath of the failure of the MAI negotiations. The accelerated pace of this investment has been due, at least in part, to unilateral relaxation of restrictions on inward direct investment by many countries worldwide.[2] To the extent that this unilateral liberalization of investment policy continues, and direct investment continues to flow at increased rates in response, the case for a multilateral approach to such liberalization is weakened. It would not be a productive use of countries' scarce political capital to negotiate a multilateral agreement that addressed a problem that does not exist.[3] In other words, if the policy environment for international investment ain't broke, countries shouldn't try to fix it.

Moreover, no one really knows exactly how great the economic benefits resulting from a multilateral investment agreement would be. There simply are no comprehensive published estimates of the costs that result from government policies that restrict or distort direct investment.[4] Indeed, one of the more perplexing aspects of the MAI negotiations was that those involved never commissioned any studies to investigate this question, either during the three years of exploratory talks at the OECD or during the three years of the negotiations themselves.[5]

To be sure, such a calculation would not be easy. One reason is that many (perhaps most) such benefits would be dynamic in nature. Among these benefits are those that would accrue from greater competition among firms with the elimination of barriers to entry to international investors and of behind-the-border policies that discriminate against these investors once they have entered a national market.[6] Other benefits include the more rapid diffusion of technology that would result from the elimination of government measures that reduce incentives for technol-

---

2. See UNCTAD (1995, 1996, 1997, and 1998); European Business Round Table (1999).

3. It would not be a waste of time, of course, to negotiate an agreement that would lock in place measures that are now applied only provisionally. Indeed, the MAI at first would have done essentially no more than this had it been concluded. However, as discussed later in this chapter, the fear of the business community is that a multilateral agreement negotiated today might lock in place standards that are *less* liberal than those actually being applied.

4. A start in this direction has been made by Moran (2000), who has released some preliminary findings.

5. In contrast, numerous times over the years the OECD Secretariat has served to advance the multilateral trade agenda by, for example, performing detailed calculations of the costs of agricultural protection and of subsidies targeted to agriculture. Liberalization of trade and control of subsidies in agriculture remain thorny issues, but negotiators in this domain can no longer be under any illusion that trade barriers and subsidies do not create real costs for the societies that impose them.

6. These barriers to entry and discriminatory policies would have been addressed largely through the national treatment provisions of the MAI. As we have seen, however, the MAI likely would have created minimal policy change, because of the large number of exceptions to national treatment that would have been registered. One exercise that the OECD Secretariat might have embarked upon, but did not, would have been an effort to generate at least crude estimates of the costs of maintaining the listed exceptions.

ogy transfer.[7] In some instances, there might also be benefits from more rapid rates of technological innovation, as liberalization increases the appropriable returns to research and development. Unfortunately, the economic tools used to calculate dynamic benefits of this kind are highly complex, and the results are inevitably imprecise and unreliable.[8]

Moran (1998), for instance, finds that the majority of performance requirements commonly imposed on direct investors by developing countries inhibit the transfer of technology to those countries. But how great are the benefits lost as a result? The honest answer is that they are almost impossible to quantify.[9] In the absence of at least some plausible estimate, however, developing countries (and, indeed, some developed countries) are likely to resist giving up their freedom to impose performance requirements. Indeed, many political leaders still see performance requirements as working to the advantage of the local economy. (See chapters 3 and 6 on this issue.) Until they can be shown convincingly otherwise, these leaders will find little reason to change.

On the other hand, not all gains from an investment agreement are so difficult to quantify. For example, it was argued in chapter 3 that investment incentives, of the kind used most commonly by the governments of developed countries (including at the subnational level), lead to investments being suboptimally located; this can include diversion of investment from developing countries to developed ones. Chapter 3 explains why this diversion reduces the overall benefits from the investment. It follows that the subsidy component of investment incentives serves to compensate investors for this loss of benefits that they would otherwise have captured. If so, then the total costs of reduced efficiency due to suboptimal investment location should at least approximately equal the subsidy value (the producers' subsidy equivalents, or PSEs) of the incentives themselves. The worldwide sum of these PSEs would then be a measure of the long-run benefits to be gained by eliminating investment incentives.

---

7. In the MAI these would have been addressed largely through prohibitions on government-mandated performance requirements (see chapter 3). Benefits from these prohibitions would largely be realized in developing countries, which, of course, were not included in the MAI negotiations (see discussion below).

8. This is true for the calculation of dynamic gains in general, not just those that might accrue to an investment agreement. It is for this reason that most calculations of the gains associated with trade liberalization are static rather than dynamic in nature. An example is the famous "Cecchini Report" (Cecchini et al. 1988), which attempted to quantify the benefits that would accrue to the measures to be taken by the EU countries in 1992 to further their economic integration. The study used static methods and did find substantial gains, but the report was criticized by, among others, Baldwin (1989), who argued that the omission of dynamic consideration caused these gains to be greatly understated. Baldwin himself produced such estimates, but these in turn were criticized on grounds that the estimation techniques were at best rather crude.

9. But, again, Moran himself attempts to do so (Moran 2000).

These PSEs are, in principle, calculable, but so far no effort has been made to actually calculate them. One reason is that detailed information on investment incentives is not generally available. For example, in the United States, most investment incentives are granted at the level of state or local government. Yet, surprisingly for a country that so prides itself on the transparency of its policies, information on the value of these incentives is very limited. There is no detailed source on the magnitudes of incentives granted that could be used to calculate their effective subsidy component. One clear implication is the need for more transparency regarding such subsidies.

Without good estimates of the costs (including the dynamic costs) to the world economy of extant policies that restrict or distort FDI, it is impossible for negotiators to know how much a multilateral agreement that would curtail these policies would be worth.[10] Perhaps worse, in the absence of plausible estimates of the gains from such an agreement, it is difficult to counter the perceptions of politicians (or of the government officials who administer the interventions) that the interventions result in local capture of some sort of benefit.[11]

To summarize, the substantive argument is sound that new multilateral investment rules would remove distortions that now reduce the efficiency of FDI and that lead to unnecessary loss of world output. However, the magnitude of this loss is unknown, and hence the strength of this argument is uncertain. Also, recent unilateral liberalization of investment policies has doubtless reduced this loss and thus weakened (but not eliminated) the case for a multilateral approach to liberalization. Indeed, the fact that FDI has burgeoned in recent years in the absence of multilateral rules has been taken as indicating that the need for such rules is actually diminishing.[12]

---

10. One can be sure, however, that this value would not be trivial. For example, if these policies reduce the annual value added by the existing stock of direct investment worldwide by only 5 percent (a guess), this lost output would amount to $130 billion per year.

11. For example, it is easy for a government official to claim that, by offering an investment incentive, the government was able to induce an investor to locate a new facility inside its territory, bringing with it jobs and creating tax revenue. The counterargument is, of course, that the investor would almost surely have placed the facility somewhere in the world even had no incentives been offered, and that another location might have created higher global benefits than the current location. But a counterargument based on the magnitude of global benefits will not play well to the residents of the country or region where the investment actually was located. Likewise, local officials can argue that a local content requirement brings a tangible gain in the form of local production of inputs and hence, again, job creation. That the opportunity cost of these jobs is excessive is, again, a hard sell at best.

12. But it is equally possible that, as a consequence of burgeoning FDI, the distortions created by subsidies and performance requirements are burgeoning as well. This underscores further the need for greater transparency and for a calculation of the magnitudes of the distortions associated with these policies.

Even if the substantive case for new multilateral rules were stronger than these arguments suggest, an international negotiation to create such rules is unlikely to be concluded successfully unless major political constituencies actively seek such rules. The next section explores whether such a constituency now exists.

Is There a Constituency for Multilateral Investment Rules?

The short answer to this question appears to be no. Indeed, the only strong call for such rules recently has come from the European Commission. The motives of the Commission are not entirely clear, but they include matters of bureaucratic politics as well as substance. Bureaucratic politics enters the picture because of the issue of which body or bodies will have authority, or "competence," within the European Union over investment policy. At present, competence for international trade negotiations in the European Union resides at the level of the Commission and the political bodies to which the Commission answers: the Council of Europe and, to a much lesser extent, the European Parliament. Competence for most other international negotiations resides at the level of the individual national governments.

The question is whether the negotiation of multilateral investment rules falls within the Commission's competence to negotiate on international trade matters. It seems that the answer depends on the venue in which the negotiations take place. As chapter 1 noted, the countries of the European Union were represented in the MAI negotiations by their national government officials. But if negotiations on the same issues were to be undertaken at the WTO, the negotiators would be from the Commission. Hence, the Commission has strong bureaucratic reasons for preferring that such negotiations take place at the WTO.

However, the Commission's preference is almost surely not motivated by this matter of bureaucratic turf alone. There is some consensus within the European business community that a multilateral agreement would be of value, and the Commission's position reflects this view. Also, the Commission doubtless anticipates that, in a future negotiating round, it will have to offer concessions on agriculture and perhaps some other issues as well. To get the EU member countries to agree to these concessions, the Commission will have to show that it has wrung concessions in Europe's favor out of other parties at the table. Conclusion of an agreement on investment could be claimed as one such concession.

As already noted, some other countries have joined the European Union in calling for investment negotiations. Among these are Japan, the Hong Kong Special Administrative Region of China, and South Korea. It is not clear, however, that such negotiations are a high priority for any of these three except perhaps Hong Kong, which is not a sovereign state but a part of China (which is not, at the time of this writing, yet a WTO member). Nor is it clear that the government of China supports the Hong Kong position on investment. For their part, although Japan and South Korea would support an investment agenda at the WTO, neither appears prepared to fight to achieve this.

As discussed in chapter 6, many developing countries today seek to attract FDI, and one consequence is a greater willingness of many of these countries to consider binding themselves to international rules than in the past. However, with the exception of a small number of countries that might bind themselves to new rules eagerly, this willingness does not go so far as to make any of these countries *demandeurs* for such rules. Indeed, some developing countries remain opposed to any such rules at the level of the WTO. Furthermore, at the WTO's ministerial meeting in Seattle, the majority of developing countries expressed the hope that existing obligations under the Agreement on Trade-Related Investment Measures might be phased in more slowly than the agreement itself calls for. This would not seem to augur well for developing-country support for the creation of new investment obligations.

Arrayed against this narrow and mostly unenthusiastic constituency for new rules are, of course, the antiglobal activists. Chapters 4 and 5 examined the positions these activists and other opponents have taken on investment liberalization and concluded that, on matters of substance, these positions are largely in the wrong. Nonetheless, it is clear that these constituencies will remain strongly opposed to the negotiation of multilateral investment rules at the WTO.

Indeed, the AFL-CIO and its affiliated unions have long sought to curtail US direct investment abroad. During the late 1960s and early 1970s, two AFL-CIO-affiliated unions attempted to use the National Labor Relations Act to challenge specific instances of US direct investment abroad, but failed because no link could be established between the foreign investment and reductions in employment in the United States (Kujawa 1981). Then, in 1971, the AFL-CIO worked with staff of the US Congress to draft the Burke-Hartke bill, which sought to impose four significant restraints on the ability of US firms to make direct investments abroad (Bergsten, Horst, and Moran 1978). The bill failed passage, although changes in US tax law in 1975 accomplished a small part of what was sought. In more recent times, the AFL-CIO has played a major role in defeating reauthorization of the fast-track trade negotiating powers of the president (Destler 1997b).

The position of most environmental NGOs remains essentially as described in chapter 5: that multilateral investment rules would serve to enrich the profits of multinationals at the expense of environmental quality. The environmentalists' main fear is that such rules would serve, in effect, to cancel out national laws and policies implemented to protect the environment. Chapter 2 argued that that this fear had some basis in the case of the MAI, because of the way that agreement might have treated regulatory takings. And although it is not entirely clear that the NGOs have fully done their homework with regard to investment issues other than regulatory takings, these groups remain stridently opposed to multilateral investment rules in the WTO.

Opposition by labor and environmental groups doubtless affected the US position on whether to seek a negotiation on investment in the WTO. This position, as already suggested, was essentially to sit on the fence. The US government did not express unequivocal opposition to such a negotiation, but it certainly expressed no enthusiasm either.

The one constituency in the United States with the means to offset the opposition and to knock the US government off the fence and into advocacy of an investment agreement is the business community. But this constituency has to date not emerged as a strong supporter of a new initiative to negotiate investment rules at the WTO. This lack of enthusiasm reflects several fears on the part of the US business community. One is that inclusion of investment issues in a new WTO round would create, as did the MAI negotiations, a new lightning rod for labor and environmental activism that could jeopardize the whole round. This might be true even if the WTO were to take up issues posed by labor and environmental activists directly, that is, if these were separated from the investment agenda and dealt with effectively elsewhere, there might still be activist opposition to new investment rules. A second fear is that, even if a negotiation to create multilateral investment rules could be launched within the WTO, the outcome might be not further liberalization but rather what the business community would see as backsliding. On this point, the US business community does not find the experience of the MAI reassuring. As noted in chapters 2 and 3, by the time the MAI negotiations ended, they had produced no new liberalization but rather only a codification of existing law and policy.

Still worse from a business perspective, some of the negotiating parties, including the US government, were pressing for additional provisions in the MAI that could be seen as *de*liberalizing. And given the greater divergence of views on investment among the member countries of the WTO than among those of the OECD, the US business community judges that a WTO negotiation would be even more likely to result in significant backsliding than occurred in the MAI negotiations.[13] Thus, especially in light of the burgeoning of FDI that has taken place in recent years, the business community has judged that a negotiation on investment at the

13. These views were expressed to the author by a senior official of an organization that speaks for US business on multilateral issues, who wishes not to be identified. This same official noted that part of the reason for the business community's attitude was mistrust of the current US administration and a fear that it might be more willing than another administration to agree to measures that business would see as deliberalizing.

WTO simply is not needed. In its view, such a negotiation at this time would pose considerable downside risk while offering relatively little prospect for actual liberalization.

This is not to say that the US business community does not seek investment policy liberalization. Clearly it does. But given the current trend for many countries around the globe to liberalize their investment policies unilaterally, from the business community's point of view there seems at present little compelling need for a multilateral agreement to achieve this same end. This would be especially so if there is some risk that such an agreement could lock into place provisions that are less liberal than those that many countries already are applying de facto.

What specific measures does the US business community seek in the domain of investment policy? The United States Council for International Business canvassed its members in late 1999 and found that the priority of most was greater transparency in investment policies and how they are applied.[14] Members also indicated a high priority for some means by which governments could be held accountable for violation of their own laws and policies. This would suggest potential support for an investor-to-state dispute resolution mechanism. But as already noted, the European Commission, the one *demandeur* for a WTO investment negotiation among the WTO members, is not pressing for inclusion of this issue on the WTO agenda. There would thus seem to be a mismatch between the priorities of those WTO members that most favor investment negotiations and those of the constituency that would be the largest potential supporter of such negotiations.

The views of the European business community, at least as expressed by the European Round Table of Industrialists (ERT), are quite parallel to those of the US community. As stated by Herbert Oberhänsli, formerly of the ERT, who has worked to help develop that organization's positions on trade and investment, the whole issue of rules on investment in the WTO is one that "can be postponed for tactical reasons."[15] But as he further elaborates, "[for the WTO] to be coherent, [investment rules] must come one day as part of the global architecture." The ERT has performed a number of surveys of investment policy in developing countries since 1987 and finds that conditions for investment have steadily improved. Thus, according to Oberhänsli, "these countries do not need guidance on best practices as defined by OECD diplomats. It would, however, be useful but not indispensable to fit . . . [investment rules] into a global framework."

The bottom line is that, except for the European Commission, there is no strong constituency pressing for negotiations on multilateral invest-

---

14. This sentiment was largely directed toward developing countries. But as suggested earlier, there is plenty of scope for greater transparency in developed countries as well, especially with regard to subsidies.

15. Interview with this author, 30 March 2000.

ment rules at present. The constituency that would seem to have the most to gain from a WTO investment agreement, the business community, is not firmly behind such a negotiation at this time. There is little perceived need for such a negotiation in light of ongoing favorable changes in the global environment for international business. On the other hand, there is fear that its inclusion in a round of multilateral trade negotiations in the near future would so galvanize antiglobal activists as to jeopardize the whole round. And without a larger constituency behind the investment negotiations on one hand, and the certainty of strong opposition on the other, the chances that a full-blown agreement on investment could soon be negotiated at the WTO seem rather slim. In light of this reality, some have proposed more limited investment negotiations at the WTO. These proposals are examined next.

Going for Less Than the Full Monty

Two proposals for limited negotiations have been advanced that are dia-metrically different from each other in substance. Neither, however, would require that WTO members authorize a new initiative to negotiate an investment agreement. Rather, each could be carried out as part of the WTO's "built-in agenda": the work already committed to under the Uruguay Round agreements to complete tasks left unfinished at the con-clusion of that round.

One proposal, offered by Moran (1998), calls for restricting the agenda largely to performance requirements and investment incentives. This, Moran argues, could be done in the context of a review of the existing TRIMs agreement. Such a review was in fact agreed to at the conclusion of the Uruguay Round and thus is part of the built-in agenda. Among other things, the review was meant to consider enlargement of the agreement.

The substantive basis for Moran's proposal rests on the fact that invest-ment incentives are used most intensively by developed countries, whereas performance requirements are imposed most often by developing coun-tries.[16] Developed countries' investment incentives adversely affect devel-oping countries if they divert investment from the latter to the former.[17] But likewise, developing countries' performance requirements can ad-versely affect developed countries if these requirements cause developed-country exports to be displaced by developing-country exports. Thus, Moran reasons, each group of countries has an interest in curtailing the

---

16. As discussed in chapter 3, in developed countries performance requirements are most often used as conditions for the receipt of investment incentives rather than as conditions for entry. In developing countries, by contrast, performance requirements often are imposed as conditions for entry.

17. The empirical evidence on whether this actually happens, however, is rather scant.

practices of the other. And this opens the way to a "grand bargain" of reciprocal concessions: developing countries would give up performance requirements if developed countries would give up investment incentives.[18]

This proposal makes eminent good sense from a substantive perspective because, even though the potential gains are not known, it is reasonable to expect that they would be quite large. But is there any chance for such a grand bargain to be concluded? For this even remotely to be a possibility, either the developing countries or the developed countries must act together as a bloc to propose the bargain to the other. Neither bloc, alas, seems to be forming. As noted in chapter 2, the United States in essence took investment incentives off the table on the grounds that the US federal government could not obligate state governments not to offer these incentives. Other federal states (e.g., Canada and Germany) might also have had problems with binding their subfederal governments to restrict incentives, and hence they tacitly approved the US move. There has been no movement on the part of other, nonfederal developed countries to counter this action, either within or outside the context of a grand bargain. In particular, the European Commission has not advanced this particular agenda. And as noted in the previous chapter, a number of developing countries remain staunchly opposed to the ending of performance requirements.

Nor is this agenda likely to be driven by the business community. Multinational firms, of course, benefit from investment incentives, and thus would not enthusiastically endorse an agenda calling for their curtailment. These firms regard performance requirements largely as a nuisance, but in the words of one executive, they are a nuisance that most firms can live with. Interestingly, constituencies that should favor the curtailment of performance requirements include labor unions and the environmental NGOs, on the grounds that these requirements might have an adverse impact on jobs in multinationals' home countries, and certainly have an adverse impact on the environment. (See the discussions in chapters 4 and 5.) Labor unions, in fact, supported the TRIMs agreement during its negotiation, but have yet to be heard from on Moran's grand bargain. However, the silence of the environmental NGOs on this issue is simply puzzling, and one reason why it seems to this author that these groups have yet to finish their homework.

The second proposal, advanced by Sauvé and Wilkie (2000), is substantively quite different from that of Moran. These authors agree that politi-

---

18. Moran also believes, largely on the basis of case studies, that most performance requirements, except possibly export performance requirements, fail to achieve their objectives in developing countries and in some cases might actually cause them economic harm. Thus there is a case for developing countries to unilaterally curtail their use of performance requirements. As developed in chapter 3, however, any case to be made for developed countries to give up use of investment incentives unilaterally is weak because of the prisoner's dilemma. A multilateral agreement might be the only effective way to achieve elimination or reduction of these incentives.

cal considerations render any grand bargain between developing and developed countries at best a remote possibility, whatever its substantive merits. They argue, however, that a politically feasible way to further liberalize investment policy through a multilateral approach would be to expand upon the obligation by WTO countries, under the General Agreement on Trade in Services, to apply postestablishment national treatment in the services sector.[19] (See chapter 3 for a detailed explanation of national treatment in this context.) Although the embryo of such an obligation already exists in the GATS, it is quite circumscribed as currently applied (see below). Sauvé and Wilkie argue that most laws and policies that are inconsistent with national treatment are in fact to be found in those service industries that are potentially covered under the GATS.[20] Thus, they argue, there are gains to be had from enlarging and deepening the coverage of the GATS.

In fact, the GATS is a rather complex agreement. It is a "bottom up" agreement, in the sense that it applies only to those activities that a country lists in the agreement (see chapter 3). A top-down agreement, in contrast, would apply to any activity that is *not* listed (i.e., as an exception). Thus, under the GATS, a service industry must be explicitly listed by a country in order for national treatment of investments (or other obligations) to apply to activities in that industry. Furthermore, even if an industry is listed, it can be subject to exceptions ("reservations") exempting the country from some obligations for some specific activities. As a hypothetical example, a country could list financial services as an industry bound by the GATS, but could exempt itself from the obligation to provide national treatment to foreign-owned banks.

The Sauvé and Wilkie proposal, then, is that countries agree to list industries and reservations such that these reflect the full extent of liberalization as embodied in law and policy toward foreign investors and their investments as currently applied. The principal goal is, to use their own words, "to secure the regulatory status quo." This might at first blush not seem like much of a step forward, but in fact countries often do not list sectors under the GATS even when these countries are open to foreign investment in these sectors and foreign investors receive national treatment (or something close). Furthermore, listed sectors are often subject to reservations that simply are not applied in practice. Thus the proposal would codify at the multilateral level the actual law and policy of countries as practiced, including their regulatory policy.

---

19. This argument is expanded in Sauvé (2000).

20. Evidence for this is, however, rather scant. Sauvé and Wilkie cite Rugman and Gestrin (1994), who examine the exceptions to national treatment for investment contained in NAFTA chapter 11, and conclude that a majority of these exceptions apply to services. NAFTA, however, covers only three countries, two of which (the United States and Canada) maintain rather few exceptions to national treatment at all. Sauvé is currently engaged in research to determine if the same results can be obtained for a larger group of countries.

Would this be useful? Business firms seem to think so. As Herbert Ober-hänsli, the former ERT official, put it, "the international institutional framework is . . . far behind business reality today." If it could catch up, it would serve the function of locking in the very considerable liberalization that has already taken place around the globe, and this would be one stopgap to prevent backsliding. However, as Oberhänsli also noted, this catch-up would be "useful but not indispensable."

Sauvé and Wilkie believe that their proposal can be carried out in the context of the ongoing GATS and GATS-related negotiations, which, like the TRIMs review, are part of the WTO's built-in agenda. What is vexing, however, is that, in these negotiations, countries have been hesitant to put into a binding international agreement those liberal practices that they have already implemented de facto.[21]

Sauvé and Wilkie also advance some other ideas for improving the "investment friendliness" of the GATS. For example, the GATS speaks of "commercial presence" and defines this so as to include most forms of direct investment. Sauvé and Wilkie believe that this definition could be clarified and broadened. They note that the investment protection provisions are commitment specific (that is, they apply only to industries that have been listed) and that these could be made into general commitments that would apply to any "commercial presence," even in an unlisted industry. They suggest that there "remains scope for much greater legal clarity, precision, and uniformity with respect to how investment-related commitments are lodged and restricted." This scope exists because significant and undesired inconsistencies can be found in different countries' schedules. That is, negotiators might have sought to have these lists provide for equivalent treatment, but in practice the inconsistencies are sometimes sufficiently great that quite divergent practices among countries could be interpreted as consistent with their GATS commitments. This leaves room for precisely the discriminatory or differential treatment of foreign investors that the negotiators had intended to eliminate.

Significantly, the Sauvé and Wilkie proposal would, if successfully implemented, primarily serve to reduce the remaining discriminatory policies that are maintained by developed countries. (The proposals would apply to developing countries as well, especially as the services sector in these countries grows in importance. But Sauvé and Wilkie suggest "sunset" provisions for these countries that would enable them to phase in

---

21. For example, this situation is mirrored in GATT Article II bindings, which place ceilings, by import category, on the tariff rates that countries may apply to imports. For many countries and many categories, these bound tariff rates are higher than the rates that countries actually apply. Exactly why countries are not willing to bind themselves to the rates they currently apply remains something of a mystery. The usual story is that countries wish to reserve the right, in some cases at least, to raise tariff rates in the future. Presumably this is to mollify protectionist interests or to preserve their options in the event of a balance of payments crisis.

obligations rather slowly.) The Moran proposal, by contrast, involves developing countries directly.

In the absence of quantitative estimates of the welfare gains that might be created by investment liberalization, it is impossible to assess which of the two proposals is to be preferred on these grounds. One suspects that the potential welfare gains from either would be substantial.[22] But as already noted, no constituency seems to be backing either proposal. In contrast, a very considerable business constituency (at least in the United States) is backing further liberalization in the services sector. Given this reality, the Sauvé and Wilkie proposals seem to stand a much better chance than the Moran proposal of actual implementation in the foreseeable future.

A Comprehensive WTO Investment Agreement: A Bridge Too Far?

Following the successful Allied invasion of Normandy in June 1944 and the subsequent breakout of Allied forces at the Battle of Falaise, the combined US and British forces attempted in September to take and secure a bridge across the Rhine at Arnhem, in the Netherlands. The ultimate objective was to attempt something of a reverse execution of the von Schlieffen plan that the Germans had used to invade France via the Low Countries in 1914 and again in 1940. The Allies' idea was to end the war quickly with a rapid sweep into Germany and encirclement of the German defensive forces.

The initial operation, conducted by about 35,000 paratroopers, succeeded in the sense that the bridge and the nearby towns were taken. But after less than a week the Germans recaptured the bridge, and the Allied forces, having suffered heavy casualties, were forced to retreat toward France. The resources squandered on the attempt at Arnhem arguably set back the ultimate Allied victory in Europe, which finally occurred the following spring.

The Arnhem operation failed largely because the forces needed to secure the bridge and the routes leading to it were unable to reach the beleaguered paratroopers in time. The failed operation was the subject of a 1970s movie, *A Bridge Too Far*, which explored whether the plan to take the Arnhem bridge was strategically correct but failed only in the execution. In fact, the movie argued, the operation failed because the resources needed to achieve the objective, given the resources that the Germans

---

22. The existing evidence indicates that the benefits from full opening of the services sector to investment and trade could be quite substantial; Warren and Findlay (2000) review some of the relevant studies.

could bring to bear to prevent it, simply were not available. Furthermore, the Allied leaders had enough information at their disposal regarding their own available resources and those of the enemy to have correctly concluded that the operation should not have been attempted at the time it was.

This chapter concludes that to seek a comprehensive investment agreement in the WTO would be, like the assault on the bridge at Arnhem, a "bridge too far." Although such an agreement might in fact increase world welfare, it is a matter of serious doubt whether it could be achieved. (One reason the issue remains in doubt is that no quantification of these benefits has ever been seriously attempted.) As at Arnhem, it is not clear that the needed resources, in this case the necessary consensus and political will among the negotiating countries, are available to achieve the objective. And meanwhile the resources that almost surely would be marshalled against such an effort are substantial and could well prevail.

No analogy should be pushed too hard, however. In the case of the Arnhem operation, there was complete consensus among the Allied commanders about the objective, the capitulation of Germany. There was also consensus that, to achieve this objective, a sweep into Germany was necessary. What went wrong was that the sweep was attempted too soon. In contrast, there is not even consensus among the WTO member countries that an agreement on investment is necessary. This bolsters the case that, even if ultimately desirable, a negotiation now would be premature. And whereas at Arnhem the identity of the enemy was clear, in the case of an investment agreement the only real "enemy" is ignorance of what might be the benefits—and the costs—of such an agreement. In particular, it is not the constituencies who oppose the agreement who are in any sense the enemy. Rather, they are simply interested parties who believe, for whatever reason, that any such agreement would create costs in excess of the benefits.

Thus, this author finds himself largely in agreement with Hoekman and Saggi (1999), who argue that:

> the major potential gain from a multilateral agreement is avoidance of wasteful competition for FDI. . . . However, to be effective, such an agreement would need to be highly comprehensive and would be costly to negotiate. At present, this does not seem like a promising prospect.

In other words, Hoekman and Saggi agree that an agreement would be, at this time, a "bridge too far." In line with Sauvé and Wilkie, they therefore call for efforts to center on further market access liberalization through the GATS.

But should work on an investment agreement stop at such efforts? Clearly it should not. The benefits and costs of a comprehensive investment agreement are largely uncharted waters. Indeed, as matters stand, debate over the desirability of an investment agreement has taken place largely in the dark. The priority now should be to obtain reasonable estimates of what the magnitudes and distributions of these benefits and costs might be. Only once these are available will it make sense for countries to attempt once again to reach consensus on an attempt to negotiate a multilateral investment agreement in the WTO, and what the priorities to be addressed by such an agreement should be.

APPENDICES

Appendix A
Productivity and Wage Determination

Much of the discussion of FDI and its effects on workers in chapter 4 is driven by the notion that workers' wages are determined by the productivity of labor. Furthermore, a firm's profits are maximized when the firm employs workers such that wage equals the value of the marginal product of an additional worker. This appendix provides elementary theoretical derivations of these notions. This entails the use of some mathematics. However, we begin by presenting the basic concepts in plain English.

The idea that wages are determined by the productivity of labor is centered on the following reasoning. A firm will hire an additional worker if and only if it expects that the additional output (the marginal product) from that worker will generate revenue at least equal to the compensation that must be paid to the worker. In other words, the marginal revenue product made possible by the additional worker must be equal to or greater than the marginal cost of employing that worker. (The marginal revenue product is defined as the marginal product times its value per unit, provided the unit value does not fall as output is increased.) Both the marginal revenue product and the marginal cost are expressed in terms of a flow of value per unit of time (e.g., dollars per hour).

A standard assumption is that there are, at least in the short run, diminishing returns to additional hires. That is, the marginal product of each additional worker begins to fall as more and more workers are added to the payroll. A moment's thought will indicate that this must in general be true. At some point, the firm cannot produce any more output no matter how many additional workers are hired, because certain constraints on output (e.g., the work space available in the firm's plants) will become binding. Thus, to maximize profit, the firm will hire additional workers until marginal product falls to the point where the marginal revenue product exactly equals the marginal cost of an additional hire. If all firms behave this way, then labor markets will clear when the marginal cost to each firm of an additional worker (i.e., the compensation paid to that worker) is equal to the value of the marginal product made possible by that worker. The marginal product, in turn, is determined by how productive the marginal worker is.[1]

These ideas can be expressed mathematically as follows. Suppose that total output is given by the following simple and standard production function:

$$Y = AK^{\alpha}L^{(1-\alpha)},$$

where Y is the total output of a firm per unit of time; K and L are inputs of capital and labor, respectively, per the same unit of time; and α is a constant with a value between zero and one. The variable A can be interpreted as the contribution of technology to output; if A rises, then, even holding K and L constant, Y will rise. All of these variables except α can be considered as time dependent, such that $Y = Y(t)$, $A = A(t)$, and so forth. For purposes of this exposition, we assume that the unit value of output (call it p; this is just the price of one item made by the plant) is independent of the level of output. In this case, total revenue R accruing to the firm from output Y will just be equal to this unit value times output: $R = pY$.

The marginal product of labor then is simply equal to the partial derivative of Y with respect to L, given by

$$Y_L = \frac{\partial Y}{\partial L} = (1-\alpha)AK^{\alpha}L^{-\alpha}.$$

The marginal revenue product MR_L made possible by the marginal worker is then given by $MR_L = pY_L$. Also, the second partial derivative of Y with respect to L is negative, implying diminishing marginal returns to labor:

$$Y_{LL} = -\alpha(1-\alpha)AK^{\alpha}L^{-(1+\alpha)} < 0.$$

---

1. A word of caution is in order here. As the mathematical exposition that follows will make clear, compensation is thus determined by the marginal productivity of labor, not by its average productivity. Official data on labor productivity, however, report average rather than marginal productivity, for the simple reason that average productivity is much easier to measure. But marginal productivity can differ substantially from average productivity. Fortunately, increases in the marginal productivity of labor, under plausible assumptions, imply increases in the average productivity in equal proportion, so that data pertaining to average productivity can be used as surrogates for marginal productivity.

To show that pY_L is equal to the compensation paid to the worker, we assume that the firm maximizes profits, letting profits be given by P:

$$P = pY - C,$$

where C is equal to total costs. C can be broken down into capital costs and labor costs. If r is the unit cost (again per unit of time) of capital and w is the unit cost of labor, then $C = rK + wL$.

Maximization of profits requires that, as a first-order condition, the first partial derivatives of P with respect to both K and L be zero. Hence,

$$(pY_K - r) = 0,$$

and

$$(pY_L - w) = 0.$$

The second of these equations implies that $w = pY_L$, the desired result.

It is useful to note that the production function specified above is linearly homogeneous in K and L, so that Euler's equation applies:[2]

$$Y = KY_K + LY_L.$$

Mutiplying by p gives

$$pY = pKY_K + pLY_L.$$

This can be interpreted as follows. Total revenue to the firm consists of two components, one of which is paid to capital (pKY_K) and the other to labor (pLY_L). Dividing the second of these by L gives the compensation per worker, which is again pY_L, or the unit value times the marginal product of labor. The result shows that if each factor of production (capital and labor) is paid at a rate equal to its marginal product multiplied by the unit value of output, then total payments to factors equal total revenues. This result is not general to all production functions, however. It follows from the linear homogeneity of this form of the production function.

Average product per worker (Y/L) is given by

$$\frac{Y}{L} = AK^\alpha L^{-\alpha}$$

---

2. A function f(x) is linearly homogeneous if the following holds: f(ax) = af(x), where a is any constant. In this instance, x can be a vector of variables, i.e., f can be a function of more than one variable. If f is a production function in two variables, e.g., f = f(K,L), then f(aK,aL) = af(K,L), implying constant returns to scale (if, say, a = 2), then the result says that doubling all factor inputs doubles output).

and is not equal to the marginal product (see note 1). In fact, for this form of the production function,

$$\frac{\partial Y}{\partial L} = (1-\alpha)\frac{Y}{L}.$$

Because the coefficient α is not dependent on time, it is clear that changes in marginal productivity over time are equiproportional to changes in average productivity:

$$\frac{\left(\dfrac{dY_L}{dt}\right)}{Y_L} = \frac{d\left(\dfrac{Y}{L}\right)}{\dfrac{dt}{\dfrac{Y}{L}}}.$$

This result, as indicated in note 1, is of importance because average productivity in practice is much more easily measured than marginal productivity.

What will increase the marginal productivity of labor and hence the compensation of workers? Chapter 2 suggests that technological advances (or simply technological improvements) can do the trick. This and a little more can be demonstrated by taking the first derivative of the marginal productivity of labor with respect to time. Recalling that all of A, K, and L are functions of time, this requires use of the chain rule:

$$\frac{dY_L}{dt} = \frac{\partial Y_L}{\partial A}\frac{dA}{dt} + \frac{\partial Y_K}{\partial K}\frac{dK}{dt} + \frac{\partial Y_L}{\partial L}\frac{dL}{dt}$$

or

$$\frac{dY_L}{dt} = (1-\alpha)K^{\alpha}L^{-\alpha}\frac{dA}{dt} + \alpha(1-\alpha)K^{\alpha-1}L^{-\alpha}\frac{dK}{dt} - \alpha(1-\alpha)K^{\alpha}L^{-(1+\alpha)}\frac{dL}{dt}.$$

Thus, the marginal product of labor, holding other variables constant, increases with technological improvements over time (dA/dt) and with increases in the stock of capital over time (dK/dt). The latter implies that the marginal product of labor increases with capital deepening (an increase in the ratio K/L). This marginal product, again holding other variables constant, also decreases with increases in the number of workers over time (dL/dt). This is simply a restatement of the point made earlier that there are diminishing marginal returns to labor.

All this simply shows that foreign direct investment to a developing country (or, indeed, to any country) will put upward pressure on wages, not the reverse. Indeed, in a sense, the theory as developed here is not needed to obtain this result. It could have been stated simply that FDI in any country will increase the demand for labor there, and when the demand for anything, labor included, increases, its price rises. And the price of labor is simply the wage paid to labor.

Importantly, what this theory also implies is that, if a firm is to maximize profits, it must hire enough workers so that the value of the marginal product of a worker is equal to the wage paid. This is important because it is widely misunderstood. For example, antiglobalist authors (see, e.g., Greider 1997) have maintained that multinational firms transfer operations to developing countries in order to combine third world wages with advanced nation productivity. The notion seems to be that the firm can make enormous profits by paying workers much less than the value of the product that they produce. This claim is a little vague. Does "productivity" mean the average product of a worker or the marginal product of the worker? If the former, the notion would apply to any production operation (the average product of a worker is higher than the wage paid to that worker in the United States as well as in Mexico; if this were not the case, then there would be zero return to capital invested in the operation). If the latter, then if the firm pays a wage that is less than the value of the marginal product of the worker, the firm simply is not maximizing profits. The firm would do better to continue to hire workers until the value of the marginal product fell to the wage level.

Appendix B
Is Foreign Direct Investment a Complement to Trade?

Erika Wada and Edward M. Graham

What is the nature of the relationship between foreign direct investment-related activities and trade (exports and imports)? Are they complements, such that, all else equal, increases in outward FDI from a home country are associated with increases in that country's exports or imports? Or are they substitutes, in the sense that, all else equal, increases in outward FDI from a home country are associated with reductions in that country's exports? (A reduction in imports is implausible in this case.) Or is there no relationship at all between FDI and trade? These questions have been around for a long time but remain subjects for debate. The reason is that the answer requires separating and assessing the impact of one factor on a variable whose value can be determined by multiple factors.

In the case of commodities, whether two goods are complements or substitutes can depend upon their relative prices. For example, when the price of butter goes up but the price of margarine does not, demand for margarine goes up, because people switch from the more expensive butter to the cheaper margarine. Thus butter and margarine are substitutes. But when the price of butter goes up, demand for bread goes down. People consume bread and butter together, so that when butter is more expensive, not only does consumption of butter fall, but so does that of bread. Bread and butter are thus complements.

It is not so easy to say whether FDI and trade are substitutes or complements. Each represents a different mode of doing business, and it is not easy to associate a single price with either mode. FDI in this instance must be interpreted to mean "economic activity generated by overseas affiliates

Erika Wada is a research assistant at the Institute for International Economics.

of firms based in the home country." However, FDI per se is not a direct measure of this activity, which could be measured in a number of ways, including sales generated by these affiliates, or value added by them, or the value of shipments generated by them. FDI itself, however, is none of these. It is simply the equity capital held by US investors in these affiliates. There is, fortunately, a positive relationship between the total stock of FDI and the economic activity that this stock generates. Therefore, in this exercise, the stock of FDI is used as a surrogate for the activity it generates. With this in mind, what we wish to determine is, in essence, whether production by affiliates of a multinational abroad substitutes for production in its home country or complements it.

The approach taken here is to extend a standard gravity model, originally developed to analyze trade activity as a function of distance, GDP growth, and population growth, to address the question just posed. The data encompass 58 countries that have engaged in significant trade and/or investment with the United States during the years 1983 to 1996.

Using the gravity model, we examine trade and investment activities between the United States and the rest of the world. We limit our examination to trade in manufactured goods and to FDI in the manufacturing sector. We do so because the distinction between the export of a service from the United States and the rendering of a service by a foreign affiliate of a US firm can often be somewhat arbitrary. Thus, a bright line between trade in services and services generated by FDI would be difficult to establish. Focusing only on the manufacturing sector thus eliminates a serious data complication, but at the expense of eliminating services, which account for a growing share of both world trade and world FDI.

The gravity model relating the FDI stock, exports, imports, and the factors that jointly determine them can be specified most simply as follows:

$$FDI_{i,t} = \alpha_1 PGDP_{i,t} + \alpha_2 POP_{i,t} + \alpha_3 DISTANCE_{i,t}$$
$$+ \alpha_4 EXPORT_{i,t} + \alpha_5 IMPORT_{i,t} + \mu \tag{1}$$

where $FDI_{i,t}$ is the stock of FDI from country j (in this case, the United States) in the manufacturing sector of country i at period t, $PGDP$ is per capita GDP of country i, POP is the total population of country i, $DISTANCE$ is the distance between the capitals of country i and country j, $EXPORT$ is the nominal level of manufactured goods exports from country j to country i, and $IMPORT$ is the nominal c.i.f. (cost plus insurance and freight) value of manufactured goods imports from country i to country j. Following standard usage, μ represents an error term with normal distribution and with mean $E(\mu) = 0$.

It is fair to question whether equation (1), a simple linear equation, correctly represents the relationships among the variables even if the variables are correctly identified. For example, one might speculate whether the impact of an increase in exports on FDI-related activities is magnified by an increase in the level of imports. Modeling such a relationship would require the inclusion of terms representing higher powers of the independent variables (polynomial terms) and/or cross-product terms. Such a model could more closely fit the data than does equation (1). There could also be a problem with endogenous effects, as discussed below.

The regression specification test (RESET) suggested by Ramsey (1969) can be used to detect the first type of specification error (nonlinear terms) in the model. The underlying reasoning of the test is simple. If the model is linear, adding any polynomial composed of the same independent variables will not increase the explanatory power of the model—any such terms will be statistically insignificant. In this case, the model can be written as

$$y = x\beta + u \tag{2}$$

$$E(u \mid x) = 0 \tag{3}$$

such that adding polynomial terms x^ℓ does not increase the R-squared statistic associated with the regression of x on y implied by equation (2). To test whether this is true, one can simply add the variable x^ℓ to equation (2) and see what the effect is on R squared. However, adding polynomial terms may create a problem of insufficient degrees of freedom. Thus, Ramsey suggested that the fitted value of the dependent variable, $\hat{y}$, can be used as a proxy for the independent variables. Using the Ramsey test, the following specification is tested:

$$\hat{y} = x\hat{\beta} + \alpha_1 \hat{y}^2 + \alpha_2 \hat{y}^3. \tag{4}$$

The null hypothesis, then, is that α_1 and α_2 are jointly insignificant. Using the standard f-test, the result for our model indicates that α_1 and α_2 are jointly *significant*, implying that some nonlinearity is indeed present. Hence, for our data, the gravity model must incorporate at least some first-order nonlinear terms. These can be added by respecifying the model as follows:

$$FDI_{i,t} = PGDP_{i,t}{}^{\beta_1} POP_{i,t}{}^{\beta_2} DISTANCE_{i,t}{}^{\beta_3} EXPORT_{i,t}{}^{\beta_4} IMPORT_{i,t}{}^{\beta_5} \mu \tag{5}$$

where μ is a log-normally distributed error term. Equation (5) can be transformed into a linear equation by taking the natural logarithms of both sides, as follows:

$$\begin{aligned} \log(FDI) = &\ \beta_1 \log(PGDP) + \beta_2 \log(POP) + \beta_3 \log(DISTANCE) \\ &+ \beta_4 \log(EXPORT) + \beta_5 \log(IMPORT) + \mu. \end{aligned} \tag{6}$$

Using RESET, we again test whether this model neglects some nonlinearity, and the result indicates that it does. To compensate for this, we then add second-order polynomials of the independent variables. This time we find that, although the second-order polynomial compounds of the log of per capita GDP, the log of population, and the log of distance are statistically significant at a 5 percent level of confidence, those of the logs of exports and imports are not. The model is therefore respecified in the following form:

$$\log(FDI) = \beta_1 \log(PGDP) + \beta_2 \log(POP) + \beta_3 \log(DISTANCE)$$
$$+ \beta_4 \log(EXPORT) + \beta_5 \log(IMPORT) + \beta_6 [\log(PGDP)]^2 \tag{7}$$
$$+ \beta_7 [\log(POP)]^2 + \beta_8 [\log(DIS)]^2 + \mu.$$

Using this specification, however, we find that the coefficients of the logs of exports and imports, β_1 and β_2 in both equations (6) and (7) are essentially the same. The standard f-test indicates no statistically significant difference between them.

Another potential complication in this model is endogeneity: trade and FDI-related activities might be jointly determined. The above specification test indicates that trade and FDI-related activities are related in a nonlinear manner. Further testing indicates that log transformation, a simple way to transform the model from linear to nonlinear form, still leaves some misspecification. This misspecification is likely caused by endogeneity. Endogeneity is a problem, for example, if a US firm at first exports cars to Mexico but later establishes an assembly plant in Mexico, which imports automobile parts from the United States and exports finished automobiles back to the United States. In this case, cause and effect are circular; FDI causes trade and vice versa.

To deal with this endogeneity we apply the instrumental variable method using two-stage least-squares (2SLS) estimation. In essence, the estimated level of trade activities instead of the actual level is used to determine the impact of trade activities on FDI-related activities. Using the estimated value of trade activity cuts the circular link between trade and FDI-related activities, so that the estimated coefficients demonstrate the pure impact of trade activities on FDI-related activities. To apply the instrumental variable method, however, at least one exogenous factor that relates only to trade activities and not to FDI-related activities should be included in the model. One potential variable is a level of tariffs or of nontariff trade barriers. One may question whether trade barriers are really exogenous, because a firm may decide to establish a facility in a country in order to get around high trade barriers there. However, even if this is the case, the impact of trade barriers on FDI-related activities is not direct but indirect through trade activities. Therefore, trade barriers can be considered exogenous from a theoretical point of view.

To measure the level of trade barriers, we use a weighted mean and standard deviation of tariff rates across all industries. Including more detailed tariff data, such as those at the three-digit Standard Industrial Classification level, would not add explanatory power, because FDI-related data at the same industrial level are not available. Instead, the standard deviation of the tariff rate is added to capture the variety of tariff rates across different goods.

To test whether trade activities are indeed endogenous, the Hauseman test is applied. The motivation for the test is that if the variable is not endogenous, coefficients from ordinary least-squares (OLS) or 2SLS regressions should differ only by sampling error. The original form of the Hauseman test is cumbersome to derive. Instead, Hauseman (1978) suggested using the following simple form. Instead of testing the coefficients from OLS and 2SLS, the simple test examines the error term from the first-stage regression.

Let us denote the dependent variable as y_1 and the potentially endogenous explanatory variable as y_2:

$$y_1 = z_1\beta_1 + \alpha_1 y_2 + u_1 \tag{8a}$$

$$E(z'u_1) = 0. \tag{8b}$$

Equation (8b) expresses all explanatory variables other than y_2 as exogenous. If y_2 is endogenous, y_1 is one of the explanatory variables. To test for this endogeneity, we first regress y_2 on all explanatory variables except y_1:

$$y_2 = z\pi_2 + v_2 \tag{9a}$$

$$E(z'v_2) = 0 \tag{9b}$$

If y_2 is endogenous, the error term from equation (8a), μ, and the error term from equation (9a), v_2, are correlated. Plugging equation (9a) into equation (8a), we get

$$y_1 = z_1\beta_1 + \alpha_1 y_2 + \rho_1 v_2 + e_1. \tag{10}$$

Note that e_1 is uncorrelated with z_1, y_2, and v_2. Since v_2 is unobservable, we can use the estimated error term from equation (9a) to test the null hypothesis: $\rho_1 = 0$ using the equation (10). The usual OLS t-statistic is a valid test. Our result shows that both export and import activities are endogenous at the 1 percent level of confidence; therefore we choose to use 2SLS.

Table B.1 shows the results of our 2SLS regression. The positive and significant coefficient indicates that exports and FDI-related activities are complements. However, imports and FDI-related activities are not signif-

Table B.1 FDI-related activities and trade (coefficient)

	All countries	Income category of host country		
		Low	Middle	High
Per capita GDP	0.99	0.21	−0.41*	−0.38**
Population	0.59	−5.02**	−0.39**	0.31**
Distance	0.93*	20.75**	0.41	0.13
Export	4.67*	1.30*	1.59**	1.59**
Import	−2.97	0.79*	0.33	−0.39**
Constant	−25.88**	−172.70**	−4.00	−0.66
Number of observations	509	38	250	221
Adjusted R-squared	—	0.70	0.30	0.85

Notes: Coefficients are estimated using the Two Stage Least Square regression. All variable are in logs.

* = indicates that the coefficients are significant at the 90 percent level of confidence.

** = indicates that the coefficients are significant at the 95 percent level of confidence.

Source: Author's calculation.

icantly related. Overall, the result implies that FDI-related activities complement, not substitute for, domestic production.

Next we grouped the sample countries by income level using the World Bank's income thresholds. (See table 4.4 for a list of these countries by income level.) Using the 1995 list of countries, our sample consists of 3 low-income countries, 20 middle-income countries, and 19 high-income countries. Table B.1 also shows the results of the 2SLS regression by income level. The results confirm that US exports and US direct investment abroad are net complements in each income category. For middle- and low-income countries, there is no statistically significant relationship (again) between US direct investment abroad and US imports. Importantly, this suggests that US direct investment in these countries does not act mainly to transfer US production abroad in order to service the US market from export platforms. However, US imports and US direct investment abroad now appear as net *substitutes* in the high-income countries. This result suggests that, as US direct investment to these countries rises, US imports from them actually decline. We know of no theoretical reason why this should happen, and the result probably is best interpreted as spurious correlation. Thus, again, the conclusion would be that US direct investment has no significant effect on US imports.

References

Aitken, Brian J., and Ann E. Harrison. 1999. Do Domestic Firms Benefit from Direct Foreign Investment? Evidence from Venezuela. *American Economic Review* 89: 605-18.

Aitken, Brian J., Ann E. Harrison, and Robert E. Lipsey. 1996. Wages and Foreign Ownership: A Comparative Study of Mexico, Venezuela, and the United States. *Journal of International Economics* 20, no. 3-4 (May): 345-71.

Amsden, Alice. 1989. *Asia's Next Giant: South Korea and Late Industrialization*. New York: Oxford University Press.

Anderson, Kym. 1992. The Standard Welfare Economics of Policies Affecting Trade and the Environment. In *Trade, Environment, and Public Policy*, eds. Kym Anderson and Richard Blackhurst. New York: Harvester-Wheatsheaf.

Anderson, Kym, and Richard Blackhurst. 1992. Trade, the Environment, and Public Policy. In *Trade, Environment, and Public Policy*, eds. Kym Anderson and Richard Blackhurst. New York: Harvester-Wheatsheaf.

Autor, David H., Lawrence F. Katz, and Alan B. Krueger. 1997. *Computing Inequality: Have Computers Changed the Labor Market?* NBER Working Paper 5956 (March). Cambridge, MA: National Bureau of Economic Research.

Axelrod, R. 1984. *The Evolution of Cooperation*. New York: Basic Books.

Baldwin, Richard. 1989. The Growth Effects of 1992. *Economic Policy* 5: 248-81.

Barnett, Richard J., and Ronald E. Mueller. 1974. *Global Reach: The Multinational Spread of US Enterprises*. New York: Simon and Schuster.

Ben-David, Dan. 1993. Equalizing Exchange: Trade Liberalization and Income Convergence. *Quarterly Journal of Economics* 108: 653-79.

Bergsten, C. Fred, Thomas Horst, and Theodore H. Moran. 1978. *American Multinationals and American Interests*. Washington: Brookings Institution.

Blomström, Magnus, Gunnar Fors, and Robert Lipsey. 1997. Foreign Direct Investment and Employment: Home Country Experience in the United States and Sweden. *Economic Journal* 107, no. 445 (November): 1787-97.

Blomström, Magnus, Robert Lipsey, and Ksenia Kulchycky. 1988. US and Swedish Direct Investment and Exports. In *Trade Policy Issues and Empirical Analysis*, ed. Robert E. Baldwin. National Bureau of Economic Research Conference Report series. Chicago and London: University of Chicago Press.

Blomström, Magnus, and Hakan Persson. 1983. Foreign Investment and Spillover Efficiency in an Underdeveloped Economy: Evidence from the Mexican Manufacturing Industry. *World Development* 11, no. 6 (June): 493-501.

Bora, B., and M. Wooden. 1998. *Human Capital, Foreign Ownership and Wages.* National Institute of Labour Studies Working Paper Series 149. Adelaide, Australia: Flinders University.

Borzenstein, E., J. de Gregorio, and J. W. Lee. 1998. How Does Foreign Investment Affect Growth? *Journal of International Economics* 45: 115-35.

Brainard, S. Lael, and David A. Riker. 1997. *Are US Multinationals Exporting US Jobs?* NBER Working Paper 5958. Cambridge, MA: National Bureau of Economic Research.

Brown, Lester R., Gary Gardner, and Brian Halweil. 1998. *Beyond Malthus: Sixteen Dimensions of the Population Problem.* Worldwatch Institute Paper 143.

Buckley, Peter J., and Mark C. Casson. 1976. *The Future of the Multinational Enterprise.* London: MacMillan.

Buiges, Pierre, and Alexis Jacquemin. 1994. Foreign Direct Investment and Exports to the European Community. In *Does Ownership Matter: Japanese Multinationals in Europe,* eds. Mark Mason and Dennis Encarnation. Oxford and New York: Oxford University Press.

Bureau of Economic Analysis, US Department of Commerce 1999. *US Direct Investment Abroad: Operations of US Parent Companies and their Foreign Affiliates.* Revised 1996 Estimates.

Bureau of Economic Analysis, US Department of Commerce. 2000. *US Direct Investment Abroad: Position on a Historic Cost Basis.* http://www.bea.doc.gov/bea/di1usd.htm #link3.

Bureau of International Labor Standards, US Department of Labor. 2000. *By the Sweat and Toil of Children, Vol. 6: An Economic Consideration of Child Labor.* http://www.dol.gov/dol/ilab/public/media/reports/main.htm.

Bureau of Labor Statistics. 2000. *National Employment, Hours, and Earnings.* http://www.stats.bls.gov.

Burtless, Gary, Robert Z. Lawrence, Robert E. Litan, and Robert J. Shapiro. 1998. *Globophobia: Confronting Fears About Global Trade.* Washington: The Brookings Institution.

Cantwell, J. A. 1991a. The International Agglomeration of Technological Activity. In *Global Research Strategy and International Competitiveness,* ed. M. C. Casson. Oxford: Basil Blackwell.

Cantwell, J. A. 1991b. A Survey of Theories of International Production. In *The Nature of the Transnational Firm,* eds. C. N. Pitelis and R. Sugden. London: Routledge.

Carson, R. T., Y. Jeon, and D. R. McCubbin. 1997. The Relationship Between Air Pollution Emissions and Income: US Data. *Environment and Development Economics* 2: 433-50.

Caves, Richard E. 1995. *Multinational Enterprise and Economic Analysis.* London: Cambridge University Press.

Caves, Richard E. 1999. *Spillovers from Multinationals in Developing Countries: The Mechanisms at Work.* William Davidson Institute Working Paper 247. Ann Arbor, MI: University of Michigan.

Cecchini P., M. Catinat, and A. Jacquemin. 1988. *The European Challenge 1992: The Benefits of a Single Market.* Aldershot, Hants, UK: Wildwood House.

Charnovitz, Steven. 1994. NAFTA's Social Dimension: Lessons from the Past and Framework for the Future. *International Trade Journal* 8, no. 1 (Spring): 39-72.

Charnovitz, Steven. 2000. World Trade and the Environment: A Review of the New WTO Report. *The Georgetown International Environmental Law Review* 2: 523-41.

Chedor, Severine. 2000. L'impact des Investissements Directs sur les Echanges et l'emploi du Pays d'origine: Une Application aux Implantations Françaises à l'étranger. Doctoral dissertation, Faculty of Economics, University of Paris I (La Sorbonne-Pantheon), January.

Cline, William R. 1995. *International Debt Reexamined.* Washington: Institute for International Economics.

Cline, William R. 1997. *Trade and Income Distribution.* Washington: Institute for International Economics.

Coase, Ronald H. 1937. The Nature of the Firm. *Economica* 4: 386-405.

Coase, Ronald. 1961. The Problem of Social Cost, *Journal of Law and Economics* 3: 1-44.

Commission of the European Union 1997. *Fifth Survey of State Aid in the European Union in the Manufacturing and Certain Other Sectors.* Brussels: Commission of the European Union.

Daly, Herman E. 1996a. Sustainable Growth? No Thank You. In *The Case Against the Global Economy*, eds. J. Mander and E. Goldsmith. San Francisco: Sierra Club Books.

Daly, Herman E. 1996b. Free Trade: The Perils of Deregulation. In *The Case Against the Global Economy*, eds. J. Mander and E. Goldsmith. San Francisco: Sierra Club Books.

Dasgupta, Susmita, Ashoka Mody, Subhendu Roy, and David Wheeler. 1995. *Environmental Regulation and Development: A Cross-Country Empirical Analysis.* World Bank Policy Research Working Paper 1448. Washington: World Bank.

De Gregorio, Jose. 1992. Economic Growth in Latin America. *Journal of Development Economics* 39 (July): 59-84.

Deardorff, Alan V. 2000. Factor Prices and the Factor Content of Trade Revisited. *Journal of International Economics* 50: 73-90.

Deardoff, Alan. V., and Robert W. Staiger. 1988. An Interpretation of the Factor Content of Trade. *Journal of International Economics* 24: 93-107.

Destler, I. M. 1997a. *American Trade Politics*, 3rd edition. Washington: Institute for International Economics.

Destler, I. M. 1997b. *Renewing Fast-Track Legislation.* Washington: Institute for International Economics.

Dollar, David. 1992. Outward-Oriented Developing Economies Really Do Grow More Rapidly: Evidence from 95 LDCs, 1976-1985. *Economic Development and Cultural Change* 40, no. 3 (April): 523-44.

Dollar, David, and Art Kray. 2000. *Growth is Good for the Poor.* http://www.worldbank.org/research. Washington: World Bank

Dua, Andre, and Daniel C. Esty. 1997. *Sustaining the Asia-Pacific Miracle: Environmental Protection and Economic Integration.* Washington: Institute for International Economics.

Dunning, John H. 1958. *American Investment in British Manufacturing Industry.* London: George Allen and Unwin.

Dunning, John H. 1988. The Eclectic Paradigm of International Production: A Restatement and Some Possible Extensions. *Journal of International Business Studies* 19, no. 1: 1-31.

Dunning, John H. 1993. *Multinational Enterprises and the Global Economy.* UK: Addison-Wesley Publishing Company.

Dymond, William A. 1999. The MAI: A Sad and Melancholy Tale. In *Canada Among Nations*, eds. Fen O. Hampson and Maureen Appel Molot. London: Oxford University Press.

Edwards, Sebastian. 1998. Openness, Trade Liberalization, and Growth in Developing Countries. *Journal of Development Economics* 39: 31-57.

Ellerman, A. D., P. L. Joskow, R. Schmalansee, J.-P. Montero, and E. M. Bailey. 2000. *Market for Clean Air: The US Acid Rain Program.* New York: Cambridge University Press.

Emmott, Bill. 1992. *Japan's Global Reach.* London: Century.

Encarnation, Dennis J., and Louis T. Wells, Jr. 1986. Evaluating Foreign Investment. In *Investing in Development: New Roles for Private Capital?* ed. Theodore H. Moran. New Brunswick, NJ and Oxford: Transaction Books.

Enrich, Peter D. 1996. Saving the States from Themselves: Commerce Clause Constraints on State Tax Incentives for Business. *Harvard Law Review* 110: 377-467.

Environmental Protection Agency of the United States (EPA). 1999. *1998 Compliance Report: Acid Rain Program* EPA-439-R-99-010. Washington: EPA.

Epstein, Richard A. 1985. *Takings: Private Property and the Power of Eminent Domain.* Cambridge, MA: Harvard University Press.

Eskeland, Gunnar S., and Ann E. Harrison. 1997. *Moving to Greener Pastures: Multinationals and the Pollution Haven Hypothesis.* World Bank Working Paper 1744.

Esty, Daniel C. 1994. *Greening the GATT: Trade, Environment, and the Future.* Washington: Institute for International Economics.

Esty, Daniel C., and Bradford S. Gentry. 1997. Foreign Investment, Globalization, and Environment. In *Globalization and Environment*, ed. Tom Jones. Paris: Organization for Economic Cooperation and Development.

European Round Table of Industrialists. 2000. *Improved Investment Conditions: Third Survey on Improvements in Conditions for Investment in the Developing World.* Brussels: European Business Round Table.

Executive Office of the President of the United States. 2000. *Economic Report of the President 1999.* Washington: US Government Printing Office.

Feenstra, Robert C., and Gordon H. Hanson. 1999. The Impact of Outsourcing and High-Technology Capital on Wages: Estimates for the United States, 1979-1990. *Quarterly Journal of Economics* 114, no. 3 (August): 907-40.

Feenstra, Robert C., and Gordon H. Hanson. 1997. Foreign Direct Investment and Relative Wages: Evidence from Mexico's Maquiladoras. *Journal of International Economics* 42: 371-93.

Frankel, Jeffrey A., and David Romer. 1998. Does Trade Cause Growth? *American Economic Review* 89, no. 3 (June): 379-99.

French, Hilary. 2000. *Vanishing Borders: Protecting the Planet in the Age of Globalization.* New York: W. W. Norton and Company.

Friedman, James W. 1986. *Game Theory with Applications to Economics.* New York: Oxford University Press.

Frischtak, Claudio. 1996. Brazil. In *National Policies for Developing High Tech Industries: International Comparisons*, eds. Francis W. Rushing and Carole Ganz Brown. Boulder, CO: Westview Press.

Ganesan, A.V. 1999. Strategic Options Available to Developing Countries with Regard to a Multilateral Agreement on Investment. *International Monetary and Financial Issues for the 1990s* 10. Geneva: United Nations Conference on Trade and Development.

Gervais, Daniel, and Vera Nicholas-Gervais. 1999. Intellectual Property in the Multilateral Agreement on Investment: Lessons to be Learned. *Journal of World Intellectual Property* 2: 257-74.

Goklany, Indur M. 1999. *Cleaning the Air: The Real Story of the War on Air Pollution.* Washington: Cato Institute.

Goldsmith, Edward. 1996. The Last Word: Family, Community, Democracy. In *The Case Against the Global Economy*, eds. Jerry Mander and Edward Goldsmith. San Francisco: Sierra Club Books.

Golub, Stephen S. 1999. *Labor Costs and International Trade.* Washington: American Enterprise Institute for Public Policy Research.

Goodland, Robert. 1996. Growth Has Reached its Limit. In *The Case Against the Global Economy*, eds. J. Mander and E. Goldsmith. San Francisco: Sierra Club Books.

Graham, Edward M. 1985. Intra-industry Direct Foreign Investment, Market Structure, Firm Rivalry, and Technological Performance. In *Multinationals as Mutual Invaders: Intraindustry Direct Foreign Investment*, ed. A. Erdilek. London: Croom Helm.

Graham, Edward. 1995. *Foreign Direct Investment in the World Economy.* IMF Working Paper 95/59 (June): 22. Washington: International Monetary Fund.

Graham, Edward M. 1996. *Global Corporations and National Governments.* Washington: Institute for International Economics.

Graham, Edward M. 1998. Investment in the WTO: Just Do It. In *Launching New Global Trade Talks: An Action Agenda*, ed. Jeffrey J. Schott. Washington: Institute for International Economics.

Graham, Edward M. 1999a. Regulatory Takings, Supranational Treatment, and the Multilateral Agreement on Investment: Issues Raised by Nongovernmental Organizations. *Cornell International Law Journal* 31, no. 3: 599-614.

Graham, Edward M. 1999b. Foreign Direct Investment Outflows and Manufacturing Trade: A Comparison of Japan and the United States. In *Japanese Multinationals in Asia: The Re-*

gional Operations of Japanese Multinationals, ed. Dennis Encarnation. Oxford and London: The Oxford University Press.

Graham, Edward, and Paul R. Krugman. 1995. *Foreign Direct Investment in the United States*, 3rd edition. Washington: Institute for International Economics.

Graham, Edward M., and Robert Z. Lawrence. 1996. Measuring the International Contestability of Markets: A Conceptual Approach. *Journal of World Trade* 30, no. 5: 5-20.

Grantham, Bill. 1998. America the Menace: France's Feud with Hollywood. *World Policy Journal* 15: 58-65.

Greider, William. 1997. *One World, Ready or Not: The Manic Logic of Global Capitalism*. New York: Simon and Schuster.

Grossman, Gene M., and Alan B. Krueger. 1993. Environmental Impacts of a North American Free Trade Agreement. In *The Mexico-US Free Trade Agreement*, ed. Peter M. Garber. Cambridge and London: MIT Press.

Hanson, Gordon H., and Ann E. Harrison. 1999. Trade Liberalization and Wage Inequality in Mexico. *Industrial and Labor Relations Review* 52, no. 2 (January): 271-88.

Hauseman, J. 1978. Specification Tests in Econometrics. *Econometrica* 46: 1251-71.

Henderson, David. 1999. *The MAI Affair: A Story and its Lessons*. London: The Royal Institute of International Affairs.

Hines, Colin, and Tim Lang. 1996. In Favor of a New Protectionism. In *The Case Against the Global Economy*, eds. Jerry Mander and Edward Goldsmith. San Francisco: Sierra Club Books.

Hoekman, Bernard, and Kamal Saggi. 1999. *Multilateral Disciplines for Investment-Related Policies*. World Bank Policy Research Working Paper 2138. Washington: World Bank.

Hufbauer, Gary C., assisted by Joanna M. van Rooij. 1992. *US Taxation of International Income: Blueprint for Reform*. Washington: Institute for International Economics.

Hufbauer, Gary C., and Jeffrey J. Schott. 1992. *North American Free Trade: Issues and Recommendations*. Washington: Institute for International Economics.

Hymer, Stephen H. 1976. *The International Operations of National Firms* (reprint of 1959 doctoral dissertation.). Cambridge, MA: MIT Press.

Hymer, Stephen H., and Robert Rowthorne. 1970. Multinational Firms and International Oligopoly: The Non-American Challenge. In *The International Corporation: A Symposium*, ed. Charles P. Kindleberger. Cambridge, MA: MIT Press.

Internal Revenue Service. 2000. *2000 International Tax Statistics*. http://www/irs.gov/tax-stats.

International Labor Organization. 2000. LABORSTA (Labor Statistics Database). http://www.ilo.org/public/english/support/lib/dblist.htm#statistics.

Khor, Martin. 1996. Global Economy and the Third World. In *The Case Against the Global Economy*, eds. J. Mander and E. Goldsmith. San Francisco: Sierra Club Books.

Kletzer, Lori. 1997. International Trade and Job Displacement in US Manufacturing 1979-81. In *Imports, Exports, and the American Worker*, ed. Susan Collins. Washington: Brookings Institution.

Korton, David C. 1996. The Failure of Bretton Woods. In *The Case Against the Global Economy*, eds. J Mander and E. Goldsmith. San Francisco: Sierra Club Books.

Krueger, Anne O. 1998. Why Trade Liberalization is Good for Growth. *The Economic Journal* 108: 1513-22.

Krugman, Paul R. 1999. *Analytical Afterthoughts on the Asian Crisis*. http://mit.edu/people/krugman/index.html.

Krugman, Paul R. 2000. Technology, Trade, and Factor Prices. *Journal of International Economics* 50: 51-72.

Kujawa, Duane. 1981. US Manufacturing Investment in the Developing Countries: American Labour's Concerns and the Enterprise Environment in the Decade Ahead. *British Journal of Industrial Relations* 19, no. 1 (March): 38-48.

Lall, Sanjaya. 1973. Transfer-Pricing by Multinational Manufacturing Firms. *Oxford Bulletin of Economics and Statistics* 35, no. 3: 173-93.

Lall, Sanjaya. 1980. Vertical Interfirm Linkages in LDCs: An Empirical Study. *Oxford Bulletin of Economics and Statistics* 42, no. 3 (August): 203-26.

Lall, Sanjaya, and Paul Streeten. 1977. *Foreign Investment, Transnationals and Developing Countries.* Boulder, CO: Westview Press.

Lalumière, Catherine, and Jean-Pierre Landau. 1998. *Rapport sur l'Accord Multilatéral sur l'Investissement.* Photocopy. Paris: La Cour des Comptes.

Lang, Jeffrey. 1998. Keynote Address at the Symposium on the International Regulation of Foreign Direct Investment. *Cornell International Law Journal* 31: 455-66.

Lang, Tim, and Colin Hines. 1996. Debate: Global Free Trade: The "New Protectionist" Position. *New Political Economy* 1, no. 1 (March): 111-14.

Langdon, S. W. 1975. Multinational Corporations, Taste Transfer, and Underdevelopment: A Case Study from Kenya. *Review of African Political Economy* 2: 12-35.

Lardy, Nicholas. 1998. *China's Unfinished Economic Revolution.* Washington: Brookings Institution.

Lawrence, Robert Z., and Matthew Slaughter. 1993. *International Trade and American Wages in the 1980s: Giant Sucking Sound or Small Hiccup?* Brookings Papers on Economic Activity 2: 161-226.

Leamer, Edward E. 1997. In Search of Stolper-Samuelson Effects on US Wages. In *Imports, Exports, and the American Worker*, ed. Susan Collins. Washington: Brookings Institution.

Leamer, Edward E. 2000. What's the Use of Factor Contents? *Journal of International Economics* 50: 17-50.

Lipsey R. E., and M. Y. Weiss. 1981. Foreign Production and Exports in Manufacturing Industries. *Review of Economics and Statistics* 63: 488-94.

Lipsey R. E., and M. Y. Weiss. 1984. Foreign Production and Exports of Individual Firms. *Review of Economics and Statistics* 66: 304-8.

Low, Patrick, and A. Yeats. 1992. Do Dirty Industries Migrate? In *International Trade and the Environment*, ed. Patrick Low. World Bank Discussion Paper 159.

Lucas, R., D. Wheeler, and H. Hettige. 1992. Economic Development, Environmental Regulations, and the International Migration of Toxic Pollution: 1960-1988. In *International Trade and the Environment*, ed. Patrick Low. World Bank Discussion Paper 159.

Mander, Jerry, and Edward Goldsmith, eds. 1996. *The Case Against the Global Economy.* San Francisco: Sierra Club Books.

Mazur, Jay. 2000. Labor's New Internationalism. *Foreign Affairs* 79, no. 1 (January-February): 79-93.

McUsic, Molly. 1996. The Ghost of Lochner: Modern Takings Doctrine and its Impact on Economic Legislation. *Boston University Law Review* 76: 650-67.

Meier, Gerald M. 1987. Infant Industry. In *The New Palgrave: A Dictionary of Economics*, eds. John Eatwell, Murray Milgate, and Peter Newman. London: MacMillan.

Ministry of International Trade and Industry (MITI), Government of Japan. 2000. *Report on the WTO Consistency of Trade Policies by Major Trading Partners.* Tokyo: Government of Japan.

Moran, Theodore H. 1976. *Multinational Corporations and the Politics of Dependence.* Princeton, NJ: Princeton University Press.

Moran, Theodore H. 1998. *Foreign Direct Investment and Development: The New Policy Agenda for Developing Countries and Economies in Transition.* Washington: Institute for International Economics.

Moran, Theodore H. 1999. Foreign Direct Investment and Good Jobs/Bad Jobs: The Impact of Outward Investment and Inward Investment on Jobs and Wages. In *Growing Apart: The Causes and Consequences of Global Wage Inequality*, eds. Albert Fishlow and Karen Parker. New York: Council for Foreign Relations Press.

Moran, Theodore. 2000. *Parental Supervision.* Photocopy (March). Washington: Georgetown University, School of Foreign Service.

Morris, David. 1996. Free Trade: The Great Destroyer. In *The Case Against the Global Economy*, eds. Jerry Mander and Edward Goldsmith. San Francisco: Sierra Club Books.

Norberg-Hodge, Helena. 1996. Shifting Direction: From Global Dependence to Local Inter-dependence. In *The Case Against the Global Economy*, eds. Jerry Mander and Edward Goldsmith. San Francisco: Sierra Club Books.

Oman, Charles P. 2000. *Policy Competition for Foreign Direct Investment: A Study of Competition among Governments to Attract FDI*. Paris: Organization for Economic Cooperation and Development.

Organization for Economic Cooperation and Development (OECD). 1995. *Meeting of the Council at Ministerial Level, Final Communiqué*. http://oecd.org.

Organization for Economic Cooperation and Development (OECD). 1997. *Meeting of the Council at Ministerial Level, Final Communiqué*. http://oecd.org.

Organization for Economic Cooperation and Development (OECD). 1998. *Open Markets Matter: The Benefits of Trade and Investment Liberalization*. Paris: Organization for Economic Cooperation and Development.

Panagariya, Arvind. 2000. Evaluating the Factor-content Approach to Measuring the Effect of Trade on Wage Inequality. *Journal of International Economics* 50: 91-116.

Pearce, R. D. 1990. *Overseas Production and Exporting Performance: Some Further Investigations*. Discussion Papers in International Investment and Business Studies 135. Reading, UK: University of Reading.

Posen, Adam. 2000. *Globalization, the NAIRU, and Monetary Policy*. Forthcoming. Washington: Institute for International Economics.

Ramsey, J. B. 1969. Tests for Specification Errors in Classical Linear Least-Squares Analysis. *Journal of the Royal Statistical Association* B, 71: 350-71.

Repetto, Robert, Roger C. Dower, and Robert Gramlich. 1993. Pollution and Energy Taxes: Their Environmental and Economic Benefits. *Challenge* 36, no. 4 (July-August): 9-14.

Reuber, G. L. et al. 1973. *Private Foreign Investment in Development*. Oxford: Clarendon Press.

Rodriguez, Francisco, and Dani Rodrik. 1999. *Trade Policy and Economic Growth: A Skeptic's Guide to the Cross-National Evidence*. Photocopy (April). College Park, MD: University of MD, Department of Economics.

Rodrik, Dani. 1997. *Has Globalization Gone Too Far?* Washington: Institute for International Economics.

Rodrik, Dani. 1999. *The New Global Economy and Developing Countries: Making Openness Work*. Washington: Overseas Development Council.

Romer, Paul. 1994. New Goods, Old Theory, and the Welfare Costs of Trade Restrictions. *Journal of Development Economics* 43: 5-38.

Rosen, Daniel. 1999. *Behind the Open Door: Foreign Enterprises in the Chinese Marketplace*. Washington: Institute for International Economics.

Rugman, Alan M., and Julie A. Soloway. 1998. Corporate Strategy and NAFTA: When Environmental Regulations Are Barriers to Trade. *Journal of Transnational Management Development* 3, no. 3-4: 231-51.

Rugman, Alan M., and Michael Gestrin. 1994. NAFTA's Treatment of Foreign Investment. In *Foreign Investment and NAFTA*, ed. Alan M. Rugman. Columbia, SC: University of South Carolina Press.

Sachs, Jeffrey, and Andrew Warner. 1995. *Economic Reform and the Process of Global Integration*. Brookings Papers on Economic Activity 95, no. 1: 1-118.

Sauvé, Pierre. 2000. *Trade and Investment at Seattle and Beyond: Scenarios for Moving Forward*. Photocopy. Harvard University, Center for Business and Government, John F. Kennedy School of Government.

Sauvé, Pierre, and Christopher Wilkie. 2000. Investment Liberalization in GATS. In *GATS 2000: New Directions in Services Trade Liberalization*, eds. Pierre Sauvé and Robert M. Stern. Washington: Brookings Institution.

Sauvé, Pierre. 1997. Q's and A's on Trade, Investment, and the WTO. *Journal of World Trade* 28: 5-16.

Schmidheiny, Stephan. 1992. *Changing Course: A Global Business Perspective on Development and the Environment*. The Business Council for Sustainable Development. Cambridge and London: MIT Press.

Schott, Jeffrey. 1996. *WTO 2000: Setting the Course for World Trade*. Policy Analyses in International Economics 45. Washington: Institute for International Economics.

Schott, Jeffrey. 2000. The WTO after Seattle. In *The WTO after Seattle*, ed. Jeffrey J. Schott. Washington: Institute for International Economics.

Selden, T. M., and D. Song. 1994. Neoclassical Growth, the J Curve for Abatement, and the Inverted U-Curve for Pollution. *Journal of Environmental Economics and Management* 27: 162-68.

Sidak, J. Gregory. 1997. *Foreign Investment in American Telecommunications*. Chicago: University of Chicago Press.

Slaughter, Matthew J. 1995. *Multinational Corporations, Outsourcing, and American Wage Divergence*. NBER Working Paper 5253 (September). Cambridge, MA: National Bureau of Economic Research.

Soloway, Julie A. 1999. Environmental Trade Barriers Under NAFTA: The MMT Fuel Addition Controversy. *Minnesota Journal of Global Trade* 8, 1: 55-95.

Stewart, Francis. 1981. International Technology Transfer: Issues and Policy Options. In *Recent Issues in World Development*, eds. P. Streeten and R. Jolly. Oxford: Pergamon Press.

Stolper, Wolfgang F., and Paul A. Samuelson. 1941. Protection and Real Wages. *Review of Economic Studies* 9: 58-73.

Swenarchuk, Michelle. 1999. *Liberalized Investment and Investor-State Suits: Threats to Governmental Powers*. Photocopy. Toronto: Canadian Environmental Law Association.

Swift, Byron. 2000. Allowance Trading and Potential Hot Spots—Good News from the Acid Rain Program. *Environmental Reporter*, 12 May: 954-63.

United Nations Conference on Trade and Development. 1994. *World Investment Report*. Geneva: United Nations.

United Nations Conference on Trade and Development. 1995. *World Investment Report*. Geneva: United Nations.

United Nations Conference on Trade and Development. 1996. *World Investment Report*. Geneva: United Nations.

United Nations Conference on Trade and Development. 1997. *World Investment Report*. Geneva: United Nations.

United Nations Conference on Trade and Development. 1998. *World Investment Report*. Geneva: United Nations.

United Nations Conference on Trade and Development. 1999. *World Investment Report*. Geneva: United Nations.

Urata, Shujiro. 1995. Emerging Patterns of Production and Foreign Trade in Electronics Products in East Asia: An Examination of a Role Played by Foreign Direct Investment. Paper presented at conference on Competing Production Networks in Asia: Host Country Perspectives. The Asia Foundation, San Francisco, 27-28 April.

Van Dyke, L. Brennan, Stephen Porter, and Bella Sewall. 1999. *Environmental Protection and Investment Rules in the Free Trade of the Americas*. Photocopy. Washington: Center for International Environmental Law.

Varley, Pamela. 1998. *The Sweatshop Quandary: Corporate Responsibility on the Global Frontier*. Washington: Investor Responsibility Research Center.

Vernon, Raymond. 1971. *Sovereignty at Bay*. New York: Basic Books.

Vitousek, P. M., et al. 1986. Human Appropriation of the Products of Photosynthesis. *BioScience* 37.

von Moltke, Konrad. 2000. *An International Investment Regime? Issues of Sustainability*. International Institute for Sustainable Development Working Paper. http://www/iisd.ca/trade.

Wallach, Lori, and Michelle Sforza. 1999. *Whose Trade Organization? Corporate Globalization and the Erosion of Democracy*. Washington: Public Citizen.

Warren, Tony, and Christopher Findlay. 2000. Measuring Impediments to Trade in Services. In *GATS 2000: New Directions in Services Trade Liberalization*, eds. Pierre Sauvé and Robert M. Stern. Washington: Brookings Institution.

Whitman, Marina v. N. 1999. *New World, New Rules: The Changing Role of the American Corporation*. Boston: Harvard Business School Press.

Wilkins, Myra, and Frank E. Hill. 1964. *American Business Ahead: Ford on Six Continents*. Detroit: Wayne State University Press.

Williamson, Oliver E. 1985. *The Economic Institutions of Capitalism*. New York: The Free Press.

World Bank. 1987. *World Development Report 1987*. Washington: World Bank.

World Bank. 1997. *World Development Report 1997*. Washington: World Bank.

World Trade Organization (WTO). 1998. *Annual Report 1998: International Trade Statistics*. Geneva: WTO.

World Trade Organization (WTO). 1999. *Trade and Environment*. Special Studies 4. http://www.wto.org/wto/environ/environment.pdf.

Zhang, Chi, Michael M. May, and Thomas Heller. 2000. *Impact of Development and Structural Changes in the Electricity Sector of Guangdong Province, China*. Center for International Security and Cooperation Working Paper (March). Stanford University.

Index

Acid Rain Program (U.S.), 154–55
activists, antiglobal
  autarky advocated by, 147–48, 161
  criticisms of multinational corporations, 5, 39
  opposition to multilateral investment
    agreements, 48–49, 191–92, 194
  See also demonstrations; environmental groups;
    labor unions; nongovernmental
    organizations; opponents of Multilateral
    Agreement on Investment (MAI)
AFL-CIO, 8, 86, 191
  See also labor unions
Agreement on Trade Related Intellectual Property
    Rights (TRIPs), 33, 57, 62, 166–67
Agreement on Trade Related Investment
    Measures (TRIMs), 61
  developing countries' participation, 174
  implementation, 191
  ongoing negotiations, 194–95
  overlap with MAI, 23
  performance requirements, 63, 194–95
agricultural chemicals, 138–39
air pollution
  automotive emissions, 140, 142–43, 162
  effects of economic growth, 136
  greenhouse gases, 137–38, 140, 155–57, 162
  market failure, 150
  optimal levels, 150–52, 151*f*
  productivity reduced by, 143
  reformulated gasoline and, 132–33, 142–43
  toxic chemicals, 148
  tradable pollution rights, 154–55, 160, 161

transferred to other countries, 137–38
  in United States, 139–40
  in urban areas, 161
  See also MMT; pollution
Aitken, Brian, 94
Alberta (Canada), 38, 39
antiglobal activists. *See* activists
APEC. *See* Asia Pacific Economic Cooperation
    (APEC) forum
apparel industry, 99*n*, 100–102, 103, 105
  See also sweatshop conditions
Apparel Industry Partnership, 105
Argentina, 10, 174
Arnhem operation, 198–99
Asia Pacific Economic Cooperation (APEC)
    forum, 174
Australia, 94
autarkic policies, 147–48, 161
automobile industry
  American, 6, 127–29, 181
  Canadian, 37
  emissions standards, 142–43
automotive emissions, 140, 142–43, 162
  See also MMT

balance of payments crises, 73, 79, 176
Bangladesh, 100–101, 105
Barshefsky, Charlene, 40
Bergsten, C. Fred, 119
Bhopal (India), 148
bilateral investment treaties, 26, 174, 176
boards of directors, 68

bonded labor, 103
Brazil, 10, 174, 179
A Bridge Too Far, 198–99
Brittan, Sir Leon, 30
Burke-Hartke bill, 191
Bush, George H. W., 17
business community
    European, 27, 190, 193
    interest in greater transparency, 193
    interest in multilateral investment agreement,
        190, 192–93, 194
    lack of support for MAI, 10, 15–17, 19, 34, 49,
        192
    OECD advisory committee, 20
    support for investment liberalization, 49
    support for NAFTA, 10
    support for trade liberalization, 10, 198
    tax issues, 27
    temporary entry of personnel, 68, 178
    in United States, 19, 49, 193
    See also multinational corporations

Canada
    automobile industry, 37
    criticism of Cuban Liberty and Democratic
        Solidarity (Libertad) Act, 28, 29
    cultural industries issue, 31–32
    debate over NAFTA, 36
    ethanol producers, 37–38, 45, 145–46
    MAI negotiations, 28, 31–32
    MMT dispute with Ethyl Corporation, 7, 37–39,
        41, 44–45, 145–46
    MMT regulations, 37–38, 47, 143
    provincial governments, 67, 195
    See also North American Free Trade Agreement
        (NAFTA)
capital movement liberalization, 22
carbon dioxide, 137–38, 140, 155–56
chemicals, toxic, 138–39, 148
children
    bonded labor, 103
    education, 100, 104
    employment of, 100–101, 104
    poverty, 101
Chile, 10, 169, 174
China
    environmental problems, 156–57, 161
    poverty, 162
    trade policies, 147
    view of potential investment agreement, 191
    wage premium at foreign-owned firms, 95
CIIME. *See* Committee on International
        Investment and Multinational Enterprise
Clean Air Act (U.S.), 132–33, 154–55
climate change, 137–38, 140, 144, 155–56, 162
Clinton, Bill, 17, 28, 36
Coase, Ronald, 152
Coase's theorem, 152
Cold War, 168–69
colonialism, 168

Committee on International Investment and
        Multinational Enterprise (CIIME), 20, 21,
        22
concessions, 71
consumerism, 134
consumers, 128
contestable markets, 125–26, 127–29, 172
Convention on the Settlement of Investment
        Disputes between States and Nationals of
        Other States (ICSID), 75
Copenhagen Declaration, 56
copyright. *See* intellectual property rights
Cornell University, 40
corporations. *See* business community;
        multinational corporations
corruption, 156
Cuban Liberty and Democratic Solidarity
        (Libertad) Act (Helms-Burton Act), 28–30,
        57
cultural industries, 11, 21, 31–33

debt of developing countries, 171–72
demonstrations
    at Geneva WTO meeting (1998), 40–41
    at OECD headquarters, 7, 12, 40, 131, 133
    at Seattle WTO meeting (1999), 8, 16, 48–49,
        131–32, 133, 186
    at UNCTAD headquarters, 10–11
developed countries
    bilateral investment treaties, 26, 174
    foreign direct investment in, 6, 9, 94
    gunboat diplomacy, 168–69
    investment incentives, 194
    positions similar to developing countries,
        166–67
    trade policies, 182
    US investment in, 106–8, 107t, 109f, 110f, 111–13,
        111f, 112f, 113f, 114
    See also labor in developed countries;
        Organization for Economic Cooperation and
        Development (OECD)
developing countries
    attitudes toward foreign direct investment,
        167–68, 169–71, 172–73
    attitudes toward multinational corporations,
        167–68, 169–70
    benefits of foreign direct investment, 5–7, 172,
        173
    bilateral investment treaties, 174, 176
    education, 100, 104
    environmental problems, 134, 137, 143, 144, 147,
        161–62
    evaluation of foreign investment projects,
        170–71
    excluded from MAI negotiations, 9, 165–66, 184
    export industries, 101–2, 105, 123
    expropriation in, 72
    foreign debt, 171–72
    government officials, 171
    greenhouse gas emissions, 155–56

import substitution policies, 84, 169
improving investment conditions, 193
income categories, 91, 107, 108*t*
income inequality, 86
interest in codes of conduct for multinational
  firms, 176–77, 183
interest in MAI, 10, 165, 174
interventionist policies, 171
local firms, 87, 88, 89, 90, 100
negotiations with foreign investors, 169–71
performance requirements, 89, 194, 195
population growth, 135, 141, 144
predicted movement of jobs to low-wage
  countries, 8–9, 81–82, 106, 113–14, 125
provisions for accession to MAI, 10, 56, 80
statements to WTO on trade and investment,
  166
tradable pollution rights, 156
trade policies, 84–85, 169, 178–79
US investment in, 106–7, 107*t*, 109*f*, 110*f*, 111,
  111*f*, 112*f*, 113*f*
views of MAI, 165–66
views of multilateral rulemaking, 166–67,
  173–75, 184, 191, 195
weak enforcement of environmental laws, 9, 156
weak environmental regulations, 9, 36, 141, 143,
  149–50
wildlife habitat, 134–36, 144, 162
See also economic growth; foreign direct
  investment; labor in developing countries
dispute settlement procedures
  arbitration conventions, 75
  expropriation cases, 38
  fears that environmental protection will be
    weakened by, 78, 132–33
  ICSID convention, 75
  in NAFTA, 37–39, 41, 45, 46–47, 52, 74, 75
  needed for environmental issues, 160–61
  in potential investment agreement, 193
  of WTO, 74, 132–33
dispute settlement procedures in MAI, 2
  concerns of MAI opponents, 78
  investor-to-state, 39, 52, 72, 74–76, 77, 78, 176–77
  potential impact, 52, 78, 80
  state-to-state, 74, 77–78
dolphins, 35–36
domestic content requirements. *See* local content
  requirements

Earth Island Institute, 35
economic growth
  contribution of new foreign investment, 85–86,
    87
  environmental impact, 134–41, 147
  export industries, 101–2
  positive effects on environment, 135–37, 162
  relationship to technological progress, 6
  waste produced, 136–40
education, 87, 100, 104
Egypt, 165

Eizenstat, Stuart, 30
employment. *See* jobs; labor
employment requirements, 69
Encarnation, Dennis J., 84
environmental groups
  belief that globalization harms environment,
    131–32, 133–34, 146–47, 162
  criticism of MAI, 131
  history of protests against international trade
    agreements, 35–39, 40
  opportunity missed in MAI negotiations,
    162–63
  opposition to multilateral investment
    agreements, 191–92
  views of NAFTA, 36, 37, 39
  See also nongovernmental organizations;
    opponents of Multilateral Agreement on
    Investment (MAI)
environmental issues
  dispute settlement procedures needed, 160–61
  effects of autarkic policies, 147–48
  efforts to include protection in multilateral
    agreements, 158–61
  failure to provide optimal level of protection,
    148–52
  fears that dispute settlement will weaken
    protection, 78, 132–33
  fears that international agreements will weaken
    protection, 39, 47, 71–72, 158–59, 191–92
  global warming, 137–38, 140, 144, 155–56, 162
  impact of economic growth, 134–41, 147
  impact of foreign direct investment, 134,
    140–41, 148–49, 156–58
  impact of trade, 134, 140–41
  international agency proposed, 160
  MAI provision to not lower standards, 71–72
  in NAFTA debate, 36–37
  reference in MAI preamble, 56
  Rio Declaration, 56
  safeguards discussed in MAI negotiations, 45,
    159–60, 162–63
  trade-off between globalization benefits and
    environmental protection, 134, 146, 147, 148
  trade-off between income and costs of
    environmental protection, 150–51, 151*f*
  tuna import restrictions, 35–36
  turtle protection from shrimp fishing, 133
  urbanization, 161–62
  wildlife habitat, 134–36, 144–45, 162
  See also MMT; pollution; regulation,
    environmental; regulatory takings
EPA. *See* US Environmental Protection Agency
ERT. *See* European Round Table on Business
Esty, Daniel C., 157–58, 160
ethanol producers, Canadian, 37–38, 45, 145–46
Ethyl Corporation, 7, 37–39, 41, 43, 44–45, 47,
  145–46
Europe
  business community, 27, 190, 193
  interest in MAI, 21, 24

investment incentives
  arguments for international rules on, 65, 66
  benefits, 65
  competition among countries, 65–66
  developing countries' views of, 177–78
  example, 63–65
  gains from eliminating, 188–89
  including in review of TRIMs agreement,
    194–95
  issue of binding subfederal governments, 26,
    67, 195
  lack of data on effects, 189
  negative effects, 63–65, 188–89
  not addressed in MAI, 3
  performance requirements linked to, 61, 63,
    66–67, 181
  subsidies, 63, 188–89
  uncompetitive investment attracted by, 84–85
  unresolved issues in MAI draft, 67
  use in developed countries, 194
  of US states, 67, 189, 195
  views of multinational firms, 195
investment liberalization
  business support for, 49
  MAI provisions, 53
  unilateral, 186–87, 189, 193
investor protection
  MAI provisions, 2, 72–74
  NAFTA provisions, 41, 45
  opposition to MAI provisions, 39, 72
  payment transfers, 73, 176
  protection from strife, 73
  See also expropriation
investors
  definition in MAI, 56–57
  freedom to transfer funds, 73
  temporary entry, 68, 178
  See also multinational corporations
investor-to-state dispute settlement procedures.
    See dispute settlement procedures
IPRs. See intellectual property rights
Iran-Libya Sanctions Act, 30

Japan, 6, 190–91
jobs
  created by foreign investment, 99
  created by outward foreign investment, 83, 106,
    116, 119, 121–22
  effects of US foreign direct investment on
    overall US employment, 114–15, 116t, 191
  eliminated by outward foreign investment, 116,
    121–22
  labor-intensive activities, 99, 113–14, 121
  predicted movement to low-wage countries,
    8–9, 81–82, 106, 113–14, 125
  quality of, 115–16
  relationship to trade, 115–16
  See also labor; wages
Jordan, Michael, 102
Jospin, Lionel, 11, 33

Korea. See South Korea
Kuznets curves, 137, 138f, 139, 141
Kuznets, Simon, 137
Kyoto Protocol, 155–56, 160, 162

labor in developed countries
  demand and supply, 115, 121, 122–24
  effects of foreign direct investment on
    bargaining power, 125–29, 130
  effects of foreign direct investment on quality
    of jobs, 115–16
  effects of foreign direct investment on
    unemployment, 106, 114–15, 116t
  effects of technological change, 122–24
  in export industries, 83, 121
  fears of jobs moved to low-wage countries, 8–9,
    81–82, 106, 113–14, 125
  skill levels, 121, 122–24
  sweatshop conditions, 100
  See also jobs; labor unions; wages in developed
    countries
labor in developing countries
  abusive treatment, 103
  benefits of foreign direct investment, 84, 85–86,
    95, 99
  children, 100–101, 104
  concern that MAI would hurt interests of, 8–9
  demand for, 86, 87, 88, 90, 95
  harm caused by investment incentives, 84–85
  human capital threshold, 87
  jobs created by foreign investment, 99
  lack of collective bargaining rights, 82, 83,
    98–99
  lack of standards, 9
  skilled, 86, 87, 95
  working conditions, 81, 82, 83
  See also jobs; sweatshop conditions; wages in
    developing countries
labor productivity. See productivity
labor standards
  Copenhagen Declaration, 56
  in developing countries, 9
  MAI provision to not lower standards, 71–72
  reference in MAI preamble, 56
  voluntary codes, 105
  See also sweatshop conditions
labor unions
  criticism of US foreign investment, 129–30, 191
  criticism of wages paid by foreign firms in
    developing countries, 86, 96, 98–99
  efforts to combat sweatshops, 104–5
  fears of jobs lost due to US outward
    investment, 81–82, 106, 121
  fears of lower wages due to foreign investment,
    82, 106, 115–16
  income inequality issue, 86
  lack of in developing countries, 82, 83, 98–99
  Mexican, 98
  OECD advisory committee, 20
  opposition to globalization, 81–82

opposition to multilateral investment
agreements, 192
in US multinational firms, 119
views of performance requirements, 195
weakened bargaining positions, 125–29, 130
See also opponents of Multilateral Agreement
on Investment (MAI)
Lall, Sanjaya, 167
Lang, Tim, 147
Latin American countries, 10, 165, 174
See also individual countries
lead, 140, 142, 143
Libya, 30
Lipsey, Robert E., 94
local content requirements, 61, 62, 63, 179, 180
logging industry, 144–45

MAI. *See* Multilateral Agreement on Investment
Malaysia, 165
managers
nationality requirements, 68
skills, 172
manufacturing
developing country exports, 123
environmental impact, 148–49, 150–52
foreign investment, 170–71
foreign investment in import substitution, 169
sweatshop conditions, 101–2
US foreign investment, 114, 114t, 208–12
US imports, 123
US trade and foreign investment, 120t, 208–12,
212t
marginal product of labor
increasing, 204
relationship to average product, 97–98
relationship to wages, 96–98, 202
See also productivity
Marine Mammal Protection Act, 35–36
Mazur, Jay, 81
Metalclad Corporation, 46n, 52
Mexico
environmental problems, 36, 37, 141
impact of NAFTA, 173
labor unions, 98
maquiladoras, 36, 94, 141
NAFTA negotiations, 17, 36–37
tuna dispute with United States, 35–36
wages, 90, 94
See also North American Free Trade Agreement
(NAFTA)
MFN. *See* most-favored-nation (MFN) obligation
mining industry, 144, 148
MMT (methylcyclopentadienyl manganese
tricarbonyl)
Canadian regulations, 37–38, 47, 143
Ethyl/Canada dispute, 7, 37–39, 41, 44–45,
145–46
monopolies, 70–71, 169, 181
Moran, Theodore H., 61, 63, 119, 180, 182, 188,
194, 198

most-favored-nation (MFN) obligation
exception for regional economic integration
organizations, 31, 59–60, 175–76
in GATS, 34
in MAI, 58, 59–60
in NAFTA investment chapter, 173
in privatizations, 69
Multilateral Agreement on Investment (MAI)
alleged secrecy of negotiations, 18–20
articles, 55
background, 20–23
beginning of negotiations, 1–2, 18, 23
bureaucrats involved, 17, 18–19
choice of OECD as venue, 9–10, 23–25, 29,
165–66, 184
core provisions, 53, 54
deficiencies, 3, 51–53, 67
definitions of investor and investment, 56–57,
182–83
developing countries not included in, 9, 165–66,
184
draft of April 1998, 51–53, 56, 71–72
environmental goals, 56
environmental safeguards discussions, 45,
159–60, 162–63
exceptions, 3, 7, 34, 51, 54–55, 78–80, 175–76
existing policies codified in, 7, 10, 51–53, 192
failure of negotiations, 10–12, 15–20, 25–35
French withdrawal, 11, 33
goals, 2–3, 24, 55–56
host country obligations, 57–72
lack of data on effects, 6–7, 187
lack of involvement by political leaders, 17, 18,
22, 25
name of agreement, 22–23
negotiation timeframe, 11–12, 24, 25
nongovernmental organizations invited to
participate, 47–48
possible deal-breakers for developing
countries, 176–77, 178–84
potential economic benefits, 3, 6–7, 187
potential impact, 52, 53, 78, 80
provisions for accession of developing
countries, 10, 56, 80
provisions likely acceptable to developing
countries, 175–77
provisions that developing countries disagree
with, 177–78
regional economic integration organization
(REIO) exception, 31, 59–60
regulatory takings issue, 45–46, 47, 48, 159–60,
176
scope and application, 56–57
as stand-alone instrument, 52–53, 55, 56
temporary safeguards, 78, 79
top-down structure, 54–55
unresolved issues, 7, 25–35, 45–46, 51, 56, 67, 69
See also dispute settlement procedures in MAI;
opponents of Multilateral Agreement on
Investment (MAI)

multilateral investment agreements. *See*
    investment agreements, multilateral
multinational corporations
    attitudes of developing countries, 167–68,
        169–70
    codes of conduct, 171, 176–77, 183
    contracts with firms with sweatshop
        conditions, 100
    criticism from antiglobal activists, 5, 39
    globally integrated operations, 121
    labor relations, 119, 125–29
    loss of rents due to globalization, 127–29
    low wages criticized, 6, 82, 86, 205
    military backing of home governments, 168–69
    nationalization of affiliates, 171
    national treatment of affiliates in European
        Union, 31
    negotiations with host-country governments,
        169–71
    oligopolistic markets, 125, 126
    outsourcing, 113–14, 121, 124, 125
    perceived as antiunion in developing countries,
        82
    predicted movement of jobs to low-wage
        countries, 8–9, 81–82, 106, 113–14, 125
    profit maximization, 95–97, 98–99
    seen as instruments of imperialism, 168
    trade with foreign affiliates, 118, 118t
    transfer prices, 181
    unionized in United States, 119
    views of investment incentives, 195
    views of performance requirements, 195
    wages paid compared to domestic average
        wage, 92–94, 94t
    wages paid in home country and developing
        countries, 91–92, 92t, 97
    See also business community; foreign direct
        investment; technology transfer
Multinational Monitor, 39

Nader, Ralph, 40
NAFTA. *See* North American Free Trade
    Agreement
NAIRU. *See* nonaccelerating-inflation rate of
    unemployment
nationalization. *See* expropriation
National Treatment Instrument (NTI), 20–21
national treatment principle
    application to environmental regulations, 35–36
    in bilateral investment treaties, 26
    developing countries' views of, 178–80
    dispute over US gasoline import regulations,
        132–33
    effort to negotiate OECD agreement, 20–21
    in European Union, 31
    in GATS, 196
    in GATT, 35–36, 132
    issue of binding subfederal governments in
        international agreements, 21
    issues in MAI negotiations, 178–80

MAI provisions, 2, 58–59, 73
    postestablishment basis, 59, 196
    preestablishment basis, 59, 178–80
    in privatizations, 69
    in services sector, 196
    tax policies, 27
natural resource industries, 168–70
    See also logging industry; mining industry
NGOs. *See* nongovernmental organizations
Nike, 102
nonaccelerating-inflation rate of unemployment
    (NAIRU), 115
nongovernmental organizations (NGOs)
    human rights-oriented, 81, 104–5
    meetings at OECD, 47–48
    opportunities missed in MAI negotiations, 46,
        47–48, 162–63
    opposition to possible multilateral investment
        agreements, 48–49, 191–92, 194
    See also activists, antiglobal; environmental
        groups; labor unions; opponents of
        Multilateral Agreement on Investment (MAI)
North American Free Trade Agreement (NAFTA)
    business support for agreement, 10
    criticisms of, 8, 39
    environmental disputes, 46–47, 52, 78
    environmental sidebar, 36–37
    Ethyl/Canada dispute, 7, 37–39, 41, 44–45,
        145–46
    impact on Mexico, 173
    investment chapter, 8, 41, 43, 173, 183
    investor-to-state dispute settlement procedures,
        37–39, 41, 45, 46–47, 52, 74, 75
    negotiations, 17, 18, 36–37
    as regional economic integration organization,
        59
    regulatory takings issue, 43, 52
    US commitment to negotiations, 17
    views of environmental groups, 36, 37, 39
NTI. *See* National Treatment Instrument

Oberhänsli, Herbert, 193, 197
OECD. *See* Organization for Economic
    Cooperation and Development
oil. *See* gasoline
oligopolistic markets, 125, 126
opponents of Multilateral Agreement on
        Investment (MAI)
    belief that business would gain from MAI, 10, 16
    criticisms of multinational corporations, 5, 39
    criticisms without basis, 9
    development of opposition, 7–9, 37, 39–40
    dispute settlement procedures issue, 78
    employment issues, 8–9, 81–82, 106
    environmental issues, 7, 9, 39, 47, 131, 158, 159
    in France, 11, 33
    human rights issues, 7
    investor protection issues, 72
    issue of yielding sovereignty to international
        body, 52

meetings at OECD, 47–48
regulatory takings issue, 43–44, 46, 47, 48, 78
role in failure of MAI negotiations, 15, 16, 48–49
Seattle city council resolution, 8
secrecy charged, 18–20
tone of campaign, 39
in United States, 40
victory celebrated, 16, 48–49
See also activists, antiglobal; demonstrations; environmental groups; labor unions
Organization for Economic Cooperation and Development (OECD)
Business-Industry Advisory Committee, 20, 56
choice as negotiating venue for MAI, 9–10, 23–25, 29, 165–66, 184
Code of Liberalization of Capital Movements, 22
Code of Liberalization of Current Invisible Transactions, 22
Committee on International Investment and Multinational Enterprise (CIIME), 20, 21, 22
demonstrations at headquarters, 7, 12, 40, 131, 133
foreign direct investment among member countries, 9
lack of expropriations, 72
meetings with NGO representatives, 47–48
ministerial meeting (1995), 18, 23
National Treatment Instrument (NTI), 20–21
Secretariat, 20
Trade Union Advisory Committee, 20
See also Multilateral Agreement on Investment
outsourcing, 113–14, 121, 124, 125
See also jobs

Papua (Indonesia), 144
payment transfers, 22, 73, 176
performance requirements
alternatives, 181
criticisms of, 60–61, 188
in developing countries, 89, 194, 195
effectiveness, 180–81
including in review of TRIMs agreement, 194–95
lack of data on effects, 188
linked to investment incentives, 61, 63, 66–67, 181
local content, 61, 62, 63, 179, 180
local equity participation, 180
MAI provisions, 2, 60–63, 180–82
negative effect on technology transfer, 89
negative effects on host countries, 61, 180–81
negative effects on jobs in home countries, 195
potential environmental impact, 195
technology transfer, 62, 89, 158, 180, 188
trade balancing, 61, 62, 181
views of multinational firms, 195
Perot, Ross, 8
personnel
employment requirements, 69

nationality requirements, 68
temporary entry, 68, 178
See also labor
pesticides, 138–39
pollution
controls to reach optimal level, 152–56
external costs, 136, 143, 151–52, 161
licenses, 152–56, 160, 161
optimal levels, 150–52, 151*f*
relationship to income per capita, 137, 138*f*, 139–40, 141
results of economic growth, 136–40
toxic waste, 136, 148
water, 136, 137–39
See also air pollution; environmental issues
population growth, 135, 141, 144
poverty
of children, 101
in China, 162
environmental benefits of reducing, 135
prisoner's dilemma, 66
privacy protection, 74
privatization, 60, 69
producers' subsidy equivalents (PSEs), 188–89
productivity
decreased by pollution, 143
increases due to technology, 6, 88–89, 128
increases in steel industry, 128
marginal, 96–98, 202, 204
relationship to wages, 89–91, 96–98, 201–5
PSEs. *See* producers' subsidy equivalents
Public Citizen Trade Watch, 40
public health laws, 42, 45, 52, 71–72

Reagan, Ronald, 17
regional economic integration organizations (REIOs), exception to most-favored-nation obligation, 31, 59–60, 175–76
regulation
of foreign investors, 181
public health, 42, 45, 52, 71–72
workplace safety, 42, 45
regulation, environmental
advantages of multilateral agreements over local rules, 159–60
Canadian MMT regulations, 37–38, 47, 143
challenges under NAFTA, 46–47, 52, 78
challenges under WTO, 35–36, 132–33
fear that companies move to countries with weak protection, 9, 36, 37, 141–44, 149–50, 159
fear that dispute settlement will weaken, 78, 132–33
fear that international agreements will weaken, 39, 47, 71–72, 158–59, 191–92
licenses (tradable pollution rights), 152–56, 160, 161
reformulated gasoline, 132–33, 142–43
trade-offs involved, 52, 134, 146, 147, 148, 150–51, 151*f*

Trade Related Intellectual Property Rights (TRIPs). *See* Agreement on Trade Related Intellectual Property Rights
Trade Related Investment Measures (TRIMs). *See* Agreement on Trade Related Investment Measures
transfer prices, 181
transnational corporations. *See* multinational corporations
transparency, 60, 71, 193
TRIMs. *See* Agreement on Trade Related Investment Measures
TRIPs. *See* Agreement on Trade Related Intellectual Property Rights
tuna, 35–36
turtles, 133

UNCITRAL. *See* United Nations Commission on International Trade Law
UNCTAD. *See* United Nations Conference on Trade and Development
unemployment
nonaccelerating-inflation rate of (NAIRU), 115
See also jobs
Union Carbide, 148
Union of Needletrades, Industrial, and Textile Workers (UNITE), 81
unions. *See* labor unions
United Kingdom, 29
United Nations, 4
codes of conduct for multinational firms, 171, 176–77, 183
Investment Advisory Service, 171
United Nations Commission on International Trade Law (UNCITRAL), 75, 76
United Nations Conference on Trade and Development (UNCTAD)
code on restrictive business practices, 171, 176, 183
code on technology transfer, 171, 176
demonstrations at headquarters, 10–11
World Investment Report, 167
United States
air pollution, 139–40
automobile industry, 6, 127–29, 181
bilateral investment treaties, 26
business community, 19, 49
campaigns against sweatshops, 104–5
Clean Air Act, 132–33, 154–55
Cuban Liberty and Democratic Solidarity (Libertad) Act, 28–30
debate over NAFTA, 36
delegation to CIIME, 21, 22
environmental regulations challenged in WTO, 35–36, 132–33
extraterritorial application of laws, 28, 29, 184
foreign direct investment in, 6
goals for MAI, 24
greenhouse gas emissions, 155
immigration policies, 178

imports from developing countries, 123
information technology, 124
international trade negotiations, 17, 18–19
investment incentives of states, 67, 189, 195
Iran-Libya Sanctions Act, 30
lack of public debate on MAI, 18
laws on government expropriation of property, 41–43
Marine Mammal Protection Act, 35–36
military interventions to protect US firms, 168–69
positions in MAI negotiations, 26–27, 31, 32, 34, 44, 56, 59–60, 71–72, 192
state governments, 26, 67, 195
steel industry, 127–29
tax policies, 27
trade involving multinational firms, 118, 118*t*
unemployment, 115, 116*t*
view of potential WTO investment agreement, 185, 192
See also foreign direct investment (FDI) by United States; labor in developed countries; North American Free Trade Agreement (NAFTA)
US Commerce Department, 35
US Congress
Burke-Hartke bill, 191
Cuban Liberty and Democratic Solidarity (Libertad) Act, 28–30
Iran-Libya Sanctions Act, 30
lack of consultation about MAI, 19
role in trade negotiations, 19
United States Council for International Business, 49, 193
US Department of Labor, 105
US Environmental Protection Agency, 132–33
US Federal Reserve Board, 115
US State Department, 40
US Supreme Court, 42, 43
US Trade Representative, 18, 40
urbanization, 161–62
Uruguay Round
business support for agreements, 10
difficulties, 18
performance requirements issue, 61
political commitment, 17, 18–19
See also General Agreement on Tariffs and Trade (GATT)

Venezuela, 94

wage premium
in developed countries, 94
evidence for, 91–95
in foreign-controlled firms, 6, 87–90
relationship to productivity, 96–98
wages
effects of oligopolistic markets, 126
increases due to technology transfer, 5, 6
relationship to labor productivity, 89–91, 96–98, 201–5

Other Publications from the Institute for International Economics

* = out of print

POLICY ANALYSES IN
INTERNATIONAL ECONOMICS Series

1   The Lending Policies of the International
    Monetary Fund*   John Williamson
    August 1982   ISBN 0-88132-000-5
2   "Reciprocity": A New Approach to World
    Trade Policy?*   William R. Cline
    September 1982   ISBN 0-88132-001-3
3   Trade Policy in the 1980s*
    C. Fred Bergsten and William R. Cline
    November 1982   ISBN 0-88132-002-1
4   International Debt and the Stability of the
    World Economy*   William R. Cline
    September 1983   ISBN 0-88132-010-2
5   The Exchange Rate System*, Second Edition
    John Williamson
    Sept. 1983, rev. June 1985 ISBN 0-88132-034-X
6   Economic Sanctions in Support of Foreign
    Policy Goals*
    Gary Clyde Hufbauer and Jeffrey J. Schott
    October 1983   ISBN 0-88132-014-5
7   A New SDR Allocation?*   John Williamson
    March 1984   ISBN 0-88132-028-5
8   An International Standard for Monetary
    Stabilization*   Ronald L. McKinnon
    March 1984   ISBN 0-88132-018-8
9   The YEN/Dollar Agreement: Liberalizing
    Japanese Capital Markets* Jeffrey A. Frankel
    December 1984   ISBN 0-88132-035-8
10 Bank Lending to Developing Countries: The
    Policy Alternatives*   C. Fred Bergsten,
    William R. Cline, and John Williamson
    April 1985   ISBN 0-88132-032-3
11 Trading for Growth: The Next Round of
    Trade Negotiations*
    Gary Clyde Hufbauer and Jeffrey R. Schott
    September 1985   ISBN 0-88132-033-1
12 Financial Intermediation Beyond the Debt
    Crisis*   Donald R. Lessard, John Williamson
    September 1985   ISBN 0-88132-021-8
13 The United States-Japan Economic Problem*
    C. Fred Bergsten and William R. Cline
    October 1985, 2d ed. January 1987
                         ISBN 0-88132-060-9
14 Deficits and the Dollar: The World Economy
    at Risk*   Stephen Marris
    December 1985, 2d ed. November 1987
                         ISBN 0-88132-067-6
15 Trade Policy for Troubled Industries*
    Gary Clyde Hufbauer and Howard R. Rosen
    March 1986   ISBN 0-88132-020-X
16 The United States and Canada: The Quest for
    Free Trade*   Paul Wonnacott, with an
    Appendix by John Williamson
    March 1987   ISBN 0-88132-056-0
17 Adjusting to Success: Balance of Payments
    Policy in the East Asian NICs*
    Bela Balassa and John Williamson
    June 1987, rev. April 1990 ISBN 0-88132-101-X
18 Mobilizing Bank Lending to Debtor
    Countries*   William R. Cline
    June 1987   ISBN 0-88132-062-5
19 Auction Quotas and United States Trade
    Policy*   C. Fred Bergsten, Kimberly Ann
    Elliott, Jeffrey J. Schott, and Wendy E. Takacs
    September 1987   ISBN 0-88132-050-1
20 Agriculture and the GATT: Rewriting the
    Rules*   Dale E. Hathaway
    September 1987   ISBN 0-88132-052-8
21 Anti-Protection: Changing Forces in United
    States Trade Politics*
    I. M. Destler and John S. Odell
    September 1987   ISBN 0-88132-043-9
22 Targets and Indicators: A Blueprint for the
    International Coordination of Economic
    Policy* John Williamson and Marcus H.
    Miller
    September 1987   ISBN 0-88132-051-X
23 Capital Flight: The Problem and Policy
    Responses*   Donald R. Lessard and
    John Williamson
    December 1987   ISBN 0-88132-059-5
24 United States-Canada Free Trade: An
    Evaluation of the Agreement*
    Jeffrey J. Schott
    April 1988   ISBN 0-88132-072-2
25 Voluntary Approaches to Debt Relief*
    John Williamson
    Sept.1988, rev. May 1989 ISBN 0-88132-098-6
26 American Trade Adjustment: The Global
    Impact*   William R. Cline
    March 1989   ISBN 0-88132-095-1
27 More Free Trade Areas?*   Jeffrey J. Schott
    May 1989   ISBN 0-88132-085-4
28 The Progress of Policy Reform in Latin
    America*   John Williamson
    January 1990   ISBN 0-88132-100-1
29 The Global Trade Negotiations: What Can Be
    Achieved?*   Jeffrey J. Schott
    September 1990   ISBN 0-88132-137-0
30 Economic Policy Coordination: Requiem or
    Prologue?*   Wendy Dobson
    April 1991   ISBN 0-88132-102-8

Toward Renewed Economic Growth in Latin America* Bela Balassa, Gerardo M. Bueno, Pedro-Pablo Kuczynski, and Mario Henrique Simonsen
1986 ISBN 0-88132-045-5

Capital Flight and Third World Debt*
Donald R. Lessard and John Williamson, editors
1987 ISBN 0-88132-053-6

The Canada-United States Free Trade Agreement: The Global Impact*
Jeffrey J. Schott and Murray G. Smith, editors
1988 ISBN 0-88132-073-0

World Agricultural Trade: Building a Consensus*
William M. Miner and Dale E. Hathaway, editors
1988 ISBN 0-88132-071-3

Japan in the World Economy*
Bela Balassa and Marcus Noland
1988 ISBN 0-88132-041-2

America in the World Economy: A Strategy for the 1990s C. Fred Bergsten
1988 ISBN 0-88132-089-7

Managing the Dollar: From the Plaza to the Louvre* Yoichi Funabashi
1988, 2d ed. 1989 ISBN 0-88132-097-8

United States External Adjustment and the World Economy* William R. Cline
May 1989 ISBN 0-88132-048-X

Free Trade Areas and U.S. Trade Policy*
Jeffrey J. Schott, editor
May 1989 ISBN 0-88132-094-3

Dollar Politics: Exchange Rate Policymaking in the United States*
I.M. Destler and C. Randall Henning
September 1989 ISBN 0-88132-079-X

Latin American Adjustment: How Much Has Happened?* John Williamson, editor
April 1990 ISBN 0-88132-125-7

The Future of World Trade in Textiles and Apparel* William R. Cline
1987, 2d ed. June 1990 ISBN 0-88132-110-9

Completing the Uruguay Round: A Results-Oriented Approach to the GATT Trade Negotiations* Jeffrey J. Schott, editor
September 1990 ISBN 0-88132-130-3

Economic Sanctions Reconsidered (2 volumes)
Economic Sanctions Reconsidered: Supplemental Case Histories
Gary Clyde Hufbauer, Jeffrey J. Schott, and Kimberly Ann Elliott
1985, 2d ed. Dec. 1990 ISBN cloth 0-88132-115-X
ISBN paper 0-88132-105-2

Economic Sanctions Reconsidered: History and Current Policy
Gary Clyde Hufbauer, Jeffrey J. Schott, and Kimberly Ann Elliott
December 1990 ISBN cloth 0-88132-140-0
ISBN paper 0-88132-136-2

Pacific Basin Developing Countries: Prospects for the Future* Marcus Noland
January 1991 ISBN cloth 0-88132-141-9
ISBN 0-88132-081-1

Currency Convertibility in Eastern Europe*
John Williamson, editor
October 1991 ISBN 0-88132-128-1

International Adjustment and Financing: The Lessons of 1985-1991* C. Fred Bergsten, editor
January 1992 ISBN 0-88132-112-5

North American Free Trade: Issues and Recommendations
Gary Clyde Hufbauer and Jeffrey J. Schott
April 1992 ISBN 0-88132-120-6

Narrowing the U.S. Current Account Deficit*
Allen J. Lenz
June 1992 ISBN 0-88132-103-6

The Economics of Global Warming
William R. Cline/*June 1992* ISBN 0-88132-132-X

U.S. Taxation of International Income: Blueprint for Reform* Gary Clyde Hufbauer, assisted by Joanna M. van Rooij
October 1992 ISBN 0-88132-134-6

Who's Bashing Whom? Trade Conflict in High-Technology Industries Laura D'Andrea Tyson
November 1992 ISBN 0-88132-106-0

Korea in the World Economy Il SaKong
January 1993 ISBN 0-88132-183-4

Pacific Dynamism and the International Economic System*
C. Fred Bergsten and Marcus Noland, editors
May 1993 ISBN 0-88132-196-6

Economic Consequences of Soviet Disintegration*
John Williamson, editor
May 1993 ISBN 0-88132-190-7

Reconcilable Differences? United States-Japan Economic Conflict
C. Fred Bergsten and Marcus Noland
June 1993 ISBN 0-88132-129-X

Does Foreign Exchange Intervention Work?
Kathryn M. Dominguez and Jeffrey A. Frankel
September 1993 ISBN 0-88132-104-4

Sizing Up U.S. Export Disincentives*
J. David Richardson
September 1993 ISBN 0-88132-107-9

NAFTA: An Assessment
Gary Clyde Hufbauer and Jeffrey J. Schott/*rev. ed.*
October 1993 ISBN 0-88132-199-0

Adjusting to Volatile Energy Prices
Philip K. Verleger, Jr.
November 1993 ISBN 0-88132-069-2

The Political Economy of Policy Reform
John Williamson, editor
January 1994 ISBN 0-88132-195-8

WORKS IN PROGRESS

**The Impact of Increased Trade on
Organized Labor in the United States**
Robert E. Baldwin
**New Regional Arrangements and the World
Economy**
C. Fred Bergsten
**The Globalization Backlash in Europe and the
United States**
C. Fred Bergsten, Pierre Jacquet, and Karl Kaiser
The U.S.-Japan Economic Relationship
C. Fred Bergsten, Marcus Noland, and
Takatoshi Ito
China's Entry to the World Economy
Richard N. Cooper
**World Capital Markets: Challenges to
the G-10**
Wendy Dobson and Gary Clyde Hufbauer
The ILO in the World Economy
Kimberly Ann Elliott
Reforming Economic Sanctions
Kimberly Ann Elliott, Gary C. Hufbauer, and
Jeffrey J. Schott
Free Trade in Labor Agency Services
Kimberly Ann Elliott and J. David Richardson
The *Chaebol* and Structural Problems in Korea
Edward M. Graham
Ex-Im Bank in the 21st Century
Gary Clyde Hufbauer and Rita Rodriquez, eds.
**NAFTA: A Seven Year Appraisal of the Trade,
Environment, and Labor Agreements**
Gary Clyde Hufbauer and Jeffrey J. Schott

Prospects for Western Hemisphere Free Trade
Gary Clyde Hufbauer and Jeffrey J. Schott
Price Integration in the World Economy
Gary Clyde Hufbauer, Erika Wada, and
Tony Warren
Reforming the IMF
Peter Kenen
**Imports, Exports, and American Industrial
Workers since 1979**
Lori G. Kletzer
**Reemployment Experiences of Trade-
Displaced Americans**
Lori G. Kletzer
**Globalization and Creative Destruction in the
US Textile and Apparel Industry**
James Levinsohn
Measuring the Costs of Protection in Europe
Patrick Messerlin
Dollarization, Currency Blocs, and U.S. Policy
Adams S. Posen
**Germany in the World Economy after the
EMU**
Adam S. Posen
**Japan's Financial Crisis and Its Parallels to
U.S. Experience**
Adam S. Posen and Ryoichi Mikitani, eds.
**Sizing Up Globalization: The Globalization
Balance Sheet Capstone Volume**
J. David Richardson
Why Global Integration Matters Most!
J. David Richardson and Howard Lewis
**Worker Perceptions and Pressures in the
Global Economy**
Matthew J. Slaughter
India in the World Economy
T. N. Srinivasan and Suresh D. Tendulka
**Exchange-Rate Regimes for East Asia:
Reviving the Intermediate Option**
John Williamson

DISTRIBUTORS OUTSIDE THE UNITED STATES

Australia, New Zealand, and Papua New Guinea
D.A. INFORMATION SERVICES
648 Whitehorse Road
Mitcham, Victoria 3132, Australia
tel: 61-3-9210-7777
fax: 61-3-9210-7788
e-mail: service@dadirect.com.au
http://www.dadirect.com.au

Caribbean
SYSTEMATICS STUDIES LIMITED
St. Augustine Shopping Centre
Eastern Main Road, St. Augustine
Trinidad and Tobago, West Indies
tel: 868-645-8466
fax: 868-645-8467
e-mail: tobe@trinidad.net

United Kingdom and Europe (including Russia and Turkey)
The Eurospan Group
3 Henrietta Street, Covent Garden
London WC2E 8LU England
tel: 44-20-7240-0856
fax: 44-20-7379-0609
http://www.eurospan.co.uk

Northern Africa and the Middle East (Egypt, Algeria, Bahrain, Palestine, Jordan, Kuwait, Lebanon, Libya, Morocco, Oman, Qatar, Saudi Arabia, Syria, Tunisia, Yemen, and United Arab Emirates)
Middle East Readers Information Center (MERIC)
2 bahgat Aly Street
El-Masry Towers, Tower #D, Apt. #24, First Floor
Zamalek, Cairo EGYPT
tel: 202-341-3824/340 3818;
fax 202-341-9355
http://www.meric-co.com

Taiwan
Unifacmanu Trading Co., Ltd.
4F, No. 91, Ho-Ping East Rd, Sect. 1
Taipei 10609, Taiwan
tel: 886-2-23419646
fax: 886-2-23943103
e-mail: winjoin@ms12.hinet.net

Argentina
World Publications SA.
Av. Cordoba 1877
1120 Buenos Aires, Argentina
tel/fax: (54 11) 4815 8156
e-mail:
http://wpbooks@infovia.com.ar

People's Republic of China (including Hong Kong) **and Taiwan** (sales representatives):
Tom Cassidy
Cassidy & Associates
70 Battery Place, Ste 220
New York, NY 10280
tel: 212-706-2200   fax: 212-706-2254
e-mail: CHINACAS@Prodigy.net

India, Bangladesh, Nepal, and Sri Lanka
Viva Books Pvt.
Mr. Vinod Vasishtha
4325/3, Ansari Rd.
Daryaganj, New Delhi-110002
INDIA
tel: 91-11-327-9280
fax: 91-11-326-7224 ,
e-mail: vinod.viva@gndel.globalnet.
ems.vsnl.net.in

South Africa
Pat Bennink
Dryad Books
PO Box 11684
Vorna Valley 1686
South Africa
tel: +27 14 576 1332
fax: +27 82 899 9156
e-mail: dryad@hixnet.co.za

Thailand
Asia Books 5 Sukhumvit Rd. Soi 61
Bangkok 10110 Thailand
(phone 662-714-0740-2 Ext: 221, 222, 223
fax: (662) 391-2277)
e-mail: purchase@asiabooks.co.th
http://www.asiabooksonline.com

Canada
RENOUF BOOKSTORE
5369 Canotek Road, Unit 1,
Ottawa, Ontario K1J 9J3, Canada
tel: 613-745-2665
fax: 613-745-7660
http://www.renoufbooks.com

Colombia, Ecuador, and Peru
Infoenlace Ltda
Attn: Octavio Rojas
Calle 72 No. 13-23 Piso 3
Edificio Nueva Granada, Bogota, D.C.
Colombia
tel: (571) 255 8783 or 255 7969
fax: (571) 248 0808 or 217 6435

Japan and the Republic of Korea
United Publishers Services, Ltd.
Kenkyu-Sha Bldg.
9, Kanda Surugadai 2-Chome
Chiyoda-Ku, Tokyo 101
JAPAN
tel: 81-3-3291-4541;
fax: 81-3-3292-8610
e-mail: saito@ups.co.jp
For trade accounts only.
Individuals will find IIE books in leading Tokyo bookstores.

South America
Julio E. Emod
Publishers Marketing & Research Associates, c/o HARBRA
Rua Joaquim Tavora, 629
04015-001 Sao Paulo, Brasil
tel: (55) 11-571-1122;
fax: (55) 11-575-6876
e-mail: emod@harbra.com.br

Visit our Web site at:
http://www.iie.com
E-mail orders to:
orders@iie.com

DATE DUE

APR	4 2001	DEC 0 4 2003	
	JUN 1 8 2001	APR 2 9 2004	
	SEP 1 7 2001		
	MAY 1 0 2002		
NOV 2 0 2002			
GAYLORD			PRINTED IN U.S.A.